LOVE'S
PILGRIMAGE

This book will make a traveler of thee
If by its counsel thou wilt ruled be;
It will direct thee to the Holy Land,
If thou wilt its Directions understand
                    —John Bunyan, *The Pilgrim's Progress*

Some men a forward motion love;
But I by backward steps would move,
And when this dust falls to the urn,
In that state I came, return.
                    —Henry Vaughan, "The Retreat"

Contents

Acknowledgments

Fᴏʀ ᴛʜᴇɪʀ ᴀᴅᴠɪᴄᴇ ᴀɴᴅ ᴇɴᴄᴏᴜʀᴀɢᴇᴍᴇɴᴛ I ᴀᴍ ɢʀᴀᴛᴇꜰᴜʟ ᴛᴏ ᴛʜᴇ sᴇᴠᴇʀᴀʟ scholars who read all or parts of this manuscript. Particular thanks go to my friends and colleagues Eve Salisbury, Clifford Davidson, Heather Addison, Elizabeth Bradburn, David Daniell, and John Saillant, as well as to my fellow participants in a seminar on sixteenth-century English provincial playing held at the Shakespeare Association of America's annual meeting in New Orleans in 2004. I particularly thank Paul White for including me in that seminar and for his comments on the portion of this book that I presented there. Thanks also to Ed Block, editor of *Renascence,* for including an early version of my study of Shakespeare and Santiago de Compostela in an issue of that journal and for allowing it to be published now herein. Papers presented at the 39th and 40th Medieval Congress at Kalamazoo greatly helped me in my quest to understand late-medieval and early-modern literary transformations of the English pilgrimage tradition. So did English 532, a course in English Renaissance literature in which, over the years I taught it, the idea for this book emerged. I thank all who studied with me in that class for helping my thoughts coalesce. I thank Western Michigan University for a FRACASF grant which helped me complete this project. Finally, thanks always to Tom Lucking for his partnership in life's pilgrimage.

LOVE'S
PILGRIMAGE

1

The Protestant Pilgrimage

The Romish doctrine concerning Purgatory, Pardons, Worshipping and Adoration, as well of images as of Relics, and also Invocation of Saints, is a fond thing vainly invented, and grounded upon no warranty of Scripture, but rather repugnant to the Word of God.

—*Articles of Religion of the English Church*, 22 (1544)[1]

Then is his pain more than his wit,
To walk to heaven, when he may sit!

—John Heywood,
The Play Called the Four PP, ll. 356–67[2]

How did english authors write about pilgrimage after the prot-estant Reformation? Through much of the Middle Ages, real and imagined journeys to saints' shrines were an important part of English life. Upper- and lower-class English people alike not only rode and walked to English shrines, like those of St. Thomas in Canterbury and St. Mary in Walsingham, but undertook perilous sea and lengthy overland journeys to Continental holy sites, most notably the shrine of St. James of Compostela in northwestern Spain.[3] As late as 1520, the Reform-minded monarch Henry VIII himself made the journey to St. Mary's of Walsingham, setting a royal standard for the observance of saint cults.[4] Even for those who stayed home, literary and dramatic representations of holy pilgrimages created imaginative pictures of travels to sacred places. Among aristocratic readers, Percival's Grail quest, recounted in Thomas Malory's *Morte Darthur* (c. 1450), both drew from and romanticized the tradition of arduous travel to holy sites to venerate saints' relics. Malory's near contemporary, the late-fourteenth-century courtier and expatriate Frenchman Jean Froissart, wrote chronicles from the English royal court recalling both his

own desire to visit the shrine of Saint James in Galicia and King Richard II's "great devotion" to make a "pilgrimage . . . to visit St. Thomas's shrine" in Canterbury.[5] Soon after the compilation of Froissart's
Chronicles, Chaucer's *Canterbury Tales* famously celebrated the English pilgrimage as a journey both social and spiritual, one that
united all cultural strata and both sexes in a communal endeavor
prompted by a mix of worldly and religious motives. Over a century
later, in the 1530s, John Heywood's popular dramatic interlude, *The
Four PP,* pondered the spiritual value of pilgrimages, providing its
audiences with a near-exhaustive list of Eastern, Continental, and
English holy sites. A key character, the Palmer, opens Heywood's
play with a sixty-odd-line recounting his journeys to "the Mount of
Calvary," "Saint Peter's shrine," "Saint Winifred's Well in Wales,"
"Saint Patrick's Purgatory," and a host of other shrines. The play
concludes with another character's judgment that the Palmer's traveling time has been "well spent" (l. 1148).

Yet, despite the English popularity of real and imagined pilgrimages, ground for Reformed England's repudiation of pilgrimage as
"a Romish doctrine" had been broken, paradoxically, by such late-
medieval and early-modern literary and dramatic representations, at
least for aristocratic audiences and other literate English people.
For Dante, the word "pilgrim" (*pellegrino*) evoked images of arduous
journey—his Purgatorial penitents are "pilgrims" bound on a "steep,"
"broken," and "tortuous way" (*Purgatorio,* canto 2, ll. 63, 65)[6]—but
the earthly pilgrimages described by English poets of the century
after Dante's were jolly outings. Chaucer famously suggested that
pilgrimages flowered as much from a primal human instinct to
shake off winter's drowse, to go forth in "Aprille" to "seken
straunge strondes," as to worship a "holy blisful martir" like
Thomas Becket, enshrined at Canterbury Cathedral. Late-medieval
skepticism regarding the religious value of the pilgrimage was both
manifested and promulgated by those widely read English texts that,
like Chaucer's, presented pilgrims as impelled by carnal or otherwise worldly motivations. "As you came from Walsingham / From
that holy land / There met you not with my true love?" ran a popular ballad.[7]

Of course, not all English authors were critical of all pilgrimages.
As late as the seventeenth century even Protestant theologians and
religious poets continued to use "pilgrimage" as a topos to describe
spiritual journeying (although they radically reconfigured that

topos, as I will shortly show).[8] However, a mark of the writings of English Reformers and their late-medieval predecessors was a perception of traditional *physical* pilgrimage—of actual travel to earthly shrines and venerated places—as a wholly carnal enterprise.

For example, in the late fourteenth century, in *The Vision of Piers Plowman*, Chaucer's contemporary William Langland wrote satirically of "pilgrimes and palmeris plighten [banding] hem togidere / For to seke Seint Jame and seintes at Rome," who "Wenten forth in here way with many wise talis [smart talk], / And hadde leve to leighe al here lif aftir [and took leave to lie about it for the rest of their lives]."

> Ermytes on an hep with hokide staves
> Wenten to Walsyngham, and here wenchis aftir.
> Grete lobies and longe, that loth were to swynke,
> Clothide hem in copis to be knowen from othere;
> Shopen hem ermytes, here ese to have.
>
> [A lot of hermits with hooked staves went to
> Walsingham, their wenches following. These
> great, long lubbers, loth to work, clothed
> themselves in clerical garb to be known from
> laymen, and styled themselves hermits, so as to
> have an easy life.]
>
> (Prologue, ll. 46–54)[9]

In Langland's account, the existence of holy shrines fosters lies about pilgrimages and concomitant garrulous sanctimony. Further, palmers, or professional pilgrims, are characterized by the deadly sins of lust (their "wenches" followed them) and sloth (they were "great, long lubbers, loth to work").

Langland's pilgrims are more harshly presented than Chaucer's, but, as is well known, several of Chaucer's characters display similarly suspicious motives. Indeed, the travelers most given to pilgrimage in *The Canterbury Tales* are also those most clearly impelled by eros or cupiditas. The Wife of Bath is an apparently incessant "holy" traveler: "thyres hadde she been at Ierusalem;" "At Rome she hadde been, and at Boloigne, / In Galice at seint Iame, and at Coloigne" (Prologue, ll. 465, 467–68). Yet her travel is described as mere "wandring by the weye" (l. 469)—a metaphor for sexual waywardness—and her "gat-tothed" (l. 470) appearance hints at an erotic agenda that the prologue to her tale confirms: "Thonked be god that is eterne on lyve, / Housbondes at chirche-dore I have had fyve / . . . . / Welcome the sixte, whan that ever he shal" (ll. 5–6, 45). As for Chaucer's Pardoner, his possession of fake relics bespeaks either his ill-inspired visits to holy shrines or his false claims that he has visited them; he carries "a gobet of the seyl / That sëynt Peter hadde, whan that he wente / Up-on the see," with which, along with a "glas" of "pigges bones," he extracts "more moneye" from poor peasants in a day than his victims can earn "in monthes tweye" (Prologue, ll. 698–99, 702, 705–6). Unlike the satirical Chaucer, Margery Kempe, in the early fifteenth century, wrote in high praise of the pilgrimage experience, speaking eloquently of the spiritual transformation wrought in her by her visit to the site of Christ's passion on Calvary. However, her account of the English reception of her purified self suggests, all the same, that her behavior after her return home bespoke a lessening of belief in the spiritual benefits of pilgrimage. Kempe's memories of her holy visit induced fits of "crying and roaring" that, felt by her to be "high contemplation," were simply "noying" (annoying) to the people of Norfolk, where she lived. She writes (speaking of herself in the third person), "some said it was a wicked spirit vexed her; some said it was a sickness; some said she had drunken too much wine," and "some wished she had been in the haven" (stayed in the port).[10]

In the 1530s, a century after the first appearance of Kempe's book, at the time of Henry VIII's break with Rome, Heywood's *The Four PP* recorded the mixed respect and scorn with which the English had by then come to regard pilgrims and pilgrimages. As noted above, Heywood's Palmer—so called because one who had visited the Holy Land carried a palm to show he had gotten there—is straightforwardly judged by a fellow character to have journeyed "for love of Christ," and thus to have "well spent" his time (ll. 1145, 1148). And indeed, the Palmer's first description of his travels suggests his piety. He is a pilgrim "of good intent" (l. 12), who offers both "prayers" and the "daily pain" of hard travel to "obtain / For [his own] salvation grace and mercy" (ll. 55–57). His prayers, furthermore, do not constitute invalid worship of saints in preference to Christ; through these prayers he merely requests saints' assistance in acquiring the help of "the Blessed Trinity." The Palmer prays "to [saints] to pray for me" (ll. 54, 53). Yet throughout the progress of the dialogue between "the four PP" (the palmer, a pardoner, a pothecary, and a peddler), the Palmer's characterization begins to conform, to an extent, to the by-then common characterization of the pilgrim as an impious erotic traveler or vagabond. "Not one good city, town, nor borough / In Christendom but I have been thorough," says the Palmer,

> And this I would ye should understand:
> I have seen women five hundred thousand
> Wives and widows, maids and married,
> And oft with them have long time tarried.
>
> (ll. 995–1000)

An earlier speech of the Palmer's foregrounded his humility, against the common stereotype of the braggart pilgrim boasting of his or her travels. Any others who had traveled to Saint Peter's shrine, the Palmer said modestly at first, could "speak as much as [he]" (l. 28). Yet here, by slyly hinting at erotic achievements with "Wives and widows, maids and married" with whom he has "tarried," the Palmer forsakes his humble persona, and begins to match William Langland's fourteenth-century description of pilgrims as lying braggarts and lust-driven libertines. The character undergoes a midplay metamorphosis, as though Heywood, staunch Catholic though he was, succumbed to the temptation to drop his moral defense of a "Romish" practice so as to mine audience laughter by parading a recognizable antipilgrim parody before his aristocratic watchers.

A more serious and sustained attack on pilgrimage, albeit an indirect one, is made when Heywood's Pardoner, much like Chaucer's of more than a century before, begins to brag of the obviously fake "relics" he carries as he walks, and claims that their power to cleanse Christians of sin exceeds even the purifying benefits of holy pilgrimage. Since pilgrims traveled to holy sites to venerate not only saints but their relics—the popular shrines of St. Barbara and St. Kelem in Worcestershire housed "silver and gilt reliquaries" containing their alleged personal effects,[11] and Erasmus, who traveled to Canterbury in 1513, speaks of the exhibit there of St. Thomas's "hair shirt," "girdle," "drawers," and "skull"[12]—Heywood's satirical representation of the Pardoner's sacred bone collection calls reliquaries and miracle-peddling con men equally into question.

And indeed, despite *The Four PP*'s concluding celebration of the virtue of all four of its represented professions, the greater part of

the play is devoted to exposing the lies typical of bad pardoners, who
falsely claim to have received miracle-working bones, teeth, and
other body parts from holy places. The Palmer's charge that "sel-
dom is it seen, or never / That truth and pardoners dwell together"
(ll. 109–10) is justified by the Pardoner's absurd claim that he carries "a buttock-bone of Pentecost" (l. 521), as well as "a box full of
humble-bees / That stung Eve as she sat on her knees / Tasting the
fruit to her forbidden" (ll. 546–49). The lack of respect accorded
relics by many early-sixteenth-century English people—even loyal
Catholics like Heywood, who remained true to the old religion
throughout his life—is suggested by the Pothecary's low-comic as-
sessment of the Pentecost buttock-bone: "This relic hath beshitten
the roast!" (l. 523).

Nor was this disdain for relics confined to those clearly fake items
peddled on the road by such as Heywood's Pardoner. Even genuine
relics are invalid objects of worship. In adoring (say) the cup Christ,
saying "This is my blood," used at the Last Supper, "palmers . . . /
kiss the pardon-bowl for the drink's sake," says Heywood's Pothecary
(ll. 568–69). In his *Colloquies* Erasmus speaks of the "horr[or]" with
which, during his visit to Canterbury, he regarded the drawers of St.
Thomas—because of their flesh-mortifying design, one hopes—as
well as the other "skulls, jaws, teeth, hands, fingers," and "whole
arms" in the reliquary. "Choice treasures," Erasmus calls these fragments, with biting sarcasm. His bitterest condemnation of the shrine
is provoked by the sight of the real treasures on display in the
church and stored in the shrine's repository: "Good Lord, what an
array of silk vestments there, what an abundance of gold candelabra!
. . . [In the shrine itself was] inestimable treasure. . . . The cheapest
part was gold. Everything shone and dazzled with rare and surpassingly large jewels, some bigger than a goose egg. . . . I've never
seen anything more loaded with riches."[13] Erasmus's journey to Canterbury, which he made in the company of the early Reformer John
Colet, seems to have been made less to venerate Thomas than to
perform fieldwork for such satirical reportage on the wasting of English money on shrines and ossuaries.

Though Erasmus's views were not everyone's, they were extraordi-
narily influential, and records of declining numbers of visits to monasteries and cathedrals in the late fourteenth, fifteenth, and early
sixteenth centuries confirm that they were increasingly shared. Not
surprisingly, reduced numbers of pilgrimages were characteristic of

Northern European countries in which Protestantism would become a strong force. Carol Piper Heming has recently chronicled the early-sixteenth-century petering-out of pilgrimages in Bavaria.[14] In England, even by the mid-fourteenth century, the shrine of St. Barbara in Halesowen, Worcestershire, had been virtually abandoned by pilgrims. As Eamon Duffy notes, devotion often shifted from saint to saint, leaving some traditional shrines abandoned while others flourished.[15] However, the overall reduction in churches' incomes from the pockets of pilgrim travelers over this century-and-a-half span implies, if not a general loss of *interest* in the shrines, a weakening of the popular belief that saints' miracles could be bought. Especially at Canterbury Cathedral, receipts in the late fifteenth and early sixteenth centuries dwindled appreciably in comparison with what A. G. Dickens calls the "golden shower of the high Middle Ages."[16] Stanford Lehmberg's extensive study of cathedral history between 1485 and 1603 records that Canterbury Cathedral's income from pilgrims fell from more than 800 pounds in 1350 to 644 pounds in 1420, then dropped sharply to a negligible amount by 1500.[17] As Erasmus testifies, the display of wealth at St. Thomas's tomb was still stunningly sumptuous in 1513, and the anonymous author of the *Rites of Durham* (not published until 1593, but written earlier in the century) suggests that Thomas's tomb was rivaled by St. Cuthbert's at Durham Cathedral: in the 1530s Cuthbert's "sacred shrine was exalted with . . . fine and costly green marble all limned and guilted with gold hauvinge foure seates or places conuenient under the shrine for the pilgrims . . . . six silver bells [were] fastned to [a] rope, soe as when the cover of the [vault] was drawinge upp the belles did make . . . a good sound."[18] Yet gifts to St. Cuthbert's shrine had also lessened during the fifteenth century, suggesting that increasing numbers of English folk had come to feel that outlay of cash and valuables for spiritual benefits at the shrines was a bad bargain, enriching only the churches (a possibility that grants a second, perhaps unconscious meaning to the *Rites* author's description of Cuthbert's shrine as "*guilted* with gold" [my emphasis]). Lehmberg concludes that "belief in miracles had declined by the early Tudor period," and that "[t]hose who still made trips to see cathedral treasures may have resembled modern tourists more than medieval suppliants."[19]

Of course, pilgrims had always visited shrines for a variety of reasons, some devoutly spiritual and some less so. In the thirteenth cen-

tury the priest Jaques de Vitry had complained about "light-minded
and inquisitive persons" who, "go[ing] on pilgrimages not out of
devotion, but out of mere curiosity and a love of novelty," distracted
the more pious travelers.[20] Thus it would be an overstatement to
claim that in the late-medieval period "simple curiosity" newly
emerged, or indeed that it entirely "displaced the intensely spiritual
feelings of an earlier age," as the historian Jonathan Sumption
writes. Still, in the fifteenth century, as Sumption acknowledges,
"[a]s traveling became easier and cheaper, tourism, lightly disguised
as pilgrimage, became extremely popular"[21]—far more popular, in
fact, than it had ever been before.

The conversion of English pilgrimage to tourism was promoted
by the pleasurable reception pilgrims received at monasteries and
cathedrals that housed sacred shrines. Although journeys to visit English saints' relics might have been arduous, especially for poorer
travelers, their successful completion was rewarded by comfortable
lodging in well-appointed guest houses. The author of the *Rites of
Durham* speaks of the "famouse house of hospitallitie" that wel-
comed all comers to St. Cuthbert's shrine. That house was "not . . .
inferior to any place in Inglande, both for the goodness of [its]
diete" and "the sweete and daintie furneture of [its] Lodginges."[22]
Canterbury also offered sumptuous hospitality, a practice supported
by the increasingly secularized living arrangements enjoyed by the
cathedral's staff. Lehmberg speaks of the increase in Canterbury of
the number of private dwellings run by the cathedral, dwellings
which, by the end of the fourteenth century, housed "the subprior,
the sacrist, the cellarer, the infirmarian, and the almoner," as well
as the "guest master." He speaks also of the numerous laymen who
lived on the cathedral premises, some of them "older men who were
maintained for life upon nomination by the king, the prior, or occasionally the pope," and quotes R. A. L. Smith's comparison of such
men to "retired civil servants," whose "stories of court life, of adventure, and of intrigue, would . . . come as a welcome relief" to the
repetitive ritual of monastic life.[23] Doubtless such secular company
would have enlivened the visits of pilgrims as well. Lehmberg's and
Smith's accounts of late-medieval life within the precincts of Canterbury Cathedral suggests that the telling of "Canterbury tales"
brightened not just the pilgrimage, but also the journey's end.

Thus, on a national scale, the diminished hope that visits to saints'
shrines could effect miracles—evident in the shrines' lessening re-

ceipts—paralleled the growing perception of pilgrimages as opportunities for worldly delight. As early as the time of Chaucer and Langland, we see pilgrimage associated with erotic adventure, a view espoused in the sixteenth century by English and Continental Reformers alike. In Germany, Martin Bucer wrote that behavior in cities that housed popular shrines was "more wicked" than that in any other,[24] while Martin Luther charged pilgrimages with "increasing drinking and fornication."[25] "Just keep an eye on sex," Luther wrote. "What were pilgrimages [under the papacy] but opportunities to get together? . . . In order that they might satisfy lust the more, well-situated places, beautiful fountains, trees, hills, and rivers were sought out for pilgrimages."[26] Luther's colleague at Wittenberg, Johannes Lonicer, asked, "Is it not a sign of Satan's work: when the youth and maids, stimulated by the devil, travel with impetuosity and fury to Our Lady in Grimmental, Felbach, Zinsbach, Aachen, Einsiedeln, Regensburg, and countless other shrines . . . ? . . . . What is the result of this journey? They amuse themselves with long-desired love."[27] Lonicer's charge brings to mind Heywood's Palmer's boast that he has "seen women five hundred thousand / Wives and widows, maids and married / And with them . . . long time tarried." By the time of the English Reformation, pilgrimages had become widely perceived as immoral or, at least, unspiritual journeys.

The far-walking pilgrim's loss of spiritual prestige both coincided with and was furthered by a phenomenon which has interested some New Historicist scholars, namely, the increasingly restrictive sixteenth-century prohibitions against vagrants in England. By 1581, constables in all English towns were authorized to "arrest such strange persons as do walke abroad in the night season."[28] As Heather Dubrow explains, citing the *OED*, "In the late sixteenth century, 'strange' could mean 'belonging to another country'" or "'belonging to some other place or neighborhood,' as well as 'unknown, unfamiliar,' and 'abnormal.'"[29] Those wayfaring to sacred locations at this point in English history would have been subject to arrest as strangers, vagrants, vagabonds, or masterless men, had there been any sacred places left for them to go.

When the shrines that made pilgrimages possible were officially dismantled, wide-scale English skepticism regarding pilgrimages' spiritual value was itself enshrined in law. In 1536 came the first formal proscription against shrines, in the royal injunction forbidding clergy to "extol any images, relics, or miracles" or "allure the people to the pilgrimage of any saint."[30] Further injunctions issued by Lord Privy Seal Thomas Cromwell in 1538 condemned "feigned images . . . abused with pilgrimages or offerings," ordered such images' removal from churches, and commanded any clergy who had "heretofore declared to their parishioners anything to the extolling or setting forth of pilgrimages, feigned relics, or any such superstition" to "openly . . . recant and reprove the same."[31] In April of that year, Cromwell's unsainting of England reached the point of absurdity when by his order a demand that Thomas Becket appear before the King's Council was read at the site of Becket's shrine. The saint was allowed thirty days to comply, but when he did not appear at his trial, he was judged in absentia, declared a rabble-rouser in life and no "holy, blisful martir." The treasures of his shrine were confiscated for the Crown, and his bones were publicly burned.[32] The official attack on Becket was soon felt throughout England, when a November 1538 proclamation charging he had defied "the wholesome laws established against the enormities of the clergy by the King's highness' most noble progenitor, King Henry II," demanded the erasure of his name from service books, the cessation of his feast day, and the removal of his picture from all churches.[33] Further dissolution of shrines followed. In 1545, Parliament passed a law authorizing the government to dispense with chantries.[34] In the early 1550s, Queen Mary undid some of the purgations at Canterbury, providing new vestments, hangings, and statues for the church, but did not restore Thomas's shrine.[35] Subsequently, Elizabeth's "visitation articles" of 1559 dictated the final abandonment of all shrines and relics.[36]

Eamon Duffy has recently argued that these proscriptions and the dismantlings of shrines constituted a violent "stripping of the altars," as the title of his massive study of "traditional religion in England" suggests. When the English government thwarted pilgrimages, Duffy argues, it robbed English people of "a ritual enactment and consecration of their whole lives" which "help[ed them] to interpret [those lives] as a journey towards the sacred."[37] And the Pilgrimage of Grace, the 1536 uprising in the religiously conservative north against the destruction of the monasteries, demonstrates that shrine dismantlement was profoundly unsettling to some.[38] However, Duffy's assertion that the dissolution of the shrines provoked general dismay among the English overlooks the fact that by the early sixteenth century, shrines were already failing to attract the right kinds of pilgrims (the ones who paid). Duffy himself concedes that "the heyday of the great national shrine at Canterbury was perhaps over by the fifteenth century, a decline attested in dwindling takings from pilgrim offerings," but maintains that "there is plenty of evidence that regional and local shrines, as well as the classic pilgrimage to Rome, Jerusalem, and Compostella, remained the focus of devotion even up to the very moment when they were outlawed."[39] Yet—leaving aside both the question of the English monarch's effective power to outlaw Eastern or Continental pilgrimages as well as the average English man's or woman's freedom to embark on such journeys—Duffy later contradicts his claim that regional holy sites flourished until the proscriptions, acknowledging that on "the eve of the Reformation there is evidence of the comparative neglect of local shrines, like those of St. Hugh at Lincoln" and "Cuthbert at Durham," as well as of "Becket at Canterbury."[40] Duffy's argument also overlooks the literary evidence that pilgrimages, while they may still have been popular in the sixteenth century, were no longer widely regarded as journeys likely to yield salvific grace to the pilgrim. The diminished interest in traditional saints' shrines indicates, to Duffy, a refocusing of attention on newer shrines that attributed healing power to national heroes, like the shrine of King Henry VI at Windsor.[41]

The datum concerning King Henry VI is significant. Duffy notes that there are "almost a third as many surviving pilgrims' badges from Henry's shrine, which lasted only fifty years [from the late 1400s until the dissolution], as from Becket's shrine, which was visited for three centuries."[42] Never a saint, although his canonization was proposed, Henry VI's shrine's popularity indicates the Renaissance rechanneling of religious pilgrimage energies toward the construction of national heroes (chiefly of the royal family) and other secular enthusiasms. Besides the veneration of English royalty, such enthusiasms encompassed the real or vicarious experiencing of New World voyaging and, again, erotic adventure.

Duffy inadvertently provides evidence of this movement toward worldly pilgrimage. He notes the resemblance between late-medieval legends like that of Saint Barbara (in fact, a false saint, who, despite her shrine, was never canonized nor existed) and "Mandeville's travels," but does so without conceding that the likeness of the miracle and travel genres for readers and hearers of these stories indicates a popular shift from religious observance to enjoyment of a pastime. Later Duffy describes the "pious wonder and simple entertainment" that late-medieval saints' stories provided for "a growing middle class audience" without acknowledging the difference between piety and a desire for entertainment. Yet there is a difference, and it was visible in the imaginative uses to which English writers and audiences put the once-holy pilgrimage during the Renaissance. One small example is the poet Michael Drayton's wry description of Spenser's fictional Colin Clout, "to fayrie [fairyland] gone a Pilgrimage" (*The Shepheards Garland*, 1593).[43]

Clearly, pilgrimage from one place to another did not die out in the English imagination, either in the sixteenth century or the seventeenth. The idea of pilgrimage did, however, undergo a profound transformation during that period. As I have suggested, notions of actual wide-ranging physical journey increasingly became secular notions (though materialistic New World voyages were supported by Protestant evangelical zeal). As Jonathan Sumption has shown, as early as the late Middle Ages opportunities for "easier and cheaper" travel in much of Europe began greatly to increase effectively secular pilgrimages: entertaining journeys undergone by those whose "predominant motive" was tourism.[44] In early modern England, the by-now-rooted idea of the secular "pilgrimage" contributed to the frequent representation of all wide-ranging geographical wanderings as picaresque adventuring—at its shadiest, criminally motivated vagrancy—or as quests for love, military conquest, and/or economic triumph. By the late sixteenth century, popular works like Robert Greene's *Conny-Catching* pamphlets (1591–92) and Thomas Harman's *Caveat of Warning, for . . . Vagabonds* (1566) disseminated satirical images of wanderers as miscreants and cozeners, those strangers from whom honest, settled townsfolk required protection.[45] Sixteenth-century increases in enclosures in the English countryside deprived numerous peasant farmers of their livelihoods—the problem is referred to both in Thomas More's 1516 *Utopia* and in Shakespeare's 1594 *Richard II*[46]—and swelled the ranks of the homeless vagrants; a large number of these turned to crime to feed themselves, and those who did not were subject to suspicion. Gámini Salgádo has sifted Renaissance texts like Greene's and Harman's to compile the vast lexicon of new terms that had sprung into being by century's end to describe such wanderers: "*Abraham man*" (a real or feigning ex-inmate of Bedlam), *"cony-catcher"* (itinerant card-hustler), *"chapman"* (peddler of shoddy goods), *"punk"* (prostitute), *"curber"* (thief), and *"Egyptian"* (gypsy) are a few.[47] That Shakespeare was influenced by such literary depictions of such characters, as well, no doubt, by real experience of such folk, is evident in his creation of *The Winter's Tale*'s roguish peddler Autolycus, who follows the "highway," whose "traffic is sheets" (business is stealing drying laundry), and whose "revenue is the silly cheat" (4.3.27–29). Shakespeare also gives us *King Lear*'s Tom O'Bedlam, a pretend madman who calls his lonely walk a "pilgrimage" (5.3.197). In an interesting late-seventeenth-century reversal of poor Tom, the real Christian pilgrims of John Bunyan's *The Pilgrim's Progress* are mistaken for "Bedlams and Mad" by the inhabitants of Vanity Fair.[48]

Such really or apparently roguish wanderers had their romantic aspect, or were granted it by Renaissance literature and the Renaissance stage. The traveling printing press of the bishop mocker "Martin Marprelate," a scandalous Puritan author of the 1580s, was jestingly called "The Pilgrim's Press."[49] One step ahead of the law that sought to censor him (and finally did), Marprelate—whose real name was Thomas Penry—was not only widely read, but a wandering hero to those of his religious persuasion. In addition, travelers' tales were as widely read as coney-catching pamphlets, and New World adventurers captured readers' imagination with their exaggerated stories about customs in Ireland, on the Continent, and even in the New World. In his seminal article "Invisible Bullets," Stephen Greenblatt shows the link between pamphlets such as Harman's *Warning for Vagabonds*, on the one hand, and Hakluyt's later *Voyages and Navigations* (1589) and Harriot's *Briefe and True Report of the New Found Land of Virginia* (1593), on the other.[50] Both types of writing stemmed from, and were popularized by, a fascination with new horizons; with the adventures of footloose wanderers. On the stage, one such wanderer, Shakespeare's Othello, spellbinds the Venetian signiory with his "travel's history," a journey among "Rough quarries, rocks, and hills," "Cannibals," and monster-men that he calls "my pilgrimage" (1.3.141–53). *Love's Labor's Lost*'s braggart Don Armado thinks to impress his hearers by calling himself "a man of travel, that hath seen the world" (5.1.107–8). Armado is foolish, and in later plays Shakespeare mocked the "traveller" Jaques, who "sold [his] own lands to see other ones" (*As You Like It* 4.1.21–23), and "brave Master Shoe-tie the great traveller" (*Measure for Measure*

4.3.16–17). However, Shakespeare's rival Ben Jonson gives the traveler some credit. The con men whom Jonson mocks in *The Alchemist* and *Volpone* are firmly resident in city houses, while adventurers like *Volpone*'s Peregrine are made to look comparatively wise and attractive as a result of their travels. Jonson himself traveled widely both in Britain, on a walking tour to Scotland in 1618, and on the Continent, in 1612, as the tutor and chaperone of Sir Walter Ralegh's son. The Continental peregrinations of Jonson, an occasional Catholic, would certainly have included visits to famed shrines like that of Santiago de Compostela had he taken his trip before the Reformation and the growth of religious and political hostilities between England and Spain. As it was, rather than kneel before the sacred images of French and Spanish cathedrals, Jonson made himself a mock-holy spectacle. Carted through the streets of Paris by young Ralegh on Mardi Gras Day, he was described by his student to watching Parisians as "a more lively image of the Crucifix than any they had."[51] The antics of Jonson and his pupil illustrate the shift of English aristocratic interests from the pious shrine-bound journey to the "Grand Tour" for (alleged) cultural refinement.

Unlike noblemen like young Wat Ralegh—not to mention his father, the New World adventurer—Queen Elizabeth remained in England. Still, she did not always stay home. Whereas her father, Henry VIII, had gone in 1520 to pay homage at the shrine of St. Mary's at Walsingham, Elizabeth a half-century later staged herself for her people's veneration on costly royal "progresses." At the lower end of the social scale, traveling players journeyed from London to Bath to Coventry and among many points in between. The number of traveling players roaming the countryside began to swell in the decades just prior to England's formal repudiation of shrines and pilgrimage,[52] and though a 1572 law requiring players to be licensed lessened their number,[53] many groups, including Catholic players in the north, still wandered, some in defiance of the statute.[54] Theirs was an example of vagabondage so magically tempting it drew Shakespeare away from his Stratford life.

The variety of glamorous wanderings available for doing, witnessing, or merely imagining by the Renaissance English included New World trading ventures, which combined commercial interests with the romantic appeal of journeys to remote places. Jean Howard has recently written of how Renaissance playwrights adapted new English interests in geography and commerce to a genre she calls "adventure plays," like Thomas Heywood's *Fair Maid of the West*, in which a woman captains a ship and makes her fortune thereby.[55] Shakespeare's *The Merchant of Venice* shares such plays' interest in lucrative journeying, and demonstrates the new literary use of the language of religious piety to describe secular ventures. Though *Merchant* is set in Catholic Italy, among its worldly businessmen, religious expeditions give way in mind and practice to commercial expeditions. "Should I go to church," the merchant Salerio asks, "And see the holy edifice of stone, / And not bethink me straight of dangerous rocks / Which touching but my gentle vessel's side / Would scatter all her spices on the stream . . . ?" (1.1.29–36). Salerio, who travels mentally while his ships venture physically forth, is the secular equivalent of the wealthy late-medieval "pilgrim" who, too busy, ill, or fearful to travel himself or herself, paid a mendicant to journey to a shrine with an offering, and thus accomplished pilgrimage and acquired spiritual benefits by proxy.[56]

Of course, as noted above, some commercial "pilgrims" performed their peregrinations in person, and thrilled readers with the stories of their experiences. I have mentioned the popularity of Hakluyt's and Harriot's travel narratives and the adventurous example set by the elder Walter Ralegh, who in 1596 published his account of his travels to Guiana. In Hakluyt's introduction to *Navigations* Hakluyt proudly characterizes the English as "men full of activity, stirrers abroad, and searchers of the most remote parts of the world."[57] The sentence brings to mind a celebrated passage in Greenblatt's *Renaissance Self-Fashioning*, where Greenblatt describes Marlowe's tragic hero Tamburlaine, who "almost ceaselessly traverses the stage," as a living symbol of English early-modern zeal for global voyaging.[58] Greenblatt does not note that such early-modern "Marlovian" restlessness was once partly satisfied by the rigors, entertainments, and even the spiritual challenges of medieval pilgrimage.

England's sixteenth- and seventeenth-century global "stirring" was unabashedly economically motivated—Hakluyt describes trade opportunities in Aleppo, Africa, and the Levant, and calls the "inland" part of the northern American continent "rich and abundant in silver mines, . . . apt and capable of all commodities"—but was religiously inspired as well. By merchant adventuring, Hakluyt writes, Protestant England may accomplish miracles: may "work many great and unlooked for effects, increase her dominions, enrich her coffers, and reduce many pagans to the faith of Christ."[59] Thus Englishmen and Englishwomen might fulfill Christ's command to all Christians, "Go into all the worlde, & preache the Gospel to everie creature" (Mark 16:15).[60] In 1609 a Virginia Company stakeholder called one New World venture "a Voyage, wherin every Christian ought to set to his helping hand, seeing the Angell of Virginia cryeth out to [England], as the Angell of Macedonnia did to *Paul, O come and helpe us!*"[61] Walter Ralegh, who staked (and lost) his fortunes, reputation, and life on a promise to find gold for the English crown in Guiana, also displays a mixture of capitalist and religious impulses in his description of his commercial pilgrimage. Guiana is "rich in gold, or in other merchandizes. . . . All places yeild abundance of cotten, of silke, of *balsamum*"; further, the country "hath yet her maydenhead": native "graves have not beene opened for gold," and their pagan "images"—a word irresistibly associated in the Protestant mind with Catholic churches—have not yet been "pulld down out of their temples."[62] The graves *will* be dug up, of course, and the images pulled down, Raleigh implies. That the replacement of pagan with Christian "temples" is part of his mercantile enterprise is clear from his apology to his readers for not having performed these desecrations already. "If wee shoulde have grieved them in their religion at the first, before they had beene taught better, and have digged up their graves, wee had lost them all."[63] Lost the natives' souls or their gold? Doubtless Ralegh means both. By the mid-seventeenth century, the championing of commerce had become part of the zealous rhetoric of the Puritans' Rump Parliament, which appointed a Council of Trade. Henry Parker, an outspoken member of that Parliament, declared in 1648, "If we have any desire to be more formidable to our [Catholic] enemies, or more aidful to our friends, . . . [commercial] traffic may be held sufficient."[64]

One might locate the origin of the Protestant economic pilgrimage prior to the Reformation, in the impulse that launched the Crusades. Indeed, Hakluyt explicitly likens the modern lust for New World conquest to a medieval impulse which united pilgrimage and Holy War: the "desire of our nation to visit the Holy Land, and to expel the Saracens and Mahometans." In this same passage, Hakluyt characterizes Virginia and Mexico as the new fields of crusading conquest.[65] Of course, Holy Catholic Spain was no less restless in its imperial energies, or in its zeal for conversion of New World natives, than was its enemy, Protestant England, during the early-modern period. Yet Spanish imperialism dovetailed with the maintenance of traditional shrines which were the longstanding goals of Catholic pilgrimage in a way not possible or even thinkable for evangelical English Protestants. Sixteenth-century Spanish Jesuit missionaries such as Antonio de Montesinos and Bartolomé de Las Casas decried the enslavement and exploitation of Indians to mine New World gold and silver[66] which was then used not only to finance Spanish wars but to refurbish shrines such as that of Santiago de Compostela.[67] Among the Spanish there was thus a divergence between evangelism and support for pilgrimage. For the English, things were different, as Hakluyt's framing of his country's religious mission suggests. For English people committed to what Steven Pincus has called the new commercial society, evangelism and a new form of pilgrimage were connected. For a nation both imperialist and Protestant, the desacralization of Jerusalem and other erstwhile holy places globally expanded the field of religious mission. If no one place was the focus of Christian conquest, many places might be subject to Christian conquest. Calvin, while condemning journeys to holy sites, yet wrote, "Christ teaches us to travel as pilgrims in this world."[68]

Travel where, specifically? Not, apparently, to the lands of actual "Saracens and Mahometans." Ironically, despite Hakluyt's comparison of the Protestant English colonial and mercantile mission to the medieval "desire of our nation to visit the Holy Land" and expel infidels, early-modern English people recognized the impossibility of controlling and converting their Muslim contemporaries, whom expanded military and economic strength in the sixteenth and seventeenth centuries had made "powerful and dangerous," in the words of modern postcolonial scholar Nabil Matar. As Matar writes, by the sixteenth century even the inhabitants of Islamic North Africa, close to Europe, were regarded by the English as "peoples they did not and could not possess"; therefore "[n]othing like the colonialist venture was ever entertained in regard to [them]."[69] On the contrary, many English sailors, soldiers, and traders who ventured near the North African coast found themselves captured and enslaved by the Moors, and for these Britons "pilgrimage" became a matter of preserving their own English Protestant faith against the temptations to be "turn'd [into] Turks" (*Othello* 2.3.170): that is, converted to what they perceived as a religion of infidels. Thousands

of Britons were taken by Barbary privateers throughout the sixteenth and seventeenth centuries, and many of these were absorbed
into the cultures that captured them, converting to Islam.[70] This
phenomenon was "destabilizing" to the "emergent national identity" of a newly Protestant country[71] whose colonialist-apostolic mission called for the conversion of others to its *own* true faith. The
popular English narratives authored by those who had escaped, or
claimed to have escaped, captivity in Islamic countries were thus aggressive literary counterattacks on the seductions of Islamic culture;
testaments to the inner steadfastness of the captured Protestant.
Such a Christian's holy "journey" was, rather than spiritual travel, a
standing of ground: a refusal to surrender to the alluring cultural
and religious influences of his exotic environment, or to budge
from his inner England. In 1680 the New English sailor Joshua Gee
referred to his captivity in Algeria as such a "pilgrimage."[72]

Among peoples less economically and militarily powerful than the
North Africans, the English were better able to combine Protestant
spiritual steadfastness with the biblical apostolic mission urged by
Calvin. For the early-modern English, such Calvinist evangelical pilgrimage was partly grounded in the older views of the Lollards, who
according to Ritchie Kendall "translat[ed] pilgrimage into a metaphor for lifelong study and *dissemination* of biblical truth" (my emphasis).[73] The early-fifteenth-century Lollard author of *The Lanterne
of Liyt* wrote that, as "pilgrimes," priests should first cleanse their
minds by journeying into the Bible, and then "hiyen hem [hie
them] fast aboute in all the brood world to dele this goostlie tresour
among this witles peple."[74] This Lollard's objective was not the reclamation of holy places, just as the goal for later Protestants was not
the repossession of a specific sacred temple through militant pilgrimage to the Holy Land. To the Protestant mind there are, again,
no sacred places, only redeemed souls. Thus new Christian soldiers
might discharge their zeal not just by creating a New Jerusalem of
saints in America, as, on the deck of a New England–bound ship,
John Winthrop urged his pilgrim flock to do in 1620,[75] but by direct-
ing—"reduc[ing]," or leading back—newly encountered "pagan
nations to the faith of Christ," to recall Hakluyt's words. In this initiative, religious, military, and capitalist motives un-self-consciously
combine. In pulling down Indian temples and digging up Indian
graves, Ralegh writes, the "common [English] soldier shall . . . fight
for gold."[76]

An entertaining passage in the writings of John Foxe shows this other English author's imaginative conversion of shrines and, implicitly, journeys to visit them to secular capitalist adventuring, and also suggests the necessary militarism of such adventuring, an aspect also noted by Ralegh. In the popular *Acts and Monuments*—twenty-eight thousand unabridged copies of which were bought by the English between 1563 and 1616[77]—Foxe speaks of a French lieutenant-general who, in an early-sixteenth-century territorial dispute between France and Spain, demanded that the Jesuit Inquisitors of Arragon yield their silver saints' images to him to be melted into money. "'[F]or,' says he [to the Jesuits], 'while you possess them in the manner you do at present, they stand up in niches, useless and motionless, without being of the least benefit to mankind; but when they come into my possession, they shall be useful. I will put them in motion, for I intend to have them coined, when they may travel like the apostles.'" The saints are not only idols, but idle. This must change. For Foxe, the hero of this dispute is not, of course, the Jesuits, but the lieutenant-general—"though brought up a Roman Catholic," a man remarkably "free from superstition"— who finally invaded the Jesuits' church, melted the saints' images into coin that could journey for God "like the apostles," and released the priests' prisoners, including "sixty beautiful young women, who appeared to form a seraglio for the three principal inquisitors."[78]

Foxe doesn't say what the soldiers did with the women. Yet his inclusion of "beautiful" females in his summary of the Frenchmen's military and religious achievement, like Walter Ralegh's description of Guiana as a "country that hath yet her maydenhead,"[79] instances the English Renaissance application of older erotic associations of pilgrimage to modern imperialist ventures. When Ralegh imagines Guiana as a woman and claims he convinced the Guianans the English had come to defend them "from invasion," he indulges a "fantasy . . . of a conquest by love rather than violence," to quote Mary Fuller.[80] Erotic pictures frequently adorned late-sixteenth-century writings that urged New World voyages; Louis Montrose notes that "[b]y the 1570s, allegorical personifications of America as a female nude with feathered headdress had begun to appear in engravings and paintings, on maps and title pages," in Europe.[81] Interestingly, it was the Protestant northern countries that applied such erotic words and images to their imperialist missions, as though in those nations the erotic wanderlust once truly or vicariously fulfilled by pilgrimages and travel tales had been displaced onto fantasies of territorial conquest.[82]

The new spirit of commercial "pilgrimage" was criticized by some early-modern English Protestants, notably Donne and Milton, whose work adapted pilgrimage to different uses. Less intent than Ralegh and Foxe's French lieutenant-general on real geographical conquest, Renaissance poets and playwrights often adapted the erotic associations of pilgrimage *exclusively* to depictions of romantic encounter. In such depictions female characters, naked or otherwise, do not symbolize unconquered countries, though unconquered countries occasionally symbolize them. John Donne once calls his mistress his "America," his "new-found land," but more frequently compares her to an enshrined saint.[83] A 1599 published miscellany of love poems by Shakespeare, Marlowe, and others was titled *The Passionate Pilgrim.* In *The Merchant of Venice,* Portia's wooers come "From the four corners of the earth / To kiss this shrine, this mortal breathing saint" (2.7.39–40). Shakespeare's women would walk "barefoot to Palestine," not for spiritual benefits, but for "a touch" of a man's "nether lip" (*Othello* 4.3.38–39). When there were no official saints, not only objects of erotic devotion but admired friends might be "canonized." Without fear of sacrilege, Robert Herrick calls his drinking companion Ben Jonson "Saint Ben" in his whimsical poem "His Prayer to Ben Jonson." "For old religion's sake, / . . . Candles I'll give to thee, / And a new altar," Herrick promises.[84] And if good friends were saints, then the physical seats of their gracious kindness enshrined them, and became, in some poems, the goals of blessed journeys. Andrew Marvell's poem to Lord Fairfax, "Upon Appleton House," predicts an "after age" when folk who have heard of the hospitality afforded at the great houses of Fairfax and others "shall hither come in pilgrimage, / these sacred places to adore" (ll. 34–35).[85]

These playful poetic framings of lovers and friends as saints, and secular journeys as pilgrimage, were the outgrowth of a Protestant culture's serious rejection not only of the worship of saints but of the idea of them as intermediaries, spiritual entities who might profitably be prayed to. It is with zealous purpose that John Foxe applauds his French lieutenant-general's destruction of saints' images in a Spanish church (and that Francis Drake, as we are told, read from Foxe's work to his saint-honoring Spanish prisoners off the Mexican coast).[86] Calvin calls the veneration of saints "stupidity."[87] The Thirty-Nine Articles of the English Church declared "Invocations of Saints" a "fond thing, vainly invented, and grounded upon no warranty of Scripture, but rather repugnant to the Word of God" (Article 22). The early-sixteenth-century Bible translator Miles Coverdale warned of the fruitlessness of all prayer aimed at all intermediaries save Christ, and the vanity of belief that one might communicate with departed human souls, beatific or otherwise. "Let no man . . . be moved by those deceitful spirits which, as they say, do appear unto men, and desire their help, praying that masses, pilgrimages, and other like superstitious ceremonies, may be done for them," he wrote.[88] As both Article 22 and Coverdale's statement suggest, the Reformers grounded their rejection of saints and pilgrimages in the English Bible. Thus in 1528 had the Protestant martyr William Tyndale repudiated pilgrimage. In *The Obedience of a Christian Man* (1528), Tyndale cited Paul's Epistle to the Romans to prove that Christians need not "run hither or thither, to Rome, to Jerusalem, or Saint James or any other pilgrimage far or near, to be saved thereby. . . . For a Christian man's health and salvation is within him: even in his mouth . . . saith Paul."[89]

The Protestant denial of the salvific value of prayers to saints and journeys to shrines led to a final permutation of the idea of pilgrimage in Protestant England. This might be called the *interiorization* of holy pilgrimage. Although pilgrimage had always been a Christian metaphor for spiritual journey, to Protestants, the *only* meaningful Christian journey is an inward one. Wrongly "ye will . . . say, that ye will go to this or that place because God hath chosen one place more than another and will hear your petition more in one place than another. . . . If thou believe in Christ, and hast the promises which God hath made thee in thine heart, then go on pilgrimage unto thine own heart and there pray," wrote Tyndale in his prologue to Numbers.[90] "[W]e are but pilgrims made, / And should in soul up to our countrey move," Philip Sidney wrote in *Astrophil and Stella*.[91] Such pilgrims, moving *only* "in soul," are a far cry from Chaucer's Canterbury-bound group, traveling by horseback to seek the "holy blissful martir." English adventurers like Walter Ralegh, and their admirers like Richard Hakluyt, thought the spiritual benefit of remote travels would accrue (and was necessary) not chiefly to the English, but to those native Americans, Africans, East Indians, or even Catholics whom the English might convert. Even the less (than Ralegh and Hakluyt) materially motivated Pilgrim Separatists, who left England starting in 1620, did not foresee spiritual progress resulting from distance traversed. (They had, of course, initially intended to go only to Holland, until their dismay at Dutch worldliness inspired their ocean journey.)[92] Those Pilgrims who went to New England found themselves, prior to departure, already inwardly transformed by Christ and spiritually placed on the hard, narrow way to which the Gospels liken salvation (Matt. 12:13).[93] Their "map" was either the Geneva or the King James Bible, and their journey one of reading and applying scripture to their lives. Certainly they traveled, and traveled far, but their removal to the wilderness to build New Jerusalem was a flight *from* the old church rather than a reverent (or even an irreverent) earthly journey *to* one of that church's sanctifying shrines. The Jerusalem that Pastor John Winthrop thought awaited his flock in America was thus not so much a place as a time. Not a site that would sanctify visitors, America was a place English settlers would, over time, sanctify. ("Come over and help us," an Indian is depicted saying on the Massachusetts Bay Company's seal.)[94] Winthrop's "city upon a hill" was one God would birth from the holy ambition the Pilgrims now bore within them. Further, the Pilgrim plantation would not be an end point of a holy journey but a model for the reverent settlements of future Protestant "pilgrims." "[M]en shall say of succeeding plantations: 'The Lord make it like that of New England,'" preached Winthrop.[95]

Of course, the Protestant redirecting of holy journey to an inward place had Catholic roots. Early Christian anchorites, in their writings, at times employed pilgrimage as a metaphor for spiritual travel, and Tertullian and Augustine frequently called the Christian a "peregrinus": a pilgrim who journeyed, not toward an earthly shrine, but to Heaven. By "peregrinus" both Tertullian and Augustine meant to suggest the Christian's status as—in Tertullian's words—"a stranger to this world and all of its customs,"[96] in conformance with Latin translations of both Peter's and Paul's letters, which called Christians "peregrinii" on earth (1 Pet. 2:11, Heb. 11:13).[97] Stephanie Hayes-Healey has distinguished between two types of pilgrimage in early-medieval tradition, "goal-oriented pilgrimage"—travel to a specific shrine to pray for a saint's assistance—and pilgrimage "not as a concrete act but a state of existence," by which devout Christians, such as the sixth-century Irish monk Columbanus, took permanently to the road as meditative ascetics, in "an extreme form of devotion."[98] Yet Hayes-Healey's distinction is too absolute, since both types of early-medieval pilgrimage were, in fact, both "goal-oriented" and "concrete act[s]": spiritual practices which bodied forth a Catholic commitment to realizing spiritual grace in the physical things of this world. Each of the types of medieval pilgrimage that Hayes-Healey discerns involved progressive physical journeys, whether its end was a shrine where a saint might be honored and supplicated, or a state of continual mendicancy, whereby Christians might physically enact their true identity as "peregrinii" and render their souls increasingly fit for the heavenly city. Purgatory, of course, was another stage of the journey as Catholics construed it, and was likewise a liminal phase in which pilgrimage was both "goal-oriented" and a "state of existence." We recall that the souls in Dante's Purgatory are "pilgrims" bound on a "steep," "broken," and "tortuous way," climbing up a mountainside to Heaven (*Purgatorio*, canto 2, ll. 63, 65). Luther and those who followed him dispensed with this phase of the holy journey as readily as they dispensed with earthly pilgrimage, when they refuted Purgatory's existence. Pre-Reformation Christians believed that through prayer, meditation, or other spiritual work—done in the cloister, on the road, or in some posthumous middle ground between earth and Heaven—one might *incrementally* approach God. That belief was denied by Protestant writers, even those who used "pilgrimage" as a metaphor for the spiritual relation between humans and God.[99]

Indeed, Protestant writers imagined the inward pilgrimage as something distinctly different from the spiritual journey envisioned in monastic writings (such as the *Institutes* of the fourth-century monk John Cassian), in the works of Tertullian and Augustine, and in Dante's *Divina Commedia*. While, as I have suggested, the *arrived* (or redeemed) pilgrim might travel to evangelize, his evangelical mission was the fruit and expression of his achieved salvation, and not a way toward it. This Christian's Protestant inward journey had been exclusively "mapped" by the Bible, and the already-saved pilgrim who followed this map resisted unscripted reflection or meditation. Following the Lollards, Protestants repudiated not only shrine pilgrimage, but mendicancy and the cloister, and championed this reformed (arrived) Christian pilgrim's evangelical witness. Such a pilgrim is akin to Plato's philosopher, who returns from the sunlit world to the dark cave to share his understanding with the be-

nighted. His sunward pilgrimage was inner; his return from it is duti-
ful work in the outer world.

In addition, English Protestants' *exclusive* religious use of the pilgrimage metaphor—when they used it approvingly—to signify inward spiritual processes was an early-modern outgrowth of late-
medieval skepticism regarding the value of outward pilgrimage to
shrines. We recall that Chaucer, who does not directly question the
sanctity of holy journey, yet makes his most carnal characters his
most inveterate pilgrims (the lusty Wife of Bath, who seeks a sixth
husband, has "thryes . . . been at Ierusalem," and has visited Rome,
"Boloigne," "seint Iame, and . . . Coloigne"). In his more harshly
satirical *Piers Plowman*, Langland prefaces his condemnation of braggart "palmeris" with praise for "ancris and ermytes that holden hem
in here sellis" and "Coveite not in cuntre to cairen aboute" [ancho-
rites and hermits that hold to their cells, coveting not in the country
to careen about] (ll. 28–29). Though fifteenth-century Lollards rejected the strictly eremitical life praised by Langland, they approvingly used the word "pilgrimes" to describe "prestis [priests] that
studien holi writ" in their own parishes (*The Lanterne of Liyt*).[100] The
German monk Thomas Kempis's *Imitation of Christ*, known abroad
by 1418,[101] also questioned the spiritual benefit of holy journeying,
reminding Christians that salvation was an inward process that
might better occur at home. "Many people travel far to honor the
relics of the saints, marveling at their wonderful deeds and at the
building of magnificent shrines," Thomas Kempis wrote. "They
gaze upon and kiss the sacred relics encased in silk and gold; and
[yet] behold, You are here present before me on the altar, my God,
Saint of saints . . . !"[102] A hundred years after Kempis was read by
English Lollards, his views were affirmed in a warning spoken in a
Renaissance play: John Heywood's Palmer is told a pilgrim's "pain"
is "more than his wit / To walk to heaven, since he may sit!" (ll.
356–57).

My intention here has been, however summarily, to acknowledge
the late-medieval roots of Heywood's skepticism about physical holy
pilgrimage, as well as the later Renaissance flowerings of secular,
commercial-imperial, erotic, and evangelical traveling. In the chapters to come I will explore various transformations of the holy journey—to amorous, military, and capitalistic adventuring and to inner
spiritual travel—as they are recorded and elaborated in the work of

five later sixteenth- and seventeenth-century English authors. Other scholars have written of the destructive effect of Reformation iconoclasm on Renaissance art.[103] My focus, to the contrary, is on the creative results of iconoclasm: on the extraordinary growth of new literary notions of pilgrimage that grew from the loss of English Catholic shrines and the pilgrimages that supported them. As David Daniell has recently written, "liberation from the threat of charges of heresy" in Reformed England "allowed . . . new powers of imagination and inventiveness that were grasped by the poets."[104] If saints to whose shrines medieval pilgrims had traveled were no longer sacrosanct, writers could do wild, irreverent things with their images in drama and literature. The notion of Purgatory has recently been shown to have undergone a like metamorphosis in the 1600s: Stephen Greenblatt has proposed that Catholic belief in Purgatory and the attendant "cult of the dead," involving prayers for the souls of the deceased, were displaced in Protestant England from religious to imaginative life, finding fanciful expression in Renaissance poems and plays.[105] I would argue that English belief in the efficacy of pilgrimage underwent a similar displacement, albeit one that was more gradual, more rooted in both medieval monasticism and late-medieval social criticism, and more supported by physical transformations of what had once been a religious practice. (By this last I mean that some Renaissance English people directed energies their forebears had spent in pilgrimage toward military, capitalist, and world-exploratory adventures.)

Book 1 of Edmund Spenser's *The Faerie Queene* (1590) is a good place to start. *The Faerie Queene* displays a rich appreciation for the world of shrines, images, and holy pilgrimage it is paradoxically compelled to destroy. Spenser's epic partly resolves that contradiction by his "narrativizing" of images: he renders idols like enshrined saints acceptable by turning them into poetry.[106] As text, they symbolize spiritual virtues realized by study of the Bible, or even Christ—the incarnate Word—himself. Still, even with images so re-sanctified (and sanitized), Spenser's Protestant transformation of shrine pilgrimage to the inwardness of Bible study coexists uneasily with his early-modern—and also Protestant—call to militant evangelical witness in the world. It is also incongruent with his duty, as a courtier and nobleman, to pay homage in *The Faerie Queene* to Queen Elizabeth's visually dazzling person and opulent court.

These competing imperatives grow partly from the general Christian struggle between worldliness and godliness, but also from the conflict between medieval Catholic and early-modern Protestant beliefs, a conflict seen also in Spenser's imposition of Protestant ideas on a Catholic medieval literary framework. Spenser draws from medieval romance the quest narrative that was itself associated with the cult of saints, relics, and shrines. Yet he inverts narratives such as Malory's account of Percival's Grail quest, making the Redcrosse Knight's journey an occasion for explicit, bitter rejection of Catholic idolatries, including pilgrimages. Furthermore, by structuring his work as an allegory, wherein the "places" to which Redcrosse goes are spiritual trials through which he passes, Spenser offers an early Protestant literary version of the pilgrimage as inward journey. Of course, spiritual transformation is a crucial outgrowth of the knight's geographical travels and physical trials in medieval romances, as well as in sixteenth-century Continental romances like Ariosto's *Orlando Furioso* (1516) and Montalvo's *Amadis de Gaul* (1505). In those Continental works, however, external travel and inner change, while related, are distinct processes, each with ontological status. In the English *Faerie Queene*, in contrast, travels and physical trials are wholly subsumed, indeed made explicable by—in a phrase, symbolic of—the spiritual changes undergone by the hero. But for the unassimilable passages when the Red Cross Knight is charged with fighting Elizabeth's foreign battles, outer landscape *is* inner landscape in Spenser's poem.

Shakespeare, like Spenser, often links characters' inner transformations to their changes in locality (Demetrius's maturation in a wood outside Athens and the growing savagery of Othello once he's left Venice for war-threatened Cyprus are comic and tragic examples). However, Shakespeare applies the language of pilgrimage chiefly to real journeys which, in themselves, work no inner changes in those who undergo them. Instead these journeys demonstrate pilgrims' willing bondage to an ideal of honor or an erotic passion that spurs them on. Unlike his contemporary Jonson, whose plays' actions were concentrated in city houses, Shakespeare used the wide public stage as a space on which playwright, actors, and audience could project a series of imagined travels: from Rousillon to Florence or England to Wales in the comedies and romances, from Eastcheap to Shrewsbury or London to France in the history plays.

Those history plays, particularly the Henry plays of the Second Tetralogy, set in the early fifteenth century, skeptically dramatize England's late-medieval redirecting of veneration from Christian to secular "saints," chiefly the royal heroes of its own military past. In so doing, the plays stage the rechanneling of pilgrimage energies into expeditions of conquest. In the sixteenth century, the grave of Edward the Black Prince replaced Becket's shrine as the end point of journeys to Canterbury Cathedral. Shakespeare's *Henry V* effaces Becket's sainthood completely, and in Becket's place elevates both the Black Prince, who is the "lion's whelp" (1.2.109), and Henry the Fifth, "mirror of all Christian kings" (2.Cho.6), for English adoration. Proper reverence towards both conquerors involves the violent "pilgrimage" of military adventure, really or imaginatively executed, a sort of "holy journey" which *Henry V* lays open to moral question.

Yet Shakespearean pilgrimage is as often impelled by love as by notions of military honor. In comedy, romance, and even tragedy, Shakespeare provides many of his global wanderers with romantic motives. Pericles sails from Tyre to Tarsus "look[ing] . . . for love" (*Pericles* 1.4.99). Following Proteus to Milan, Julia is a "true-devoted pilgrim," empowered "To measure kingdoms with [Love's] feeble steps" (*The Two Gentlemen of Verona* 2.7.9–10). *All's Well That Ends Well*'s Helena disguises herself as a palmer bound for Compostela, but in fact heads for Florence to pursue a wayward husband. The dressing of lovesick characters with the language or garb of pilgrims is a literary tradition that dates back at least as far as Petrarch, and yet Shakespeare uses the conceit quite differently than did the Italian poet. When Petrarch writes of love's pilgrimage, he contrasts his enslavement by Eros, fictive divinity, with the appropriate servitude he should grant God. In one sonnet, his quest for Laura's "blessed image" feels like an old man's journey to Rome to seek God's likeness, but is not the same (Sonnet 16). The old man's pilgrimage is the real and valid one. In another sonnet, "a passing pilgrim [leads his] heart astray / Because she b[ears] Love's colors in her face," but the poet stops following her when God reminds him "How many steps [he's] wasted in the wild" (Sonnet 54).[107] This religious dimension, so strong in Petrarch's work, recedes in Shakespeare's love pilgrimages, which become, if not wholly secular, wholly erotic. Eros replaces rather than wars with God. In Shakespeare there is no sense that traditional pilgrimages are being wickedly diverted to the pursuit of carnal love (we are glad the disguised Helena ends up in Florence rather than Compostela). In the comedies and romances, the worship Shakespeare's passionate pilgrims bestow on their lovers is nearly always undeserved, but the pilgrims' journeys, so far from being wrong, help reform the inadequate lovers (if not the pilgrim), and are essential to the comic result.[108] Only in a tragedy such as *Othello* does Shakespeare explore the self-damaging potential of erotic idolatry, and even there he does not, like Petrarch, negatively oppose such idolatry to traditional Catholic forms of religious reverence. In plays of comic or tragic eros, the idea of Christian pilgrimage is wholly subdued by Shakespeare's romantic conceit.

While Shakespeare's actors physically enact erotic pilgrimage on the stage, John Donne uses written verse to create love pilgrimages exclusively in words. I have mentioned Donne's likening of lovers to saints, as he does most famously in "The Canonization." There the passion that binds Donne to his lover inspires a wholly secular withdrawal into a "hermitage" shared by two (line 38). This retreat, imaginatively constructed by means of the poem, is a flight from outward paths which are no less secular: the busy world's concern with "ruined fortune," "arts," and court "place" (ll. 3–5).[109] Yet Donne playfully imagines folk of the outer world forsaking such pursuits and remaking his "hermitage" into an erotic shrine. "[A]ll shall" reverently travel to him and his lover to request their intercession with a God who wants to improve everyone's erotic practices ("'beg from above / A pattern of your love!'" [ll. 44–45]). Perhaps better than any other literary or dramatic work, "The Canonization," with its elaborately eroticized vision of the holy journey, reveals the complete desacralization notions of traditional pilgrimage had undergone by the early seventeenth century in England.

Yet Donne's sacred verse shows the power that the pilgrimage trope, reconstituted to convey a Protestant religious sensibility, still held to evoke a sense of spiritual struggle. Donne's religious poetry describes Christian journey as a paradoxical *anti*pilgrimage: a quest to return home from the paths of waywardness; to enter the doorway of salvation that is present and at hand. As we have seen, some earlier, Catholic authors like Thomas Kempis proposed that stationary reverence had a spiritual value superior to that of physical pilgrimage. "You are here present before me on the altar, my God, saint of saints!" Kempis wrote. Yet by the early seventeenth century, English writers influenced by Calvinist theology lacked Kempis's confidence that one might *be* comfortably at home with Christ simply by staying put and in a state of grace. According to Calvin, salvation is available only to the elect, whom God has called, and "it daily happens that those who seemed to be Christ's, fall away from him again, and hasten to destruction."[110] Donne's poetry uses the conceit of pilgrimage to figure the soul's own tendency so to "fall away," to depart onto wrong inward pathways. In Holy Sonnet Number 4 Donne likens his "black soul" to "a pilgrim, which abroad hath done / Treason, and durst not turn to whence he is fled."[111] Here pilgrimage is a metaphor not for spiritual purification, but for a fall from grace. It signifies sin. The pilgrim's journey abroad has been criminal rather than blessed. Travel has facilitated his treason, or betrayal of his true country—implicitly associated with Heaven—and has made the salvific journey home impossible on his own strength.

When we turn from Donne to Milton, we see in the later, Puritan author's work a heightened interest in both the pilgrim's Christian conversion and the complications of erroneous spiritual traveling. For Milton, proper inward pilgrimage is related to reading, to intellectual work. The replacement of the shrine-bound palmer by the pilgrim reader may perhaps be expected in an age for which the new "saints," so commonly called, were martyred Bible translators like William Tyndale and the posthumously burned John Wycliffe.[112] For such a reader, Milton's prose and poetry are presented as powerful complements to and even extensions of scripture that, properly digested by reason, lead the sinner to conversion. Paradoxically, *Paradise Lost* means to convert what Brian Hampton[113] calls the "pilgrim reader," first through a graphic depiction of diabolical pilgrimage. In *Paradise Lost,* the initial sin—here not Adam's, but the erring angels'—is punished by a painful vertical journey that is memorably evoked by references to both time and space. Lucifer is "Hurled headlong flaming from th'ethereal sky / . . . To bottomless perdition," where he lies "Nine times the space that measures day and night" (book 1.45–50).[114] For Milton, sin—in punishment or commission—is involved with travel, and with insistence on going alone, or disdain for community. The antipilgrimage from God is a flying away, an alienation of the soul from its proper place. Curiously, this is so even when Satan's voyage to Eden takes him physically upward from Hell and in closer proximity to Heaven. The mission which brings him geographically closer to God only intensifies the two's spiritual separation. Further, Satan's circuitous flight track demonstrates the crookedness of his purpose, and bodies forth his tortured, reticular reasoning, as "horror and doubt distract his troubled thoughts" (4.18–19). In Satan's progress—better termed a regress—Milton represents both ill-motivated physical journeying and spiritual waywardness. Fittingly, as Satan approaches a portion of Hell "since called the Limbo," as Milton's introduction says,[115] he encounters other errant travelers whose mazy wanderings are described as pilgrimages. In this province of the damned "pilgrims roam, that strayed so far to seek / In Golgotha him dead, who lives in Heav'n" (3.476–77). Here Milton likens Catholic pilgrimage to Mary Magdalene's fruitless search for Christ in the tomb from which he is risen. Milton's lines echo the question the angels ask Mary at the grave, "Why do you seek the living among the dead?" (Luke 24:5). Yet in Milton's conceit, the papist pilgrims do not even get so far as the tomb, but haunt Golgotha, the hill of Calvary, drawn towards Christ's death but shareless in the resurrection. Their wanderings end at the Place of the Skull.

This, finally, is where travel threatens to end in Bunyan's *The Pilgrim's Progress*, the most famous English work treating of pilgrimage since Chaucer's *The Canterbury Tales*. In part a coda to Reformation literary treatments of the holy journey, Bunyan's Restoration work recapitulates themes important to the pilgrimages described by various late-sixteenth- and earlier seventeenth-century English authors. Though his most profound textual influence was the Bible, Bunyan was also a student of Spenser. He assumes Spenser's allegorical method and, while discarding the chivalric conventions of *The Faerie Queene*, revisits much of that epic's first book's spiritual territory, including the province of Despair, wherein the pilgrim Christian finds his journey halted. Bunyan's dream narrative also repeats, in a more serious register, the references to sainted idol-kings with which Shakespeare sported in his Henry plays, and passes judgment (as, to an extent, did Shakespeare and Donne themselves) on the erotic pilgrimages celebrated in both Shakespeare's romantic plays and Donne's profane verse. Bunyan's work also recalls Milton's epic poem and his prose work *Areopagitica* in its emphasis on the importance of shared spiritual journeying and communal dialogue.

Finally, like Spenser, Donne, and Milton, Bunyan invokes the transformational power of blessed reading, but also makes the danger of inward spiritual wandering his argument. As Stanley Fish says, Christian's walk is "anti-progressive,"[116] a series of threatened slippings-away from Christ's dwelling into the slough of despond and other traps of despair. What Bunyan calls his hero's "pilgrimage" is "a desperate venture,"[117] an effort to return himself to the road he could see, by the light of scripture, from the outset of his travels. Continually distracted by tempting pathways, he strives to move not forward, but back. His salvation, through Christ, is given and assured; his sense of constant threat, paradoxically, as much evidence of that salvation as the godly evangelical work he performs on his way. By fearing the damnable traps that the earthly pilgrimage offers, and accepting repeated redirection to the "King's Highway," Bunyan's Christian avoids the complacency that is the hallmark of false, effectively Hellbound pilgrims.

The work of Bunyan and the other Protestant religious writers treated herein reminds us that to the Protestant mind, salvation is not a progress. Protestantism offers no purgatorial journey to be rehearsed (and shortened) in life by physical acts of pilgrimage. "[T]o believe that God will be sought more in one place than another, or that God will hear thee more in one place than in another . . . is a false faith, and idolatry, or image-service," Tyndale wrote.[118] "See him plaguing himself," Luther says of the sinner, "going on pilgrimages to St. Iago. And yet it is in vain; with all these works he will merit nothing but hell-fire. He will not find Christ, who alone reconciles the father to us, forgives sin, brings God's grace, and leads us from hell to heaven."[119] As Luther elsewhere writes, journeys to shrines, like other works, are distractions from faith and repentance, for God saves the sinner "not according to [his] . . . running." Such movement "beat[s] the air only."[120]

Thus the Protestant pilgrimage in English Renaissance literature is either desacralized—transformed to erotic, military, or commercial adventure—or turned back on itself, so it becomes an inward spiritual struggle against our own alienation from God, who is our home. Properly understood, the Protestant "pilgrimage" is no pilgrimage at all, but a cessation of flight along worldly physical *and* spiritual paths. The maverick Milton, as we will see, gives some credit to the pilgrim for his work, but for most Protestant authors, even the pilgrim's regress is accomplished not by the Christian's own efforts, but by God, who—in the words of John Donne—"like adamant" draws the sinner's "iron heart."[121] In George Herbert's terms, the weary Christian's very exhaustion will "toss him to [God's] breast."[122] The trajectory of that homeward spiritual movement has been memorably traced in the lines of a twentieth-century English poet: "the end of all our exploring / Will be to arrive where we started / And know the place for the first time."[123]

2

Protestant Pilgrimage and Secular State in Book 1 of Spenser's *The Faerie Queene*

[N]ext care in religion is to build upp and repaire all the ruined
Churches. . . . to have them builte in some better forme accordinge to the Churches of Englande.

Edmund Spenser, *The Vewe of the Present State of Ireland*[1]

MIDWAY THROUGH BOOK 1 OF SPENSER'S *THE FAERIE QUEENE*, THE HERO-
ine Una meets a man Spenser calls "the Pilgrim" (1.6.38).[2] He walks
"in simple weedes forworne, / And soild with dust of the long driéd
way," and wears "sandales" that are "with toilesome travell torne."
He bears a "Jacobs staff." With his staff, worn shoes, and threadbare
garb, his face "tand" by the summer sun, he fits the conventional
description of the wide-ranging palmer, wearied by travel in the East
(he looks "as he had traveild . . . / Through boyling sands of Arabie
and Ynde" [1.6.35]). And, not surprisingly in a late-sixteenth-
century Protestant epic, this Catholic pilgrim turns out to be no holy
man, but a treacherous magician, one Archimago, who has earlier
brought division between Una and her Redcrosse Knight, and now
seeks to pain her further by telling her (falsely) that Redcrosse is
dead.

The trusting Una and the rustic Satyrane, her present companion,
believe the lie of the Pilgrim (a deceiver who also haunts book 2 of
the epic). But the very road dust that bespeaks Archimago's "holy"
wanderings makes him suspect to Spenser's Protestant readers. This
is a character who seeks the living among the dead. He venerates
shrines, images, relics, and earthly *places*, and does not follow the
inward, scripturally guided path to salvation.[3]

Yet an interpretive problem arises. How can pilgrimage to earthly
places be wrong, when four cantos later the Redcrosse Knight himself is told his "painefulle pilgrimage" to the new "Hierusalem," or

Heaven, must be earned through an earthly journey to "Cleopolis" (1.10.61, 59)? In canto 10, instructed by a genuinely holy "agéd man" (1.10.59), an opposite to the disguised Archimago, Redcrosse is promised sainthood only if he arrives at the earthly "Hierusalem" (Cleopolis), which is the Faerie Queene's glorious court and an image of London, Queen Elizabeth's seat of power. The holiness so earned will also be curiously earthbound, or regional. Following the knight's service to Cleopolis, his "owne nations frend, / And Patrone" he "shalt calléd bee, / Saint George of mery England, the signe of victoree" (1.10.61).

The contradiction is unresolvable in the poem. It cannot be vanquished by *The Faerie Queene*'s dominant definition of pilgrimage as spiritual journey mapped by the Bible, nor fully explained by its expected Protestant emphasis on spreading the word on earth, because the "Hierusalem" passage is tied to the glorification of a particular queen and city. That passage, along with subsequent ones in canto 12 which glorify Elizabeth's court, shows the poem's double consciousness. Here secular, state-driven ideology intrudes on the poem's inward-looking Calvinist vision. Inner landscape becomes, briefly, outer world, and Protestant pilgrimage idolatry.[4]

If the thematic shape of Redcrosse's journey in book 1 were sketched on paper, the resulting image might be of an hourglass turned on its side, with the right-hand portion of the vessel smaller than the portion on the left. For the first ten cantos Redcrosse travels inward. His conflicts with Archimago; the adversarial knights Sans Foy, Sans Loy, and Sans Joy (Faithless, Lawless, and Joyless); and Despair allegorize his spiritual difficulties. Those difficulties are resolved by his reunion with Una in canto 9 and sojourn in the House of Holiness in canto 10, and culminate in his vision of Heaven and its earthly image, Cleopolis, also in 10. After this point the eleventh and twelfth cantos express Redcrosse's journey outward, using allegory to signify events and enemies that exist, or are prophesied to occur one day, on the material plane. In these cantos Redcrosse engages the fearsome dragon of Catholic rule.[5] He then travels back to Cleopolis, or London, from whence, it is foreseen, he will again go out into the world at large to fight "six yeares in warlike wize" against "that proud Paynim king" (1.12.18): a phrase that rhetorically fuses England's Catholic enemies with Eastern pagans. (This fusion has been predicted earlier by the Catholic "pilgrim's" appearance, which has bespoken travels not to Compostela or Jeru-

salem, but to "Arabie and Ynde.") The whole of Redcrosse's pil-
grimage, inward and outward, will make him a saint ("Saint
George"). While traditionally such canonization would result in
Redcrosse's own enshrinement, making him the end point of pil-
grimages, Spenser is able to sanitize this "Catholic" reading because
of George's fully symbolic status. Spenser's contemporary Gerard de
Malynes could religiously refer to the "invented historie of S.
George" and call him a champion "under [whose] person . . . our
Saviour Christ was prefigured."[6]

Yet allegory does not resolve a fundamental incongruity between
the inward and outward journey book 1 describes. The problem,
again, lies not in the holy man's or, later, the redeemed Adam and
Eve's act of turning Redcrosse from an inward road onto the outward paths of Protestant evangelism. As my first chapter discussed,
and as I note above, the embrace of the great apostolic commission,
to fight error by sharing the gospel, was a duty of the redeemed or
"arrived" Protestant pilgrim. The difficulty here derives from the
violent character of the pilgrimage—it is war—and, again, from
Spenser's locating war-pilgrimage's starting inspiration not in Christ
(figured by Saint George) but in the city of Cleopolis and the person
of the queen. Spenser's doing so renders Redcrosse's final mission—the duty to return to Cleopolis and fight pagans—seem more
like a medieval Catholic enterprise than the Protestant reader has
been led to expect. The Catholic Crusades, in contrast to Protestant
holy wars, were tied to conventional pilgrimage, connected as they
were to the reclamation of holy places. That connection is made explicit in the introduction to Tasso's 1581 *Jerusalem Delivered*, where a
Christian bound to "free the mighty Sepulchre of Christ" is called
not only "knight" but "pilgrim" (canto 1, verses 1, 4).[7] As we have
seen, Protestants, unlike Tasso, refuted the belief in holy places like
"the mighty Sepulchre of Christ," and instead located sanctity in the
grace-dispensing word. Yet Spenser, though such a Protestant, stalls
himself with a paradox. Book 1 of *The Faerie Queene*, while denying
the blessedness of traditional shrines and sacred cities, still claims a
paradoxical holiness for Cleopolis. Thus for the Redcrosse Knight
holy pilgrimage is finally not a transformation of physical into spiritual Crusade, but a version of the traditional Crusade. Redcrosse will
not reclaim the Holy Land of Jerusalem but will extend England's
earthly holiness into other lands by defeating their Catholic sover-
eigns. Christopher Hodgkins has argued that English authors like

Spenser who spread the ethos of Protestant imperialism championed, not the reconquest of *special* cities or sites, but the general rescue of all whom Protestants saw as infidels, in *every* earthly place, from "spiritual and political bondage."[8] This was to be done by what we might call the "Englishing" of foreign lands: the extension, into far places, of the Protestant English cultural center. In book 1 of *The Faerie Queene*, Saint George, now the symbol of Christ, exists to glorify the imperial Protestant city, rather than the other way around.

When, in this book's next chapter, we examine Shakespeare's history plays, we will see this view of imperial pilgrimage made religiously innocuous by its relegation to a long-ago time, and to a field of theatrical fantasy. But Spenser's work, addressed to the queen and descriptive of England's present political situation, resists such Shakespearean playfulness. Committed to the present veneration of Elizabeth and the hope of English empire, Spenser discloses the ill fit of secular imperialism to the Protestant spiritual journey.

This dissonance, or tension, is implicit in Spenser's own explicit likening of *The Faerie Queene* to both Homer's *Odysseus* and Virgil's *Aeneid*, a comparison echoed in 1596 by Charles Fitzgeoffrey and in 1607 by Sir John Stradling.[9] *The Odyssey* is a tale of nostalgia and ultimate homecoming. In Odysseus's return to Penelope Spenser could see prefigured the alienated sinner's spiritual homecoming to God. *The Aeneid*, on the other hand, is an epic of empire, recounting a journey of physical conquest. In Virgil's work the climactic event is not the rejoining of parted lovers but the building of an earthly city, and, by implication, the extension of that city's sway over the world. As English Virgil, Spenser offers Protestant England, centered (in his description) in London, as not only "Troynovant" but the new Rome. But in shifting the imperialist locus from Catholic Rome to Protestant England, he taints England, and Elizabeth's court specifically, with the "Catholic" vice of place-centered reverence. In *The Faerie Queene*'s tenth canto, Elizabeth's court becomes a shrine.

How does Spenser use Catholic images and practices against themselves, in a way that glorifies Protestant empire? Partly through what Judith Dundas describes as the textualizing of Catholic images.[10] Spenser's transformation of Catholic images and relics to words makes thrifty Protestant use of the broken "fragments of the medieval church" (to use Maryclaire Moroney's phrase).[11] My conclusion, indicated here, will be that the image of a sacred queen and city cannot finally be textualized and thus accommodated to the vision of Protestant pilgrimage elaborated by most of book 1. Yet fully to demonstrate that, I must first disclose the process by which some medieval "fragments" *are* aptly transformed by Spenser into Protestant spiritual "relics."

Let us begin, then, with the objects carried by book 1's devilish or misguided characters. When Archimago first appears to Una and Redcrosse as a hermit, in canto 1, he bears, like the pilgrim he later pretends to be, the physical signs of Catholic superstition. These mark him as one who ostensibly seeks the sacred but really busies himself with the profane. The book which Archimago wears hanging from his belt "should be the Bible," as John King writes, "but his practice of telling tales of 'Saintes and Popes' suggests instead that he reads from a collection of legendary lives of the kind that were banned under Edward VI and Elizabeth."[12] He spends the day telling rosary beads (1.1.30), which, from a Protestant perspective, means fingering a token fetishistically rather than applying his mind to prayer. Spenser attacks beads in more detail in his portrayal, in canto 3, of the blind old woman Una meets who crouches in a dark corner, spasmodically and repetitively telling her rosary and reciting "Nine hundred *Pater nosters* every day" (1.3.13). In both these instances, beads are standard Catholic "costume accessories" that figure the maliciousness or error of those who use them.

We are, then, surprised when we find in the House of Holiness a dignified and gracious dame, "the Ladie of the place," "busy at her beades" (1.10.8). Nor is this venerable lady the only beads-person of the holy house. Later in the canto, another "auncient matrone" (1.10.34) leads Redcrosse "unto an holy Hospitall / . . . In which seven Bead-men . . . / Did spend their days in doing godly thing" (1.10.35, 36, and ensuing passages). Curiously, beads signify not superstition but right religion when they appear in the House of Holiness. The seven men, whose description as "Bead-men" initially suggests stationary prayer, in fact do not tell rosaries but perform services Christians are biblically told to do, feeding the hungry (Rom. 12:20), helping the sick (Matt. 10:8), and donating their own clothing to those in need (Matt. 5:40). Elsewhere in book 1 we see similarly paradoxical repudiations and redemptions of the tokens of Catholic ritual and practice. The word "reliques" or "relicks" is critically applied to those characters associated with wayward Catholicism, like the "griesly" queen of Night whom false Duessa reveres: "Up then, up dreary Dame, of darknesse Queene, / Go gather up the reliques of thy race," Duessa urges her (1.5.24). Yet Redcrosse's sword, spear, and shield are sacred "reliques of his powre" (1.7.48) and unambiguously holy.

The Faerie Queene's contradictory dismissals and retentions of these marks of Catholicism have been thought to betray Spenser's mind's own split between Protestant iconoclasm and an artist's love of images, between a post-Reformation disdain for tokens of religious "superstition" and a poet's awareness of the power of symbols. As King writes, "Spenser shares the early Protestant assumption that iconoclasm involves a complex dialectic in which attacks on 'false' images"—among which we may include sacred objects—"are connected to a countervailing effort to construct acceptable forms of 'true' literary and visual art."[13] Yet what would such forms be? Or, as Maryclaire Moroney puts it, how might the "ruins" of Catholicism "be accommodated within the imaginative economy of the later sixteenth century"?[14]

One way this might be done was, again, by turning images and objects into text. Thus the poem's occasionally positive representations of rosary beads and "reliques" accomplish these objects' translation through narration. Profane things earlier in the poem, they are now made sacred by their use as poetic representations of abstract spiritual states.[15] While the disguised Archimago and the benighted old woman are the "real" devil and a "real" person bearing "real" beads, the gracious old bead-telling woman in the House of Holiness is a textual representation of a spiritual quality. She is "Mercie" (1.10.34), and her beads, correspondingly abstract, are concomitantly acceptable. Redcrosse's "reliques," chiefly his shield, are likewise redeemed as relics because they so clearly represent spiritual qualities and experiences. Ernest Gilman points out that Redcrosse's shield is "scor'd" rather than "painted" with an image of the Cross, which means the shield is "incised with a sharp instrument as in a woodcut or metal engraving, crisscrossed by sword cuts, scratched out, or even scourged, marked with the cuts of a lash."[16] (Shakespeare's Falstaff uses the word in this sense when, fleeing the battle at Shrewsbury, he complains, "Here's no scoring but upon the pate" [*1 Henry IV* 5.3.31].) "These deeper implications wipe away any sense of a pleasingly decorated surface that might otherwise have been contained in the prospect of a painted shield, and they recast the shield as a symbol of spiritual militancy rather than as an objet d'art," Gilman adds.[17] The shield with the scored cross, part of the "armour of a Christian man specified by Saint Paul,"[18] in Spenser's words, is "a commemoration rather than an image of Christ" which "points back to the enduring *word* of salvation," as Gilman says (my emphasis).[19] To quote Spenser himself in *The Vewe of the Present State of Ireland*, by changing things not just to words but to *right* words—indeed, to reflections of *the* word—*The Faerie Queene* rebuilds the remains of "the Ruined Churches . . . in some better forme accordinge to the Churches of Englande."

So with pilgrimage. Healing wells were sites of pilgrimage which Spenser condemned when he was a colonial administrator in Ireland in the 1580s. But Spenser redeems the image of the healing well in *The Faerie Queene*, incorporating it into the narrative of Redcrosse's journey. During his climactic struggle with the Dragon in canto 11, Redcrosse stumbles luckily backward into a "Well of Life" (1.11.29) which "unto life the dead . . . could restore / And guilt of sinfull crimes cleane wash away, / Those that with sicknesse were infected sore, / It could recure. . . ." The well is the "fountain of life" to which Calvin has referred.[20] Like Redcrosse's shield with its scored image of the Cross, and indeed like each virtuous relic, thing, and place in book 1, it is a verbal symbol of both Christ the embodied word and the word that makes Christ accessible. It is the unlooked-for goal of Redcrosse's pilgrimage.

Redcrosse's stumble into the Well of Life is significant, for it underscores a vital distinction between the Protestant spiritual pilgrimage toward Christ and the profane pilgrimage to earthly places—the latter represented by the disguised Archimago, (apparently) "wearied by boiling sands of Arabie and Ynde." Pilgrimage to *places* is intentional. The Catholic pilgrim sets forth for Canterbury or Compostela, if not with a map, with a settled resolve to reach a particular shrine. Yet Redcrosse's journey throughout book 1 has been haphazard, accidental, shifting in focus and goal, in ways apt to the "clownishe . . . man" (or ignorant rustic) Spenser described him as being.[21] Redcrosse is wayward, misled, and in frequent need of spiritual rescue. His haphazard travels exemplify Calvin's claim that salvation is granted by God's grace, not achieved through human works: that "man is so held captive by the yoke of sin that he can of his own nature neither aspire to good through resolve nor struggle after it through effort."[22] In Luther's terms, man does not save himself by his own "running."[23]

Thus the willful "running" of Redcrosse is presented as erroneous wandering. In his abandonment of Una, "Will was his guide, and griefe led him astray" (1.2.12). Such variants of the word "stray" and others of "wander" repeatedly describe his movements and those of Una once she is forsaken by him (1.3.3, 1.3.4, 1.5.18, 1.6.2, 1.7.28, 1.7.50); the word "fall" is also used ("Ay, me, how many perils doe enfold / The righteous man, to make him daily fall?" [1.8.1]). A knight errant, Redcrosse is also an erring knight, whose steps go outward from an ideal place whose distance from the knight is not physically measurable. Unlike, for example, Ariosto's *Orlando Furioso* (trans. 1591), whose heroes range among the specific geographies of France, England, and Scotland, *The Faerie Queene* constructs an allegorical plane (in part, a plain) for Redcrosse's adventures that is oddly surreal. At the start of canto 1 Redcrosse is already "pricking on the plaine" (1.1.1), an unlocalized plane of spiritual adventure. His starting point and ending point are remote in the poem, known "only in memory and expectation," in the words of Jeffrey Fruen.[24] Thus geography itself is outside the poem's borders. The absence of place in the poem intensifies our sense that Redcrosse's travels *take* him nowhere, but rather *do* something to him, inflecting his spiritual condition. They tangle him in sin, and untangle him into redemption.

The language with which Spenser describes the knight's first journeys stresses their inwardness, waywardness, and mazy, tangled movement. Redcrosse's companion Una, grieved by the bondage of her parents (Adam and Eve), looks "As one that inly mourned," seeming to hold "in heart some hidden care" (1.1.4). The forest Redcrosse and Una initially encounter leads "inward farre" (1.1.7), and when they enter it they "wander too and fro in wayes unknowne, / Furthest from end then, when they neerest weene" (1.1.10). The wood is like a "labyrinth" (1.1.11). In it they encounter a female monster—a precursor of the monstrous Sin, "portress of Hell gate," in Milton's *Paradise Lost* (2.746)—whose self-coiling around Redcrosse, no less than her repetitive birthing and swallowing of her offspring, figures the confinement of the wayward spiritual traveler in "Errours endlesse traine" (1.1.18, 15). The superstitious, rosary-holding blind woman Una meets soon after this, in canto 3, wishes that Una might be caught eternally in such "traynes," "And that in endlesse error she might ever stray" (1.3.24, 23), lost in perpetual aimless activities like mindless bead-telling and the saying of "Nine hundred *Pater nosters* every day." From a Protestant perspective, such rotely pious actions, the dark fruit of error, reveal "no life, but lively form of death."[25]

The repetitive, restricted activity of error is paralleled by the circuitous paradoxes with which Duessa, the allegorical representation of the Church of Rome, and her ally, the queen of night, describe Duessa's deceptiveness. In canto 5, when Duessa visits Night to beg help in misleading Redcrosse, she boasts, "I that do seeme not I, Duessa am" (1.5.26). To this Night replies, "In that faire face / The false resemblance of Deceipt, I wist / Did closely lurk" (1.5.27). The phrase "false resemblance of Deceipt" is either a redundancy, as "false lie" might be, or a term rendered meaningless by its self-cancellation. Duessa, who leads Redcrosse astray, is a vacuum who absorbs her victims into the nothingness of aimless journeying. Her self-cancelling self-descriptions are appropriate expressions of her own nothingness. She is "all that [is] not" (1.7.35). Appropriately, even in her disguise, she—like the false Archimago—appears as the sort of misguided pilgrim Protestants imagined and disdained, one drawn by death instead of the spiritual water of life. Duessa's earlier mournful tale to Redcrosse of her loss of a "Prince so faithfull and so faire," who "fell . . . / Into the hands of his accursèd fone," presents in allegorical terms the story of the Crucifixion, but not of the Resurrection. "[F]orth I went his woefull corse to find," she laments, "And many years throughout the world I straid" (1.2.24). Designed though it is to provoke unmerited pity, this story is yet revealing of Duessa's true character. She is a failed Magdalene who, seeking a dead body, has somehow missed her encounter with the risen Christ.

Duessa's vain search for her prince's "woefull corse" registers the Protestant view that the Catholic pilgrim indulges a morbid and spiritually moribund interest in bones, tombs, and the relics of suffering. Margery Kempe's famous fifteenth-century account of her pilgrimage to Jerusalem might be seen to exemplify this interest, for in it she speaks at length of her visit to the Mount of Calvary, where she "saw verily and freshly how our Lord was crucified,"[26] but makes no mention of the empty tomb or of Bethany, where Christ ascended. Luther thought the Catholic Mass itself a perverse celebration of a perpetual "human sacrifice," which confined worshipers to a continual and fixed celebration of Christ's physical suffering without acknowledging his—and their—liberation from death.[27]

Duessa's aimless mistreadings are like the paradoxical animate paralysis of such Christians, and like Spenser's allegorical representation of the Christian caught in "Errours endlesse traine" (the episode in which Redcrosse is gripped by that monster, prior to his first meeting with Duessa). Both Duessa, the false woman and church; and Redcrosse, the Christian misled by false doctrine in Errour's den, are confined to reiterated, purposeless movement. Their wayless way is distinct from the proper path that, rightly retraced, leads the sinner back to the heavenly starting point, Jerusalem's earthly reflection (Redcrosse's quest has begun at Cleopolis, the Faerie Queene's court). The nature of Redcrosse's and Duessa's erring, limited motion is expressed at separate points in book 1 by images of physical constriction: Redcrosse bound by snaky Errour and, later, the man Ignaro (Ignorance), servant in the Palace of Pride, who moves backward and forward at the same time ("For as he forward mooved his footing old, / So backward still was turned his wrincled face" [1.8.31]).

Escape into freer spiritual movement is possible. Backtracking from error releases sinners from trapped action-in-paralysis, just as patient untangling frees thread from its knottedness. When, in the den of Errour, Redcrosse "with the Lady backward [seeks] to wend" (1.1.28)—that is, breaks free of the monster and moves out of the trees, back to the lighted country—his proper pilgrimage is temporarily restored. "[O]ut of the wood," he is "forward on his way (with God to frend)" (1.1.28), though this "forward" movement has in fact been a physical regress—and though, of course, he is immediately distracted by a new bypath, proposed by the "hermit" Archimago whom he and Una next meet.

Restorative pilgrimage in *The Faerie Queene* has a larger, more circular sweep than do the motions of sinful entrapment, though its final goal—God—is not a new place, but the spiritual home from whence pilgrims began. To figure the redemptive circular journey, Spenser invokes the homeward travels of Odysseus, applying them, intriguingly, to Redcrosse's lost companion Una, who goes in quest of him, rather than to the knight himself. Una seeks Redcrosse "With paines farre passing that long wandering Greeke, / That for his love refuséd deitie" (1.3.21). Her refusal to let the rustic, adoring wood nymphs and satyrs of canto 6 "ma[k]e her th'Image of Idolatryes" [1.6.19]) recalls Odysseus's choice to keep traveling rather than to accept godhead as gift of the nymph Kalypso. Likewise, Una's reaction when, deceived by Archimago, she thinks she has found her knight parallels Homer's description of Odysseus restored to Penelope. Una's "joy" (1.3.32) is like that of

> . . . the beaten marinere,
> That long hath wandred in the Ocean wide,
> Oft soust in swelling Tethys saltish teare,
> And long time having tand his tawney hide
> With blustring breath of heaven, that none can bide,
> And scorching flames of fierce Orions hound,
> Soon as the port from farre he has espide. . . .

(1.3.31)

Near *The Odyssey*'s conclusion, Odysseus hugs Penelope

> as sad men at sea, when shore is nigh,
> which long their hearts have wish't (their ship quite lost
> By Neptune's rigor, and they vext and tost
> Twixt winds and black waves, swimming for their lives . . .)
> Crawle up to land
> With joy

(Bk. 23, ll. 362–68)[28]

A personification of faith and "true love" (1.3.30), Una appears immune to the temptations of pride, lust, and despair which impede her knight's progress. Therefore, Spenser's association of her with the wandering, much-tempted Odysseus rather than faithful Penelope is noteworthy. One suspects that, cloistered in passive virtue in her bedroom in Ithaka, Penelope was a model too evocative of the monastic life to bear comparison with Una, a Christlike performer of virtuous work in the world. ("Were not the battles and wars of David better than all the fasting and praying of the best and most pious monks?" Luther asked.)[29] Una's task is not eremitical but evangelical. Her own salvation is justified and made manifest by her quest to redeem Redcrosse from error—by her spiritual militancy, her active aid and direction, which assists his own journey to a right spiritual home.

This journey, again, is an inward pilgrimage, of the sort to which Philip Sidney ruefully alludes in *Astrophil and Stella*: "[O]n earth we are but pilgrims made, / And should in soul up to our countrey move" (sonnet 5).[30] Yet, as we have seen already, the truly holy walk is not subjectively willed, planned, mapped, or purposeful. Red-crosse's volitional spiritual journey is a series of erroneous entangle-ments: with Errour, with Duessa, with Despair. He embarks on proper pilgrimage only late in the epic—in the House of Holiness in canto 10—and only as a result of divine rescue and unmerited healing at the hands of others.

Thus canto 8 finds Redcrosse a passive prisoner in the House of Pride and Una and Prince Arthur performing his militant libera-tion, as representatives of "heavenly grace" and "stedfast truth" (1.8.1). At the rescuers' approach, the doors of the prison "of free-will open flew" (1.8.4), a paradoxical assertion that presents human choice as an effect of God's grace (a Lutheran doctrine elaborated on by Calvin).[31] Spenser is detailed and emphatic in his description of Redcrosse's absolute immobility and impotence at this juncture, and the contrasting arduousness of Prince Arthur's work to free him. "After long paines and labours manifold, / He found the meanes that Prisoner up to reare / Whose feeble thighes, unhable to uphold / His pinéd corse, him scarse to light could beare" (1.8.40). Thus "this good Prince redeemd the Redcrosse knight from bands" (1.9.1). The pure grace the redemption exempli-fies—in fact, the blood of Christ—is figured in the "drops of liquor pure" Arthur gives Redcrosse after the rescue; the gift frees and makes useful the holy "booke, . . . his Saueours testament." Red-crosse presents that booke to Arthur, who, now armed and identi-fied with this "worke of wondrous grace," may new "soules . . . save" as he has saved Redcrosse (1.9.19). Later in the canto, vanquished and powerless in the cave of Despair, Redcrosse is as dependent on Una's intervention as he has been on Arthur's. There, Una prevents his suicide ("Out of his hand she snatcht the curséd knife, / And threw it to the ground" [1.9.52]). Both the redemption episodes of canto 9 are designed to demonstrate the vanity of belief in humans' power to work their own salvation through conventional acts of spiri-tual purification, even if those acts are not vain pilgrimages to "Ara-bie" or "Ynde" but inward "journeys" of prayer. *All* such works are vanity. "If any strength we have, it is to ill, / But all the good is Gods, both power and eke will" (1.10.1).

What, then, is proper pilgrimage? What is the spiritual pathway granted to the Christian elect?

The pains Spenser takes in book 1 to turn traditional religious *ob-jects* into religious *text* prepares us for the answer, which is indeed

given by Calvin: "Scripture is needed as guide and teacher for any-
one who would come to God the Creator."[32] "[W]hatsoever is required to the salvation of man, is fully contained in the Scripture of
GOD," says an official English homily book of the early seventeenth
century.[33] The Bible is the Protestant pilgrim's road.

That scripture is the armor of the Christian knight is suggested
not only by Spenser's description of Redcrosse's shield, which (recalling Gilman's words) "points back to the enduring word of salvation," but also by that of Prince Arthur's, a diamond that shines with
"blazing brightness" (1.8.19) and in which the giant Orgoglio
(Pride) can "*read* his end" (1.8.21, my emphasis). The image of the
sparkling jewel and the book are combined in Spenser's description
of Fidelia, whom Redcrosse meets when he comes to rest in the
House of Holiness. Like the diamond shield that blinds Orgoglio,
Fidelia's "Christall" (gemlike and Christlike) face shines with
"sunny beames . . . / That could have dazd the rash beholders sight"
(1.10.12), and she carries "A booke, that was both signd and seald
with blood, / Wherein darke things were writ, hard to be understood" (1.10.13). The paradoxical description of scripture as a light
containing darkness, a sun that can blind, joins the message of
Psalm 119, "Thy word is a lamp unto my feet" (v. 105), to Second
Peter's reference to the "things hard to be understood" contained
in the Bible (3:16). The journey of the Christian pilgrim now becomes lexical: a gradual accustoming of his eyes to the light, signify-
ing an engagement of his reason with biblical text. This is the
process of Protestant penitence. In Calvin's terms, "no one can embrace the grace of the gospel without betaking himself from the errors of his past life into the right way, and applying his whole effort
to the practice of repentance"—a repentance which "has its foundation in the gospel."[34] Like the late-medieval Lollards, the sixteenth-
century Reformer and Bible translator William Tyndale held that
"the Christian believer [must] take an active part in reading and
interpreting" scripture:[35] must "seek out the law that God will have
[him or her] to do, interpreting it spiritually."[36] Canto 10's account
of Redcrosse's gradual understanding of the sacred words Fidelia
reads him bears out this early Protestant emphasis on this pilgrimage of the mind.

Yet here again we encounter a Spenserian paradox. For despite
canto 10's concern to render holy "pilgrimage" (1.10.61) the reasoned work of reading scripture, Spenser here takes pains to under-

score, at the same time, the passivity of Redcrosse's engagement in this pilgrimage. The allegorical distinction between Redcrosse's frail soul and his strong female guides—among them Fidelia (Faith), who reads to him; Una, who "schoole[s] him" (1.10.32); and "Mercie," who assists "his weaker wandring steps" on the "ready path" (1.10.34, 33)—reminds us that salvation is rescue, or a spiritual *change* wrought by God upon the sinner, rather than a *place* achieved through the initiative of the holy traveler. After all, "[n]one could read [scripture] except [Fidelia] did them teach" (1.10.19). Thus John King is correct when he says that Redcrosse must *be transformed* from illiteracy to understanding.[37] The agent of the transformation is not Redcrosse himself, but Faith, a gift of God, which makes scripture intelligible to him (as it was not to Orgoglio, the giant Pride, who was only blinded by it). For Redcrosse, the House of Holiness is a place of "kindly rest," where, to apply the words of the seventeenth-century Puritan pastor William Perkins, his "labor" is, paradoxically, "to be settled" in faith.[38] Thus the knight dutifully attends to the teachings of Fidelia, without whom he cannot even raise his lids ("she . . . / . . . opened his dull eyes, that light mote in them shine" [1.10.18]).

That Redcrosse is a mere vessel for the containment of scriptural understanding, poured into him by the action of Faith, Mercy, and Love, is emphasized by Spenser's stress on the knight's aural reception of the word. Hearing strengthens his sight. Besides the humbling of Redcrosse's pride, what keeps him from being blinded by Fidelia's "Christall face," as Orgoglio has been by Arthur's diamond shield, is her voice, which, articulating scripture, mediates the word for him. (Again, "none could read, except she did them teach.") Unseen, intangible, heard words are the Protestant response to the highly visual, physical character of the Palace of Pride. That place of imprisonment is graphically rendered through descriptions of the palace's "resplendent gold," the "bloud of guiltlesse babes" on its floore (1.8.35), and the "marble stone . . . / . . . Altare" in its midst, "carved with cunning imagery" (1.8.36). While King, Gilman, and many others have written of the iconoclastic impulse underlying the Palace of Pride's description, I would add that the palace is distinct from the House of Holiness—which is its "antithesis," to use King's word[39]—not just in its rich ocular deceptions but in its stone solidity, its *place*-ness, which suggests its profane status as a physical site of erroneous pilgrimage. Like Rome, a major goal of Catholic pilgrimage, the Palace of Pride is a location to which "Great troupes of people traveiled / Both day and night, of each degree and place"; upon arrival they find themselves trapped in worldliness rather than spiritually purified: "few returned" (1.4.3). Against this palace of carnal pleasures (through which the Seven Deadly Sins parade) Spenser sets the more ethereal, less geographically situated House of Holiness, where things heard are more important than things touched or seen. The House of Holiness is not reachable, as is the palace, by a "broad high way" (1.4.3), but has a location vaguely described as "not farre away" (1.10.3), a direction which bears out the earlier cantos' representations of travel itself as erroneous wandering from home. Salvation is not a place to be journeyed to, but a spiritual condition that is always at hand.

Again, salvation's wholly internal, spiritual process is emphasized through the greater attention Spenser pays in its description to things intangible, spoken, and heard (despite the admittedly arresting visual images of Fidelia's face, of the "sacred Booke" itself "with bloud ywrit" [1.10.19], and finally of Cleopolis). Whereas "sumptuous shew" (1.4.7), "royall robes," and the maiden queen's "gorgeous array" first seize Redcrosse's attention in the Palace of Pride, in the House of Holiness words are his welcome. Lengthy greetings are delivered by the place's holy residents (the "Ladie of the place'"'s address to Una is eighteen lines long). Redcrosse makes "cry and rore" in the pain of his repentance (1.10.28), and the high mount from which he sees Cleopolis is like musical Parnassus, where "three learned Ladies play / Their heavenly notes" (1.10.54). The most dramatic of sounds is, however, Fidelia's scripture-reading voice, "For she was able, with her words to kill, / And raise againe to life the hart, that she did thrill" (1.10.19).

While, since Fidelia allegorically represents Faith, her oral presentation of scripture might easily symbolize a Christian's silent reading of the Bible, her spoken witness also invokes and derives from a Renaissance Protestant homiletic tradition which stressed the importance of preaching the word. Bryan Crockett has written extensively of the popularity of Elizabethan pastors whose speech, filled with "verbal pyrotechnics," was, like Fidelia's, a "wonder" (*FQ* 1.10.19).[40] "Popery is a religion for the eye; ours for the ear," said the Puritan pastor Ralph Brownrig. Calvin himself indirectly proposes the power of what I have elsewhere called Protestant "verbal theater."[41] In his *Commentaries on Exodus*, Calvin writes, "[T]here is much . . . force in the language when [Moses] introduces the Egyptians as speakers, . . . for thus does the marvellous catastrophe more strikingly affect our minds."[42]

"Force," "speak," "strike," "affect": all these words convey Calvin's sense of the outward imposition of grace, through the faith-mediated word, on the passive elect Christian, whose work is to accept rather than to effect salvation—to travel nowhere, to no *place*, but to allow himself to be led to his spiritual home, "not farre away." Redcrosse is such a Christian, made fit for redemption through his humble acquiescence in the process of salvation. Hence even the inward journey that proper pilgrimage becomes in *The Faerie Queene* is a submission to guidance rather than an independent spiritual achievement. Both salvation's inward placelessness and its bestowed character are shown in the account of Redcrosse's upward travel to the mount from which he sees the new "Hierusalem." The knight is assisted by Mercie and, subsequently, by an "agéd . . . man" (1.10.46); though one guide is female (and presumably weaker, according to social and literary convention) and the other old, they are better able to climb the "steep and hy" hills (1.10.46) than is the young knight, a fact which underscores the obvious fact that this journey is not physical in nature. Further, the hills which lead up to the sacred mount are not reached by leaving the House of Holiness and venturing back onto the plain, though Redcrosse will finally be instructed to make such an outbound journey. Instead, the high hills on which Redcrosse begins his "painefull pilgrimage" seem to lie deep inside the House of Holiness itself. That House provides access to the vision of Jerusalem and, presumably, the final ascent to it, so when Redcrosse, following the old man's instruction, returns from the holy mount, he finds himself back at the portals of the House of Holiness, with Una waiting. Only then does he take leave of the place which, in its surreal containment of a larger world, has annihilated all earthly locations.

Except one. Redcrosse's vision of Jerusalem is inseparable from his tie to Cleopolis, its earthly reflection. Gazing at the "new Hierusalem" that is Heaven, Redcrosse thinks of London. He tells his guide, "Till now . . . I weenéd well, / That great Cleopolis, where I have been, / In which that fairest Faerie Queene doth dwell, / The fairest Citie was that might be seen" (1.10.58). The old man responds that despite Heaven's superiority, Cleopolis—again, the metaphorical representation of the site of Elizabeth's court—is "for earthly frame, / The fairest peece, that eye beholden can," and then instructs Redcrosse to turn back from Heaven, return to Cleopolis, and "haunt" the place, there doing "service to that soveraigne Dame," Elizabeth (1.10.59).

The link this passage forms between the celestial and the earthly city returns us to what I have earlier called the poem's double consciousness. In the last cantos of book 1, Spenser reverses his hero's inward spiritual track so that Redcrosse is propelled outward into the physical world, toward a "soveraigne Dame" and away from a sovereign God, to seek a place of "earthly frame" rather than a heavenly destination. Thus Spenser incorporates into his poem two distinct visions of English pilgrimage: the quest for reunion with God and the quest for glorification of the Protestant state. When, on the holy mount and in sight of the heavenly city, Spenser's holy old man turns Redcrosse around, the man's words speciously unify the two visions, presenting the knight's new direction as simply the next phase of the spiritual journey to the new Jerusalem that he has lately begun. But this new path will be puzzlingly retrograde, as well as repetitive. "[T]urne againe / Back to the world," the old man says, "And shortly backe return unto this place" (1.10.63, 64).

In fact, this new journey is profane rather than sacred. It is secular in a way that defies accommodation to the religious allegory that Redcrosse's sojourn in the House of Holiness has presented. That sojourn has been a paradoxically passive journey, or resting pilgrimage, whose character was introspective and whose steps involved Redcrosse's gradual spiritual purification by means of an administered diet of scripture. The House of Holiness is not a place but a spiritual condition, and the "new Hierusalem," deep in the bowels of that house, is by implication no location but a state of oneness with the Creator, which Redcrosse nearly achieves. His next prescribed pilgrimage will be, in contrast, aggressive, militant, and geographically aimed. As he later says, he has been directed not only to Cleopolis, but to other realms ruled by that "proud Paynim king" (1.12.18), a phrase that makes the common Protestant association between England's Catholic ruler-enemies and Islamic "infidels."[43] The new Crusades will be fought in Europe, with Catholics for Saracens.

Throughout book 1, Spenser's most blatant poetic fusion of these two rival faiths, Catholicism and Islam—faiths that were rivals, that is, to Protestant Christianity, though in fact sixteenth-century Catholic Europe was itself at war with the Islamic Ottoman Empire—has been the alliance between Duessa, symbol of the Catholic Church, and her "cruell Sarazin" lovers Sans Foy, Sans Loy, and Sans Joy, "proud paynim[s] all" (1.5.4, 1.3.35). When in the book's final canto Redcrosse speaks of his own obligation to battle a "Paynim" who clearly signifies England's (Catholic) enemies, we see a poetics of English statecraft obfuscating what were the real facts of international conflict in late-sixteenth-century Europe. In reality, the most bitter sixteenth-century European enemies of Islamic nations were Spain, Austria, Venice, and the Papal States themselves, who united in the Christian League to defeat the Turks at Lepanto in 1571 (in a battle which Shakespeare's *Othello*'s fight between Turks and Venetians seems to recall). Not only did England never join the Catholic states to resist the Turkish "proud paynim," England plotted against those states in a way that implicitly aligned England with Islam. Nabil Matar has recently shown that in the 1590s Queen Elizabeth entertained diplomatic efforts from the predominantly Muslim nation of Morocco to draw England into an alliance with the North Africans against England's predominant foe, Spain.[44] Though the alliance did not materialize, Elizabeth's friendliness to the Moroccan ambassador renders transparent the religious language which, in an English Protestant epic, overlies a secular concern for national defense and expansion. Spenser's use of "paynim" for "papist" reflects and promotes an early-modern English politics in which real theological issues were muddied by the pragmatic considerations of nationhood, and even of empire.

Thus does Redcrosse's charge to fight Catholic enemies distort the apostolic commission, wherein Christ bids Christians to go "into all the worlde, & preache the Gospel to everie creature" (Mark 16:15). Spenser's linking of imperial expansion to forced religious conversion has roots, paradoxically, in earlier Protestant thought (though this linkage was by no means peculiar to Protestants). Proto-Protestant Lollard doctrine, as we saw, held that the Christian "pilgrim," once transformed by his own faith-driven encounter with scripture, must journey into the world to redeem others with the gospel. Calvin allowed that civil force might be helpful in this endeavor, and goes beyond—or against—gospel teaching so to argue. In his *Institutes*, Calvin first champions the biblical distinction between what wasn't and was Caesar's, between "spiritual freedom" and "civil bondage," but later grants "civil government the duty of rightly establishing religion," saying that Christians must be free to

"go as pilgrims upon the earth while [they] aspire to the true fatherland."[45] In other words, in Calvinist terms, though the true nation
or "fatherland" is heaven, the state must safeguard spiritual travel
toward it. It follows that when the state is imperial and globally ex-
pansive, it must everywhere protect pilgrims' journey toward the
new, invisible Jerusalem. Ironically, this requires, among other
changes, the outlawing of earthly journeys toward the old, visible Jerusalem, as well as toward other holy sites.

By poetic sleight of hand, Spenser therefore transforms the holy
task of his redeemed Christian pilgrim. In biblical terms, that task is
to preach the gospel. In the Calvinist terms of the Protestant state,
the task is rather to make the world safe for such preaching—which
means, ultimately, the protection of the gospel's hearers from the
temptations of erroneous faiths. This requires the defeat of "paynim" enemies and the control of their churches, as well, inciden-
tally, as their territories. The result of the slippery logic is that for
Spenser's Redcrosse Knight, giving Caesar what is Caesar's becomes
venerating Caesar. Extending Caesar's empire becomes, as in Virgil,
holy work. As Patrick Cheney writes, *The Faerie Queene* is devoted to
"reconstructing the Empire of Augustus in Queen Elizabeth's English yard";[46] Spenser's epic is also consecrated to the expansion of
that yard.

Were book 1 of *The Faerie Queene* separable from its historical context, it might end, as it began, as spiritual allegory. After all, most of
the battles fought in book 1 make only metaphorical reference to
arms, as does Paul when he speaks of Christian armor, in the letter
to Ephesians Spenser cites when describing Redcrosse's shield.[47]
Prince Arthur's defeat of Pride and rescue of Redcrosse in canto 8
clearly occur on the metaphorical plane, and signify Christ's rescue
of the hapless sinner from his own self-love. Even Redcrosse's defeat
of the dragon in canto 11, with the monster's papist significance,[48]
might suggest the virtuous Protestant's personal resistance to Catholic superstition, once his spirit has been strengthened and purified
by the word. But the specific direction given in canto 10 to Redcrosse to fight for Elizabeth forces the reader's attention to the real
territorial battles in which England was engaged in the last decades
of the sixteenth century. To "doen service to that soveraigne Dame"
was to uphold England's material extension. In 1586, four years before *The Faerie Queene*'s first publication, Spenser's contemporary
Philip Sidney had died at Zutphen trying to secure the Lowlands for

English rule; at about that same time Spenser himself, as Crown dep-
uty in Ireland, was involved not only in the destruction of Irish
shrines but in "the manipulation of treason charges so as to facili-
tate the [English] seizure of lands," to quote Stephen Greenblatt.[49]
The work of Elizabeth was the work of empire, and the strengthen-
ing of empire becomes therefore the specific task of the redeemed
knight in book 1's eleventh and twelfth cantos.

Thus in these parts of the poem, as we might expect, Spenser's
allegorical valence becomes mixed. The Well of Life into which Redcrosse falls represents salvation by the word—it is a concrete sign of
an invisible condition—and yet some symbols that had been, up to
this point, physical referents to spiritual things are now reversed,
and become poetic referents to physical things (or to people). In
canto 1, a narrated monster symbolized the abstract quality of error.
In canto 11, a narrated monster suggests the reigning pope.[50] In
canto 12, Redcrosse begins his journey back to the Faerie Queene,
or Elizabeth, in Cleopolis, or London. Redcrosse's pilgrimage, then,
is turned inside out, redirected from an inward path of spiritual
change to an outward path of imperial celebration and aggression.
Changed from Christian to civil soldier, Redcrosse is charged with
"rightly establishing religion," or with the defeat of Catholic enemies so that, in Spenser's own words from *The Vewe of the Present State
of Ireland*, churches might be rebuilt "accordinge to the Churches of
Englande."

Where is Cleopolis, the earthly reflection of heaven, situated in
this altered pilgrimage? Here again the ground of pilgrimage is slippery. Cleopolis, as we have seen, is first offered in canto 10 as Redcrosse's earthly destination. As he regards the new Jerusalem, the
knight is told by the old man to "haunt" the earthly city of Cleopolis. This presentation of Cleopolis as the earthly site of the English
Christian's spiritual passage might cohere with the poem's initial
representation of pilgrimage as spiritual journey were we to interpret Cleopolis as a Neoplatonic way station, a poetically rendered
ideal whose contemplation assists our understanding of heaven.
And in fact, the Cleopolis of *The Faerie Queene* is in some ways such a
Neoplatonic ideal, wholly constructed as it is by narrative, by verbal
description which tames its dangerous visual glory by making it text.
Prince Arthur speaks "Of Gloriane great Queene of glory bright, /
Whose kingdomes seat Cleopolis is *red*": that is, "read" (1.7.46, my
emphasis).[51] By turning Cleopolis to words and (in Jeffrey Fruen's

words) "making [Elizabeth] the focus of a Bible-like typology," Spenser "puts his poem forward as a complementary scripture,"[52] or an induction to the Bible. Its readers become, like Redcrosse, journeyers—"jolly Mariners," Spenser calls us in the poem's final canto (1.12.42), Odysseuses who at the poem's end have safely "seiséd the shore" (1.12.16). For us Cleopolis and the Faerie Queene are symbols rendered in language. And indeed, for many English women and men, Elizabeth's court and herself were such unseen ideals, known, if not through Spenser's poem, by what was said about them.

But for Spenser, two things must have complicated the transformation of Cleopolis, and Redcrosse's journey there, to a narrative way station designed to lead to holy scripture. The first would have been Spenser's own knowledge of the hard, glittering reality of the court for which Cleopolis stands. The physical seat of Elizabeth's power was not, in fact, allegorically "red" by Spenser, by others who "haunt[ed]" it, or by those who witnessed the queen's royal progresses. It was seen. The visual opulence of her court might indeed have inspired Spenser's description of royal Lucifera in the House of Pride:

> A Mayden Queene, that shone as Titans ray,
> In glistring gold. . . .

(1.4.8)

> As faire Aurora in her purple pall,
> Out of the East the dawning day doth call:
> So forth she comes: her brightnesse brode doth blaze;
> The heapes of people thronging in the hall,
> Do ride each other, upon her to gaze:
> Her glorious glitter and light doth all mens eyes amaze.

(1.4.16)

Not only was Elizabeth herself visually dazzling in the way suggested by this passage, her idealized likeness was publicized in sketches and portraits which emphasized her glory. The famous "rainbow portrait" of the queen, in which her red and gold gown is stitched with images of eyes and ears,[53] in fact brings to mind Spenser's description of Lucifera "adornéd all with gold" and drawn by "Pecocks" with tails "full of Argus eyes" (1.4.17). The stunning opulence of Elizabeth's court and its pictorial representations could not have been far from Spenser's mind when he composed the description of proud Lucifera, "royall Dame," and of Lucifera's lords and ladies, who "frounce their curléd haire in courtly guise" and "prancke their ruffs" (1.4.14). Far less is the Elizabethan court invoked in Spenser's description of the virtuous attendants who surround the redeemed Adam and Eve: "A noble crew about them waited round / Of sage and sober Peres, all gravely gownd" (1.12.5). Thus the actual court which Spenser allegorically instructs the Christian knight, or "noble person,"[54] to honor was one which, by his epic's own suggestion, needed "sage and sober" moral correction.

A second problem arises when the reader attempts to regard Cleopolis as a secondary reflection of the heavenly Jerusalem. In such a Neoplatonic system, one would expect Cleopolis, the "earthly frame" that mirrors Heaven, to be more clearly pictured in the poem than is Heaven itself, since it is physically closer to Redcrosse and to Christian readers. Yet the opposite is true. In his vision in the House of Holiness, Redcrosse sees (albeit from a distance) "a goodly citie," which Spenser renders in some detail: its "wals and towres were builded high and strong / Of perle and precious stone"; it is a "stately building" that "high extend[s] / [Its] loftie towres unto the starry sphere" (1.10.55, 56). Although Spenser here claims that "earthly tong / Cannot describe" the place, he in fact presents a more vivid picture of "Hierusalem" than he does of "Faerie lond," or Cleopolis, its earthly image (1.7.36). Indeed, Cleopolis is never even distantly glimpsed in the poem. As Suzanne Wofford writes, *The Faerie Queene* presents a "periphery," with Cleopolis as its "absent centre."[55] If this is so, then Heaven/Hierusalem, literarily pictured in the poem, belongs to that periphery, while the invisible Cleopolis does not. Thus a curious inversion takes place. In an idolatrous switch, the unpictured, faraway Cleopolis becomes the pilgrim's remote goal, and Heaven appears the closer destination. Ostentatiously and profanely real in the experience of the English courtier, the Elizabethan court is made virtuous by its invisibility, its lack of hard presence, in *The Faerie Queene*.

It may be that Spenser's long years as an administrator in remote Ireland, far from the seat of England's power, shaped the longing for Cleopolis that is so powerfully rendered in this poem. It is certainly true that in an epic dedicated to the glorification of a "fanatically idealized" Protestant queen,[56] the physical opulence of that queen's actual court had to be effaced. Spenser sanctifies Elizabeth's court by presenting it obliquely, as an undescribed, hinted-at ideal, even while he reproves its excesses in his description of Lucifera and the Palace of Pride. By withholding Cleopolis from the reader's perception, Spenser allows the city to arrogate the reverential longing that might otherwise be directed toward God.

This redirecting of desire affects, or is designed to inspire, the English reader (or "jolly mariner"), just as it inspires book 1's hero. Redcrosse is charged with the duty to "haunt" and serve the earthly court of Cleopolis as a means of approaching Heaven, but—as I have earlier shown—the shape of the narrative argues for a different journey, before diverting him, and us, from it. Redcrosse is already close to Heaven, and must turn his back on it to approach the place of the Faerie Queene. The road to Cleopolis takes him out of the celestial and into the profane, or earthly, realm. Deceptively, by its very absence from the narrative, that earthly realm's center—Elizabeth's court—displaces the heavenly city as Redcrosse's ideal destination, the place to which he belongs and owes ultimate reverence.

Since Cleopolis's holiness depends on its absence from the poem, and since reverence to the seat of empire is paid by performing abroad the work of empire, book 1 does not describe Redcrosse's return to the Faerie Queene's court. His arrival there is unnarrated, and the book ends with him launched aggressively outward, beyond Cleopolis, into other parts of a world that has become recognizable as Europe. Una, the spirit of truth that guided him to salvation in the House of Holiness, is once more left bereft and mourning (1.12.4). The epic departs from its moorings. Projected unity is no longer the joining of the private Christian to God, but unification, the profane combining of lands by imperial conquest, in realization of what Suzanne Wofford calls England's "national prophetic destiny."[57] In the quest to fulfill this destiny poetry itself becomes an aggressive instrument. As Spenser's contemporary Charles Fitzgeoffrey bragged, "England['s] poet"'s narrative of the Redcrosse Knight "singly challenges the world's wide coasts."[58]

Book 1 of *The Faerie Queene* thus plays its part in one variant of the early-modern reconstitution of traditional pilgrimage, namely, the rewriting of pilgrimage as imperial endeavor. In my first chapter I argued that in the late sixteenth and early seventeenth centuries, religious concepts of spiritual pilgrimage existed side by side with secularized versions of holy travel. Here we have seen an instance of this coexistence in a single work. In part one of his epic, Spenser refashions pilgrimage in an attempt poetically to accommodate a profane to a sacred vision of the blessed journey. Yet the two visions are imperfectly harmonized. Their disjunction reveals the contradiction that arose when Calvin's framing of spiritual pilgrimage, and the state's duty to safeguard it, was embraced by a state committed to self-expansion.

Were spiritual and imperial pilgrimage more happily married in the work of Spenser's poetic contemporaries? It would be more accurate to say they were more happily divorced. To show this, I will in my next two chapters examine Shakespeare's literal "play" with notions of pilgrimage on the Elizabethan and Jacobean stage. More detached than Spenser from England's national ambitions, Shakespeare staged imperial pilgrimage in a way that invited audiences to question such military endeavors' holy claims. In time Shakespeare found the idea of pilgrimage more apt for erotic than imperial story, and directed holy travel toward the private realm, adapting the conceit of pilgrimage to dramas of marriage, which he rendered in both comic and tragic registers. In creating erotic stage journeys, as we will see, Shakespeare discarded the religious assumptions of pilgrimage completely.

3

Imperial Pilgrimage on Shakespeare's Stage

> . . . for miracles are ceas'd;
> And therefore we must needs admit the means
> How things are perfected.

> —*Henry V* 1.1.68–70

WHEN ST. THOMAS BECKET'S SHRINE WAS DISMANTLED IN 1538 BY ORDER of Thomas Cromwell, workmen took from Canterbury Cathedral "nearly three hundredweight of gold, the same amount of silver, almost twice as much silver gilt, and innumerable precious stones." The historian John Phillips records that "[t]his spoil filled two great chests, so heavy that six or seven strong men could barely carry one out of the church."[1] The money and jewels, which went straight to the coffers of Henry VIII, bespoke the devotion of late-medieval and early-sixteenth-century English pilgrims, of whose contributions this wealth was largely composed. But Phillips's catalogue of gold, silver, and precious stones also reveals the spectacular quality of the shrine itself, and suggests that visits to the "holy, blissful martyr" at Canterbury offered pilgrims ocular entertainment as well as spiritual sustenance. A Venetian ambassador's description of St. Thomas's shrine in 1500 is entirely devoted to its visual splendor: "the tomb . . . is entirely covered over with plates of pure gold, but the gold is scarcely visible from the variety of precious stones with which it is studded, such as sapphires, diamonds, rubies, balas-rubies, and emeralds, and on every side that the eye turns, something more beautiful . . . appears."[2] Erasmus's description of Canterbury Cathedral in 1513 makes clear that the precious things consecrated to St. Thomas were themselves made part of his shrine, and these, as well as the ossuary at Canterbury, contributed to the dramatic aspect of a visitor's experience. Erasmus expresses the horror he felt at the "skulls, jaws, fingers," and "whole arms" arranged near the shrine, and of the place's opulence writes, "Good Lord, what an array of silk vestments there, what an abundance of gold candelabra! . . . [In the shrine itself was] inestimable treasure. . . . The cheapest part was gold. Everything shone and dazzled with rare and surpassingly large jewels, some bigger than a goose egg."[3] In my first chapter I suggested that this account of the (to Erasmus) ghastly bone display and the dazzling shrine, a description amusing in its own right, showed that as a Canterbury visitor, Erasmus—along, presumably, with his traveling companion John Colet—was more tourist than palmer. We need only slightly to expand our understanding of early-modern Canterbury tourism to impute to such travels to the saint's shrine the satisfaction of another impulse: the desire for entertainment.

Certainly, as I have earlier argued at length, by the early sixteenth century in England pilgrimages were widely perceived as occasions for various sorts of delight. In *The Canterbury Tales*, Chaucer gave his readers fanciful representations of the *narrative* entertainment English pilgrims enjoyed, but Chaucer's characters also enjoy impromptu *shows* even before they arrive (as they never do) at Thomas's shrine. Before the Miller begins his tale, he makes a spectacle of himself, sitting "pale" from "dronken" (drunkenness) "upon his hors" and swearing "in Pilates vois"—that is, in the raucous voice of a conventional Pilate in the mystery plays.[4] Arguments enliven the journey for all riders, and the Host repeatedly likens the tale-telling contest itself to a "playe,"[5] a word which in the fourteenth century meant "game" but also "dramatic entertainment."[6] In 1998 I witnessed a group of players realize the dramatic potential of Chaucer's narrative, as, portraying the Wife of Bath, the Host, the Pardoner, and others, they led an audience of tag-along pilgrims through the streets of downtown Toronto, hilariously enacting the *Tales* as they went. The interchanges between the fictional pilgrims have their own drama, and in the late fourteenth, fifteenth, and early sixteenth centuries Chaucer's *Tales* contributed to a popular idea of pilgrimage as traveling fun which doubtless exceeded the facts. Still, the descriptions of English shrines recorded by Erasmus and others leave no doubt that whatever their roadside experiences, when pilgrims arrived at the more famous holy sites, the reverence they showed their saints was rewarded, if not by answered prayers, at least by a satisfying visual and sometimes auditory experience. Anne

F. Harris has recently shown that from the late twelfth through the early sixteenth centuries, stained-glass windows in Canterbury's Holy Trinity Chapel helped compose a "theater of memory" for enthralled pilgrims by providing a stationary "reenactment" of Becket's murder and subsequent miracles.[7] We recall that visitors to St. Cuthbert's sumptuous shrine at Durham Cathedral were granted "seates or places . . . under the shrine," from which they could serve as attentive audience as the cover of Cuthbert's vault was raised by a belled rope ("[T]he belles did make . . . a good sound," a sixteenth-century observer recorded).[8] The reliquary, or feretory, at St. Thomas's (also belled)[9] tomb was likewise hidden under a cover that was raised for pilgrims' viewing by ropes and a pulley,[10] a contraption that dimly foreshadowed the stage trap and flying harness of the Renaissance stage, used to present underworld horrors or heavenly gods to the audience's view. Actual medieval and pre-Reformation sixteenth-century saints' plays formed a stage (pun intentional) in the redirection of English pilgrimage from such shrines to early-modern playing places. Clifford Davidson has written of the spectacular representations of martyrdoms and miracles in plays such as the lost play of St. Denys mentioned in the will of Robert Lasingby of York in 1455, and the play of St. Erasmus (no relation to the humanist) shown at Perth between 1484 and 1534.[11] The literal staging of saints' lives by local players was an elaboration of the theatrical presentation of popular saints' tombs and relics at the original shrines. In some such plays, notably the infamous (to Reformers) play of the Rood of Grace at Boxley, shrines and dramatic entertainments fully joined. Brian Spencer records badges received by early-sixteenth-century pilgrims who visited Boxley to see the dramatic display of a Cross which (mechanically manipulated) could be seen to move.[12] Indeed, by the early sixteenth century, the language used to describe saints' shrines had merged with that used to describe theatrical entertainments. Paul White has discovered that civic expenditures in Chagford, Devon, in 1513 included an outlay for fourteen "pageants" which were apparently not plays, but "shrines or tabernacles for saints permanently housed in the parish church."[13]

Although the intake from pilgrims' pious offerings to English shrines declined in the fifteenth and early sixteenth centuries from "the golden shower of the high Middle Ages," to recall A. G. Dickens's phrase, no records demonstrate that the visits themselves diminished in number. Even if we grant (against Eamon Duffy)

Stanford Lehmberg's argument that by the sixteenth century English pilgrimage had become tourism,[14] we are left with the question of what English tourists went to see after their shrines were finally and fully dismantled under Elizabeth.

Canterbury Cathedral itself provides one answer, for it housed another venerable tomb, and this one was not dismantled. Just south of the shrine of St. Thomas lay the tomb of Edward the Black Prince, in the chapel of the Holy Trinity, "high aloft in the sacred space behind the altar," as Arthur Stanley writes. Stanley adds, "no other corpse had been admitted within this venerated ground" when Edward was buried there.[15] From 1376 through 1538, the prince's and Thomas's tombs were twin attractions for Canterbury pilgrims, who in the late-fourteenth century purchased Edward-funerary badges and Thomas-pilgrim badges from the same artisan-booths outside the cathedral.[16] Richard II went to Canterbury "to visit St. Thomas's shrine, and also because the prince his father was there buried," in the words of the courtier Jean Froissart,[17] and when Thomas's shrine was demolished the prince in the chapel remained.

The prince's black-armored effigy must have looked unassuming near the colorful jewels that bespoke the holiness of St. Thomas. Yet the Black Prince's presence by Thomas's tomb suggests the competition dead English royalty waged with saints during the century preceding the Reformation. More specifically, the armoring of Edward's image indicates the religious reverence the English had begun to accord the imperialist, soldiering royal hero. At the close of that historical pathway stood the men who cheered their armored Queen, Elizabeth, who had ridden to Tilbury to bless them before an expected battle with Spain, in 1588.[18] The Virgin Queen's journey to bolster her troops' morale was a neat secular inversion of her father's pre-Reformation pilgrimage to honor an enshrined Virgin at Walsingham. It was also an exercise in theater. Only a few years later, thanks largely to Shakespeare, as I will show, the actual theater had become the venue in which fantasies of imperial pilgrimage, inspired by the memory of royal military heroes, could be best entertained and vicariously satisfied.

The stage as end point for military pilgrimage was prefigured not only in Elizabeth's role-play but earlier, in the theatrical aspects of provincial "shrines" like Edward's at Canterbury in the early sixteenth century. Yet the cult of royalty that was integral to war-pilgrimages began not just as theatrical play, but as genuine popular

belief in the sanctity of kings, or of some kings. Through much of
the Middle Ages king worship was a religious movement that was at
times indistinguishable from or identical with the real veneration of
saints. English reverence for "sacred monarchy" was evident as early
as the twelfth-century reign of Henry II, the first English monarch
known to have practiced touch-healing for scrofula. Indeed, King
Edward the Confessor, who was later canonized, is thought by Marc
Bloch to have begun that healing rite even earlier in England, in the
eleventh century.[19] Late-fourteenth-century Canterbury pilgrims'
badges picturing both Edward the Confessor and Thomas Becket
show the conscious attempt of the then-reigning king, Richard II, to
link holiness and royalty by harnessing the canonicity of an antiroyal
saint. The main patron of Canterbury Cathedral during his reign,
Richard meant, by supporting its shrine and such badges, to promote an awe for the king equal to that already accorded Thomas[20]
(though a final Thomas-like "martyring" was surely not in his plan).
By the end of Richard's time, and partly through his efforts, English
veneration of royalty had paradoxically expanded to include not just
celebration of monarchs' (like Edward's) healing powers, but of
royal heroes' battlefield victories. We see this in the honors accorded the Black Prince, for a "Life of the Black Prince," similar in
form to a saint's life, was composed (anonymously) in Anglo-French
soon after his death, in praise of his war achievements.[21] The blood
of Thomas Becket, spilled in defense of the Catholic Church, was
giving way in English importance to the blood of princes and monarchs spilled in defense—or aggressive expansion—of their country.
In the early fifteenth century, even soldierly Plantagenets less venerable than Edward were housed on sacred ground at Canterbury Cathedral and elsewhere. In 1413 the corpse of Henry IV joined
Edward's within the gates of the chapel that housed Becket's tomb.[22]
Henry VI, buried at Windsor, was visited far more often than was
Becket in the fifty years before the outlawing of holy pilgrimage.[23]
Miracles were attributed to Henry VI, though he was never canonized, and one such reputed miracle suggests the gradual supplant-
ing of saints by kings in the reverent English imagination. Eamon
Duffy records a story of a baby who choked on a St. Thomas Becket
pilgrim badge he'd been given to play with. The child's life was de-
spaired of until the father prayed to Henry VI, whereupon the child
coughed up the badge. The father then took the Becket badge to

Windsor, "where it was hung over Henry's tomb, one of the spoils of holy war."[24]

Gentle Henry VI is not the Plantagenet we most readily link with imperial conquest, though Shakespeare makes Henry VI's father dream his boy will one day "go to Constantinople and take the Turk by the beard" (*Henry V* 5.2.208–9). Still, we may note that the real or mythic regurgitated Becket badge, placed at Henry VI's grave, was considered "one of the spoils of holy war." That circumstance suggests that just prior to the Reformation, the English associated their venerable past kings with a religiously righteous conflict between England and its enemies, and accorded them a more tenacious reverence than that given to traditional saints. In 1559 Henry VI's shrine was dismantled with the others, but he, unlike Thomas Becket, soon found a new locus of veneration, where takings surpassed the old offerings to Thomas at Canterbury, and pilgrims exceeded in number even travelers to the tomb of the Black Prince. Fewer than fifty years after the final destruction of shrines, the ghosts of Henry VI, Edward Plantagenet, and others of their royal relatives were being widely visited and loudly applauded in the theaters and provincial playing places of England.

Thus when we read Victorian author Arthur Stanley's claim that only Admiral Nelson "fill[s] in [English] minds the place of the Black Prince,"[25] we may wonder how responsible Shakespeare was for widening that mental place by elaborating Edward Plantagenet's and other princes' myths in the history plays. For it is in those plays, particularly *Henry V*, that Shakespeare most fully exploits the shift of Protestant England's reverence from Catholic saints to royal military heroes and the redirection of English wanderlust from provincial pilgrimage to imagined imperial endeavors. This redirecting of pilgrimage was one way in which, as James Shapiro has recently observed, Shakespeare's theater "absorbed social energies that had become unmoored in a post-Reformation world."[26] By Shakespeare's time, even Edward the Confessor, a genuine Catholic saint and a king who, like Henry, was known as a gentle healer, could be presented on stage as national genius of a country of warring invaders. In an odd passage in *Macbeth*, Malcolm, rallying Macduff for the English assault on Macbeth's Scotland, pauses in his war talk briefly to describe this eleventh-century King Edward's "most miraculous" touch-healing work (4.3.147): the scrofula-curing tradition that was still (though reluctantly) practiced by King James, and before James by Queen Elizabeth, on provincial progresses.[27] Although English royal touch healing ended with James, it was retained by the Shakespearean stage, but recontextualized within a dramatic celebration of war, as were some other Catholic traditions. In *Henry V*, to inspire his invasion of France, Henry is urged to make pilgrimage, not to the Holy Land as his father wished to do (*Richard II* 5.6.49), but to English churches closer at hand, to supplicate holy men far more militant than Christ. "Go, my dread lord, to your great-grandsire's tomb, / From whom you claim; invoke his warlike spirit, / And your great-uncle's, Edward the Black Prince," says the Archbishop of Canterbury (1.2.103–5). Such "mighty ancestors," the archbishop implies (1.2.102)—speaking outside his fifteenth-century moment— are the new Canterbury saints.

We might locate the start of the history plays' exploitation and encouragement of traditional saints' replacement by royal warriors in *1 Henry VI*'s reductive treatment of Joan of Arc. In the last act of this play, Joan de Pucelle tells her English captors she is "chosen from above, / . . . To work exceeding miracles on earth" (5.4.39–41). But the reliability of her claim is immediately undercut by her ensuing prevarications. She claims to be "a virgin . . . / Chaste and immaculate," then says she is bearing a Frenchman's child (ll. 50–51, 73). Her lack of dignity and her defensive untruths in what might have been her scene of martyrdom render her, if not the "sorceress" York calls her (5.4.1), a merely typical woman, frail and unsanctified by special grace. In its presentation of Joan, *1 Henry VI* is an antimiracle play that bears out the dictum of the twenty-second of the Thirty-Nine Articles of the English Church: "The Romish doctrine concerning Purgatory, Pardons, Worshipping and Adoration, as well of Images as of Relics, and also Invocation of Saints, is a fond thing, vainly invented." Of course, there is a martyr in the First Tetralogy, who superficially inherits the miracle-working powers the Reformed English thought impossible for Catholic saints. It is Henry VI, whose hands, like those of earlier kings, were believed to cure scrofula during his life.[28] In *Richard III*, dead Henry VI is "dear saint" (4.1.69) and "holy Harry" (4.4.25), and his corpse miraculously bleeds in the presence of Richard, the Duke of Gloucester (1.2.56). Yet the blood that comes from holy Harry's "cold and empty veins" (1.2.59) is more a proof of warlike Richard's diabolism than of Henry's saintliness: "[T]hou lump of foul deformity, / . . . 'tis thy presence that exhales this blood," spits Lady Anne (1.2.57–58). And in *3 Henry VI*,

Henry VI's healing powers are symbolic rather than literal. It is this English king's "pity" that hath been balm to heal [the people's] wounds" (4.8.41).

In the Henry plays of the Second Tetralogy, even traditional English saints are presented or invoked in ways which place them in the shadow of the true miracle worker, the "warlike Harry," Prince Hal, later King Henry V (*Henry V* Pro.5). Recent scholars have discussed how Falstaff parodies the historical image of the proto-Protestant "saint," the Lollard John Oldcastle, for whom Falstaff was originally named.[29] Prince Hal, Falstaff complains, could "corrupt" this "saint" (*1 Henry IV* 1.2.90). "Blown Jack'"'s battlefield miracles—his alleged defeat of Hotspur and his own resurrection—are deceptions to which the audience is privy. The real wonder-worker is, of course, Prince Hal, whom we see kill the glorious Percy (*1 Henry IV* 5.4). To Falstaff's degraded saint, crowned Henry is a Christ, echoing Christ's dismissal of sinners in "I know thee not, old man" (*2 Henry IV* 5.5.47, Matt. 25:12) and presenting the image of Christ's anguish in Gethsemane as he prays alone on the eve of Agincourt (*Henry V* 4.1.289ff.). Though never historically canonized, Henry V is described by Shakespeare's Chorus in terms which approach hagiography. He is "the mirror of all Christian kings" (2.Cho.4), an epithet evocative of what Catherine Sanok calls "exemplarity": the use of saints, in books chronicling their lives, as models to inspire Christian behavior.[30] Still, as King Henry's image is glorified, the Old Church economy of saints and chantries is mocked.[31] The scheming prelates of *Henry V* remind the Elizabethan audience of the worldly use the late-medieval church made of English monies. In complaining that Henry would strip the Church of "temporal lands" left them by "men devout," Canterbury appears a greedy landlord, while the king, who would use the money to support all Englishmen (from earls to "lazars" and "indigent faint souls past corporal toil") seems the true Christian leader (1.1.9, 13–16). Before Agincourt Henry reminds God that he has built "[t]wo chauntries" and hired priests to pray for the release of Richard's soul from Purgatory, but acknowledges the pointlessness of the exercise: "[A]ll that I can do is nothing worth, / Since that my penitence comes after, / Imploring pardon" (*Henry V* 4.1.301–5). These lines make no sense if we read them as a claim that repentance after sin—here, Henry's repentance for his father's murder of Richard II and his own royal accession—is worthless; certainly from both Protestant and Catholic perspectives, repentance *should* follow sin, rather than precede it. The lines acquire meaning when we regard them as Shakespeare's post-Reformation denial, through Henry, of the existence of a Purgatory from which Richard's soul might graduate, and thus of the validity of bought prayers for the dead. Henry's purchased pardon for Richard's sin, coming as it does after Richard's death, avails Richard nothing, despite Henry's Christly intentions. As the early-sixteenth-century Reformer Miles Coverdale warned, the doctrine that "masses, pilgrimages, and other like superstitious ceremonies, may be done for [dead men]" is "deceitful."[32]

The devaluing of Catholic practices, including prayers to canonized saints, is pervasive throughout *Henry V*'s representation of the English campaign in France. Foxe, we recall, applauded the French lieutenant-general who mocked the silver saints' images in churches because they did no useful work; less directly, Shakespeare also alludes to the dormant wealth idling in Catholic churches. To the French the English horsemen look "liveless," like a church's "fixed candlesticks" (4.2.55, 45) (of course, the French are fooled: the English *are* alive). As for saints, St. Denis doesn't help the French fight or Henry speak French (5.2.184–87), and even St. George's name ranks below Henry's as inspirational battle cry. At Harfleur, Henry shouts "God for Harry, England, and Saint George!" (3.1.34), revising the name order given by *Richard III*'s Richmond ("God and Saint George! Richmond and victory!" [5.3.270]. St. George's influence is, in any case, null in *Richard III*; Richard III prays to him, too, and loses [5.3.301, 349]). St. David's Day is a mere commemorative marker of past Welsh battles fought on England's behalf (4.7.98–103). Before Agincourt, Henry V converts Saint Crispin's Day to an occasion for his own future commemoration—on future saint's days, he pledges, "shall our names, / . . . Harry the King, Bedford and Exeter," be "freshly remembered"—and for veneration of stigmata earned by his soldiers, who will "show [their] scars" (4.3.51, 53, 47). When Henry offers his "joints" to the French as relics, he is mocking the Catholic practice of displaying saints' body parts in return for pilgrims' money.[33] "Bid them achieve me, and then sell my bones!" he taunts them (4.3.91). But battle-bruised bones won't be worth much, Henry suggests; they'll "yield [French Catholics] little" (4.3.123–25). Of more profit is Henry's living body, to be spent fighting. Henry's taunt proclaims to Shakespeare's audience that, to dignify Wat Ralegh's later jest about sprawled, drunken Jonson in his Paris cart, the king is "a more lively image of the Crucifix than any [the French] had."

As moving, talking, working king, Henry embodies blessed qualities, displaying, as Canterbury notes, his sudden "reformation"—a word that appears frequently in the second Henriad, and one whose association with English church reform has been demonstrated by Maurice Hunt.[34] Speaking, Henry fosters "wonder" among his audiences (1.1.53); leading troops, he facilitates the miraculous Agincourt triumph, called by Exeter "wonderful" (4.8.112). Graham Holderness has written that Shakespeare's Lancastrian kings "ritualistically appropriat[e]" the myths of medieval culture.[35] Agreeing, I would suggest that chief among these reworked myths is that of saints' miracles and intercession. In *Henry V* the monarch, a Christlike intercessor, pleads directly with God for his soldiers' victory, and his prayer is granted.

There is irony, of course, in Shakespeare's presentation of a king who is holier than the saints because he is like Christ. For warlike Harry is in many ways Christ's antithesis. (In an obvious example, Christ would not, one assumes, have ordered the slaughter of captured Frenchmen, as Henry does at 4.6.37.) Henry is alone in his anguish before Agincourt, like Christ in Gethsemane, but his prayer is quite different than Christ's in his sacred moment. Rather than pray for the strength to submit to death, Henry prays for the will to inflict it, asking a "God of battles" to "steel" (steal?) his "soldiers' hearts" (4.1.289). Not just saints' stigmata but Christ's nail wounds are imaginatively replaced by battle scars when Henry predicts that the English warrior will "strip his sleeve and show his scars" on Crispin's day (4.3.47). For Christ's passively shed blood, Henry offers the blood of fighting men, whose wounds will be celebrated in a secular communion whose description evokes the Reformed sacrament: he who "sheds his blood" with Henry will in future "flowing cups [be] freshly *remembered*" (4.3.61, 55, my emphasis).[36] Late-medieval Canterbury pilgrims drank drops of St. Thomas's blood in water;[37] early-modern English drinkers will toast the blood of the soldier-saints who replaced Thomas. This whimsical adaptation of the myths and rituals pertaining to Christ's Crucifixion, and to Becket's martyrdom, to a battle-avid king suggests that Reformation Shakespeare found once-sacred activities—the Catholic Mass, bleeding images of Christ, and saints' blood and stigmata—available for play. Henry's suiting of Christ's passion, as represented in the Mass and by Catholic images, to English war-aims participates in his play's high-spirited transformation of holy pilgrimage to imperialist military campaign. Instead of the shrine-reaching pilgrim's palm or badge, the English warrior will have scars to show for his successful journey. As James Shapiro notes, "Only in a post-Reformation world" would such claims "have been imaginable."[38]

Intrinsic to Henry V's Protestant reworking of Catholic pilgrimage is the dynamic whereby sacred destination is replaced by sacred starting point. When there are no blessed foreign locales, England itself, the place from which warriors depart, assumes a "holy" topical identity. While Spenser's *Faerie Queene* makes serious claims for the holiness of England, and of the radiation outward of the Protestant imperial center, Shakespeare is characteristically ironic in his staging of the migration of holiness from Holy Land to England.

England's assumption of holiness is gradual in Shakespeare, and is accomplished over the course of the entire second-tetralogic cycle. Early on, at the close of *Richard II*, Shakespeare seems to affirm the old tradition of pilgrimage from England to a holy place to expiate wrongs. Then, as I noted earlier, Henry IV vows to make such a "voyage" to the Holy Land, and so to perform an act of penitence which will "wash [Richard's] blood off from [his] guilty hand" (5.6.49–50). This public promise is publicly reaffirmed at the start of *1 Henry IV*, when Henry IV makes clear that his expiatory act will be a warlike crusade to recapture "the sepulchre of Christ" from "pagans" (1.1.19, 24). Holy pilgrimage, now described as a pilgrimage of war, still depends on an Old Religious faith in the sanctity of places. In the Holy Land are "holy fields, / Over whose acres walk'd those blessed feet / Which fourteen hundred years ago were nail'd / . . . on the bitter cross" (1.1.24–27). Yet in *2 Henry IV*, the king privately reveals to Prince Hal the political scheming that always underlay his thwarted promise to reach those "holy fields." Henry IV confesses he "had a purpose . . . / To lead out many to the Holy Land / Lest rest and lying still might make them look / Too near unto my state" (4.5.209–12). In other words, the crusading pilgrimage to the east was to be a feint to distract rivals like the Percys from a more local conquest: the capture of the English throne. Henry's skeptical undercutting of the holy pilgrimage is implicitly confirmed by God, who collaborates in the relocation of holy land to England. Henry is taken to die in a "Jerusalem, / Which vainly [he] supposed the Holy Land," but which is in fact a room in his castle (4.5.237–40).

Yet before he dies, the king passes his politic mission to his royal son, explicitly charging him to fulfill his own original purposes of converting holy pilgrimage to outwardly directed foreign conquests. As it was mine, he suggests, "Be it thy course to busy giddy minds / With foreign quarrels" (4.5.213–14). The site of these quarrels' bloody resolution is no longer specific. With the king's revelation that his purpose was never to achieve holy ground but to provide a military distraction, one foreign locale seems as good as another for English invasion. Destinations are thus stripped of special sanctity.

Fictively, half that sanctity is displaced onto England itself, as though the energies inspired by and spent on pilgrimage, including crusading pilgrimages, could not be easily desacralized. In the Second Tetralogy there are no more holy places to go, but the sanctity of English purposes blesses the place from which soldiers start. England itself is "other Eden, demi-paradise." It is a "plot" that is "blessed" because it is the "teeming womb of royal kings / . . . Renowned for their deeds as far from home . . . As is the sepulchre in stubborn Jewry," as the dying Gaunt says in *Richard II* (2.1.42, 50–55). Gaunt's parallel syntax suggests not just that England's kings are renowned as far as Christ's tomb, but that they are as renowned as the tomb. Such a claim would have been blasphemous for the real John of Gaunt, but wasn't for a Gaunt reconfigured for the post-Reformation English stage. In the early fifteenth century, a few decades after John of Gaunt's death, the English mystic Margery Kempe wrote movingly of her visit to the site of Christ's Passion in Palestine, in a passage we have lately discussed. There in a vision she saw "freshly how our Lord was crucified."[39] But nearly two centuries later, when fictively recreating Kempe's late-medieval era, Shakespeare thought it more affecting to characterize *England* as Calvary. Thus two acts after Gaunt's dying speech *Richard II*'s Bishop Carlisle envisions his own war-torn land as a future "field of Golgotha" (4.1.144).

Shakespeare's transferral of sanctity's aura from traditional holy sites of pilgrimage to England itself was possible, even inevitable, in an era when shrines had been dismantled and journeys to holy places officially condemned. Local ground, made holy by Christ or the saints who walked there, is now imaginatively sanctified not by traditional individual saints, but by a Protestant community of saints. The "commonwealth" is "a saint," to quote *1 Henry IV*'s Gadshill (2.1.80). In *Richard II*'s third scene Shakespeare seems particularly concerned poetically to reinterpret holy ground as England itself, a land graced by its blessed monarchs. The word "pilgrimage" appears thrice in this scene, once as Gaunt's description of life itself (1.3.229),[40] and twice as a metaphor to describe an English subject's relation to his country and king. Preparing for a joust that he hopes will prove him loyal to Richard II, Bolingbroke describes the impending fight as "a long and weary pilgrimage" (1.3.49). When the joust is thwarted and Bolingbroke banished from England to Continental lands which Shakespeare's audience associated with Catholicism, Bolingbroke foresees his coming travels not as a blessed but as "an enforced pilgrimage" (1.3.264). Damnably, these wanderings will take him from the seat of all blessedness, which is England itself. Other places are hellish. Mowbray too turns "from [his] country's light / To dwell in solemn shades of endless night" (1.3.176–77). For the old man, John of Gaunt, "pilgrimage" is similarly a journey of exile from England, which time, leading him toward death, enforces in his aging body (1.3.230). Gaunt's ensuing description of England as "other Eden, demi-Paradise" (2.1.42) curiously depicts his own dying as a journey away from rather than toward Heaven.

What makes England so blessed in Shakespeare's histories? As Bolingbroke's description of valiant battle as "pilgrimage" suggests, its military success has much to do with its special status. Chief among England's saints are kings who have appropriated the Holy Land's sanctity for their own country by successful acts of war performed abroad. England, again, is "blessed" because (as dying Gaunt says) its royals are "Renowned for their deeds . . . far from home": deeds of conquest, such as those done in France by "the hand / Of that black name, Edward, Black Prince of Wales," as the French king shudders to recall in *Henry V* (2.4.55–56). In Shakespeare's *King John*, Richard Cordelion is briefly honored—significantly, not by an English character, but by French King Philip—for having "fought the holy wars in Palestine" (2.1.4). But *Henry V*'s warring king, looking back to later royal "lions" Edward III and the Black Prince (1.2.109), does not lead followers to reclaim a holy place. Instead, as Spenser's Redcrosse Knight is bade to do, Henry V performs an inverted pilgrimage, extending native English holiness outward through imperialist expansion. Victory in France absorbs France into the "other Eden" that is England, enlarging the "world's best garden" (*Henry V* Epi.7). By this process, Frenchness becomes Englishness. As Henry tells the French princess Katherine, whom he will wed, "when France is mine and I am yours, then yours is France and you are mine" (5.2.174–76). Henry's pronouncement superficially resembles the Reformer William Tyndale's vernacular adaptation of Galatians 3:28, "In Christ there is neither french nor english, but the frenchman is the englishman's owne selfe, and the english the frenchmen's owne selfe."[41] But Henry's vaunt reverses Tyndale's egalitarian Christian message, not only omitting reference to Christ but favoring, preserving, and expanding English claims. "I will not part with a village of [France]," Henry tells Katherine. "I will have it all mine" (5.2.174–75).

In the play's last scene Henry, imaginatively characterizing Katherine and himself as embodiments of their national saints, plots the further extension of England through the pair of them. "Shalt not thou and I, between Saint Denis and Saint George, compound a boy . . . that shall go to Constantinople and take the Turk by the beard?" (5.2.206–9). Here, proposing a new Crusade led by a yet unborn son, Henry reiterates his father's pledge to travel eastward, "chas[ing] pagans" (*1 Henry IV* 1.1.24). This proposed eastward expansion recalls Redcrosse's pledge to enlarge the Faerie Queene's territory by vanquishing "that proud Paynim king" (Spenser, *The Faerie Queene*, 1.12.18). Yet Henry V's shift of goal from the Holy Land to Constantinople—in 1599 a rich commercial center and the seat of Ottoman power—lays bare the raw imperialist purposes that always underlay "holy" journeying in this cycle of plays. Here we may recall Richard Hakluyt's explicit linking of past English Crusades in Palestine to new commercial missions to Aleppo, Africa, the Levant, and finally the New World. In his 1593 *Voyages and Discoveries*, Hakluyt tells readers that the past "desire of [the English] nation to visit the Holy Land" may now be satisfied by conquest of America, "rich and abundant in silver mines."[42]

Was *Henry V*, then, like Spenser's *The Faerie Queene*, a call to arms for Shakespeare's audience? Did the play promote English global imperialism by imaginatively transforming Canterbury pilgrimage and Jerusalem Crusades to general war campaigns, and religious icons to sacred, sword-waving kings?

If it did not, it is because these transformations were wrought and restricted by playing. In *Henry V*, King Henry offers his living, fighting, speaking, royal body as a moving icon, superior to the dead "joints" available for worship in a Catholic reliquary. Yet the real Henry V is now dead, and his play takes pains to accentuate the difference between him and the actor playing him. The play begins,

> O for a Muse of fire, that would ascend
> The brightest heaven of invention!
>
> . . . .
>
> *Then* should the warlike Harry, like himself,
> Assume the port of Mars. . . .
>
> (Pro., 1–6, my emphasis)

The unreachable *then* that makes sacred kingship possible is not England's future, but its past.

It is true that *Henry V* records a popular shift, evident as early as the late-medieval period the play represents, of reverence from Catholic saints to English monarchs who were also military leaders. It is also true that through its scheming prelates and references to ineffectual chantries and valueless relics, the play exploits anti-Catholic ideas of Shakespeare's own time[43]—indeed, that Shakespeare's post-Reformation moment enabled him, as it did Spenser, religiously to mock relics and demote saints while proposing the conversion of once-holy pilgrimage to English imperial conquest. Still, the religious language with which the plays describe imperial endeavors—as well, no doubt, as the plays' practical military influence—was undercut by the several techniques by which Shakespeare called attention to the imaginary, theatrical character of the wars presented.

One such technique was his putting into the mouths of his characters eloquent descriptions of how the "holiness" of war was a theatrical effect (whether the war was waged by prelates or "holy" Protestant—or proto-Protestant—princes). In *2 Henry IV*, Morton speaks of how the Archbishop of York, who has joined Northumberland to fight the king, "[t]urns insurrection to religion / . . . Derives from heaven his quarrel and his cause" (1.1.202, 207) (and Morton is on York's side!); later in that play, Westmoreland distinguishes between the civil sphere, which handles war, and the religious, which should remain committed to peace (4.1.41–52). Costumed in his "white investments" (vestments), which should "figure innocence" (4.1.45), the deceptive archbishop gains followers in his militant cause. Unlike Spenser, who in *The Faerie Queene* attempts to fuse imperial aggression and Protestant religion, Shakespeare here slyly draws attention to war's essentially profane or secular character.

Another technique by which Shakespeare relegates "holy war" to the province of the imagination is his location of English Continental and proposed Eastern victories in the unrecoverable early 1400s. In the 1590s, when the second *Henriad* was first staged, Shakespeare's audience knew that Henry V's triumph in France had been brief, and that English claims there were ultimately lost, or if they did not know it, the play's epilogue told them. Audiences knew also that Henry's son did not "go to Constantinople and take the Turk by the beard"; in fact that Protestant England had not even made one of the Catholic Christian League that defeated the Turks at Lepanto in 1571, in recent English memory. By the late sixteenth century, England's more local quarrels with Catholic Spain had eclipsed its hostility towards Islamic nations, as I discussed in my last chapter. We may recall Nabil Matar's recent discovery that diplomatic efforts were made by Morocco to align with Elizabeth in the anti-Spanish cause in the 1590s.[44] In such a revised political context, an English assault on Constantinople must have seemed an enjoyable fantasy best relegated to a prior century. James Shapiro may have been right when he suggested that *Henry V* was seen by some as a "belated Armada play," meant to inspire warlike defensiveness against renewed threats of attack by what one Elizabethan subject called "the Hotspurs of Spain."[45] But still, home defense from invasion is not the outward-pushing expansion the play seems to recommend, and besides, the threat of a renewed Armada assault quickly fizzled in 1599. Shakespeare himself may have been thinking more of Ireland than of Spain when writing this play, as Shapiro has more lately concluded.[46] *Henry V*'s Chorus does associate great Henry—"by a lower . . . likelihood"—with Elizabeth's general Essex, who in 1599 was attempting to secure English control of Ireland by quelling rebellion there (5.Cho.29–32). But in all post-1600 performances of the play the audience would have known that Essex had failed and the reference to his glory would therefore have been omitted.[47]

I am suggesting that the glorious imperial "pilgrimage" the play dramatizes was for its audience an imaginary journey, celebrated as such. Again we may recall Stephen Greenblatt's recent proposition that the banished Catholic practice of prayers for the dead found imaginative life on the Renaissance stage. The energies once satisfied by another Catholic practice, English pilgrimage, were perhaps not so easily contained—in an earlier chapter I have suggested that some of these energies found outlets, as the travel author Hakluyt proposed, in New World exploratory, military, and commercial projects—but one use that was made of them was theatrical. Shake-

speare's company and others toured the provinces when they were
not playing in the city. Nonprovincial audiences, for their part,
crossed the Thames, and from thence embarked on imaginary travels. *Henry V*'s Chorus claims the playhouse as powerful locus of fictive voyages, urging audiences to

> . . . think
> [They] stand upon the rivage and behold
> A city on th'inconstant billows dancing;
> For so appears [Henry's] fleet majestical,
> Holding due course for Harflew. Follow, follow!
>
> (3.Cho.13–17)

In *Henry V* Shakespeare famously calls attention to the wires and mirrors that grant fictive life to performance: the "four or five . . . ragged foils" with which players mock battles (4.Cho.50), and the
audience's thoughts, invoked above. This metatheatrical comment
has its complement in the play's revelation that Henry's own saintly
transformation, heralded as miracle, has in fact been staged. In the
play's first scene Ely tells Canterbury what audiences who had seen
the *Henry IV* plays already knew: that the king's apparently wondrous
reformation was plotted long in advance, in private, and achieved by
a process of "obscur'd . . . contemplation" in an Eastcheap tavern.
Canterbury agrees, "It must be so; for miracles are ceas'd; / And
therefore we must needs admit the means / How things are per-
fected" (1.1.63, 67–69). This Catholic bishop's deeply Protestant
comment leads us to credit imagination's role in the construction of
even royal saints, a thing the Chorus also urges us to do. "'[T]is
your thoughts that now must deck our kings" (Pro.28). *Henry V* suggests that the means by which kings are made holy, and fit to inspire
reverent soldiering, are like the means by which playgoing is turned
into warfare. Both means are theatrical.[48]

Shakespeare's audience's willingness to engage in theatrical play
with saints and shrines, and imaginatively to reroute holy pilgrimage, was supported by Protestant England's earlier official redefin-
ing of intercessory saints as hoaxes. Doubtless the early Reformers
disliked that keepers of the more celebrated shrines, when those still
operated, used tricks of stagecraft to enhance the shrines' appeal.
Erasmus's descriptions of the severed limbs he saw in Canterbury
Cathedral, and other accounts of the dramatic raising, by ropes and

pulleys, of the lids over the sparkling jewels at both Cuthbert's and Thomas's tombs, may suggest to us today the wax body parts that horrify Webster's Duchess of Malfi, or the glittering treasure over which Marlowe's Barabas gloats. The ludicrous ceremony with which Lord Privy Seal Thomas Cromwell "proved" Becket's lack of sanctity in 1538, and with which Cromwell accompanied the dismantling of Becket's shrine, was an action designed to expose not just such stage management of the shrines, but the unreality of the saint himself: his purely theatrical existence. Cromwell, we recall, gave Becket thirty days to appear before the King's Council to answer charges. Too dead to comply, St. Thomas was condemned as a fraud, and his bones—once relics, now useless joints—were publicly burned.

As the martyr who defended the pope's authority against the monarch's, Thomas was fittest for repudiation in a ceremony which exalted a king at a saint's expense. Cromwell's 1538 proclamation declared that Thomas Becket had resisted "the wholesome laws established against the enormities of the clergy by the King's highness' [Henry VIII's] most noble progenitor, King Henry II."[49] In Shakespeare's *Henry VIII* (1613), the sanctity of Becket, who in 1170 fell from stab wounds in Canterbury Cathedral, is in 1613 imaginatively displaced onto Lord Cromwell himself and made conditional to Cromwell's subservience to the monarch. For in *Henry VIII* Cardinal Wolsey tells Cromwell that if he "Serve the king" and fall, he will fall "a blessed martyr" (3.1.448–50). In Shakespeare's history plays, kings and even lesser lords can displace saints because saints are officially illusions. Yet *Henry V* suggests that sacred kingship is also a staged thing.

In the past twenty years the assertion that the stage contributed vitally to the widespread English demystifying of the monarch, and led within a half-century to a king's formal execution, has become almost a critical commonplace. Theatrical deconsecration led to decapitation, Franco Moretti wrote in 1982.[50] I am less confident than some in our ability, as students of literary and dramatic texts, to assign simple cause to such complex historical outcomes. Like Shakespeare scholars, audiences see what they like to see,[51] and make of plays what they will. One early-modern subject might have been moved to reverence for all monarchs by the image of Henry V praying before Agincourt like Christ in Gethsemane. Another's adoration might have been tempered when he heard the praying king address God as "God of battles," and recalled that the divinity with whom the Chorus had most explicitly linked Henry was Mars (Pro.6). By the same token (or relic), a Protestant playgoer in London might have laughed wisely at Henry V's mockery of saints' bones. On the other hand, had *Henry VIII* been staged in the provinces, a Catholic in Warwickshire might have heard regret for the loss of Becket's shrine in Wolsey's claim that if Cromwell serves the king he "fall[s]"—fells?—"a blessed martyr." Not only faith but class differences very likely resulted in differing audience responses to saint references in Shakespeare. In her exhaustive study of Saint George's representation in literature and art, Samantha Riches notes that

> [t]he concept of St George as a warrior-saint [rather than a figure of Christ] would undoubtedly have appealed to men who were themselves soldiers, and perhaps especially to the aristocratic elite who fought in armor and on horseback, a guise in which the saint is often presented. He may have been less appealing to the bowmen and the foot soldiers, who saw only a vague reflection of their own experience of combat in the image of this dragon-slaying knight. How much less meaningful would this figure have been to the rest of the English populace . . . [?][52]

Thus Henry V's "Cry, God for Harry, England, and Saint George" must have stirred varying degrees of reverence, as well as none, among audiences.

We cannot rightly gauge the cultural impact of such dramatic effects, or determine from them whether Shakespeare himself revered saints or kings. A half-century after *Henry VIII*'s first performance, Milton was far more direct in his rejection of the theatrical apparatuses used to sanctify both saints *and* kings: in *Eikonoklastes,* he describes a portrait of King Charles as "drawn out to the full measure of a Masking Scene" to "catch fools and silly gazers," and adds that "quaint Emblems and devices begg'd from the Old Pageantry of some Twelf-nights entertainment at *Whitehall,* will doe but ill to make a Saint or Martyr."[53] Compared to Milton the firebrand, Shakespeare is disinterested. What *he* shows us, most plainly in *Henry V,* is that England's dismantled shrines and desacralized pilgrimages provide rich materials for dramatic play.

4

For Fidelia, Fidele:
Compostela and Erotic Pilgrimage in *All's Well That Ends Well, Cymbeline,* and *Othello*

Sancho replied, "I would like your grace to tell me why Spaniards, when they do battle calling on Saint James the Moor-Killer,
say, 'Sant Iago, and close [ranks for] Spain!'"
                        —Miguel de Cervantes Saavedra, *El Ingenioso
                        Hidalgo Don Quijote de la Mancha*[1]

FOR SHAKESPEARE, PLAY WITH PILGRIMAGE WAS NOT LIMITED TO HISTORI-
cal theater set in the medieval English past and primarily addressing
political themes. Indeed, it is Shakespeare's plays of romantic passion—including comedy, romance, and tragedy—that most fully celebrate and redirect the English pilgrimage, turning it fully into what
its early discounters, like William Langland, had accused it of being:
a quest for erotic fulfillment. In *Henry V,* as we have seen, eros is subsumed to the royal imperialist drive. Henry addresses French Katherine in a lover's vein, yet reveals his hope that their marriage will
finally serve to expand English empire, by producing a son who will
"go to Constantinople and take the Turk by the beard." Yet, when
released from the warlike imperatives of the Henry plays, Shakespeare lets eros reign, and sends his characters on love pilgrimages,
to joyful or destructive ends.

Some of Shakespeare's early and middle plays show the connection he habitually made between eros and pilgrimage. In *The Two
Gentlemen of Verona,* Julia, following her lover Proteus to Milan, calls
herself a "true-devoted pilgrim," "not weary / To measure kingdoms" with her "feeble steps" (2.7.9–10). In *A Midsummer Night's
Dream,* Hermia rejects the "maiden pilgrimage" (1.1.75) of cloistered prayer for a more strenuous journey with Lysander through

the Athenian woods. In *Romeo and Juliet* the young lovers develop a sustained metaphor by which they and Romeo's lips become "blushing pilgrims" as the two prepare to kiss (1.5.95–107). *The Merchant of Venice*'s Bassanio has sworn a "secret pilgrimage" to Portia, whom he will woo (1.1.120). And in *As You Like It*, Orlando, pinning verses on trees, argues the superiority of love poems to "Rosalinda" to conventional satirical maxims that called life an "erring pilgrimage" (3.2.130). That "erring pilgrimage" was a hackneyed phrase in 1599 suggests that the association between Catholic pilgrimage and religious error was by 1600 a commonplace which justified Shakespeare's easy application of the word "pilgrimage" to erotic quest. Yet it is Shakespeare's post-1600 plays which most elaborately develop the erotic pilgrimage, finding inspiration from a curious source: the famous legends surrounding the shrine of Santiago de Compostela, in northern Spain.

Shakespeare's interest in Santiago, Spain's patron saint, is manifest in three post-1600 plays of distinct genre: the comedy *All's Well That Ends Well*, the tragedy *Othello*, and the romance *Cymbeline*. Each of these plays sports with ideas about pilgrimages and miracles, themes which Reformed English sensibilities now associated primarily with Catholic holy sites such as Spain's Compostela, where the apostle James was reputedly buried. As he plays with these themes, Shakespeare not only makes use of Saint James's name (which appears in French, Spanish, and Italian in the three plays), but also borrows from the specific legend of Santiago, adapting aspects of the saint's myth to stage action in ways calculated to satisfy audience expectations for erotic plots in tragedy, comedy, or romance.

In a fourth play written close to the turn of the seventeenth century, *Hamlet*, mad Ophelia associates Compostela pilgrims with eros, singing, " 'How should I your true love know / From another one? / By his cockle hat and staff, and his sandal shoon" (4.4.23–26). The lost song, doubtless familiar to Elizabethan playgoers, suggests that the traditional accouterments of the Compostela pilgrim, the staff and the cockle (seashell) pinned hat, marked a lover. By analyzing this common English prejudice, the long-standing legend of Santiago Matamoros, and the dramatic use Shakespeare made of both prejudice and legend, I hope to demonstrate that in *All's Well*, *Othello*, and *Cymbeline* Shakespeare subordinated Greco-Iberian myth, Catholic notions of pilgrimage and miracle, general cultural prejudices regarding Mediterranean peoples, and even English anti-

Semitism to his overriding dramaturgical purposes. Specifically, I want to show that in these three plays he stripped the Santiago myth, as well as English prejudices against Jews and Spaniards, of topical religious significance. In exchange he invested those myths and prejudices with erotic significance, and did so in ways fitted to the comic, tragic, or romance enactment of love relationships.

When Shakespeare linked the pilgrimage to Compostela with comic, tragic, and tragicomic eros, he was—as Ophelia's song suggests—assisted by the reputation the Santiago pilgrimage already had in England. The pilgrimage was considered a sexy expedition even before Reformation edicts reconstrued all pilgrimages to saints' shrines as vanity. As Colin Smith writes, since the mid-twelfth century, when the *Liber Sancti Jacobi* proclaiming the miracles of Santiago was widely translated and propounded from European pulpits,[2] travel to Spain had been associated by the English with exotic entertainments which sometimes included, "despite warnings, indulging in a little light-hearted dalliance away from the constraints of home." Smith also comments on the "folkloric and pre-apostolic associations" with Venus worship suggested to the English (and other Europeans) by the seashell, the badge of the successful Compostela pilgrim.[3] Of course, as I have suggested, the example of Chaucer's Wife of Bath, who joins the Canterbury pilgrims to seek a husband, shows that the English association between pilgrimage and erotic quest did not only pertain to pilgrimages on foreign soil. But the English vision of the Mediterranean world as a hotbed of sensual intemperance[4] made a journey to Spain seem an especially likely occasion for romantic dalliance. And in fact, English skepticism regarding the spiritual motivation of some Compostela pilgrims was well founded. In their two-volume history of Compostela, Vázquez de Parga, Lacarra, and Uría Ríu attest to the existence of many pleasure-seeking "pilgrims" for whom the journey to Galicia was "little more than a pretext for the satisfaction of curiosity to encounter people and strange lands to satisfy the unquiet traveler's humor":[5] a worldly restlessness, if not, strictly speaking, an erotic one. An episode in the second part of Cervantes' *Don Quijote* bears out the claims of Vázquez de Parga, Lacarra, and Uría Ríu. There Sancho Panza meets a Moor who has disguised himself as a pilgrim in order to "see it all," and who begs money as he travels.[6] Luis Andrés Murillo writes that such false Compostela pilgrims were many and that they usually were "single men and women claiming to be married"[7] and thereby giving a religious color to their clandestine dalliances.

As my first chapter suggested, suspicions about pilgrims abounded in England even before the sixteenth-century English Reformers' general condemnation of pilgrimages and shrines. A Jacobean audience thus might not have been surprised when *All's Well That Ends Well*'s Helena claimed to be setting out for the shrine of "Saint Jaques," or Santiago (3.3.4–17), but then turned up far out of the way in Florence, spending her energies on a plot to dupe her wayward husband into consummating their marriage.[8] Shakespeare's audience might also have thought of wander-lusty pilgrimages to the shrine whose name Iago bore when Roderigo called Othello an "extravagant and wheeling stranger / Of here and everywhere" (*Othello* 1.2.136–37), or when Othello himself recounted his "pilgrimage" to strange lands where men's heads "grow beneath their shoulders" (*Othello* 1.3.130–53). Indeed, Othello's stories would have reminded literate playgoers of the popular late-medieval *Mandeville's Travels*, wherein accounts of pilgrimages are mingled with fantastic tales of folk in Mauritania, where Iago claims Othello will go (*Othello* 4.2.224) (Mauritanians "han but o [one] foot . . . so large that it schadeweth all the body agen the sonne whanne thei wole lye and rest them").[9] Similarly, audiences would have been primed to accept Imogen's journey to Milford Haven as a love pilgrimage (though a licit one). In *Cymbeline* Milford Haven is a Welsh outpost whose location in Britain is analogous to the site of Santiago de Compostela in a place called "Land's End" in Galicia, western Spain.[10] But Imogen, of course, does not go to this British "Land's End" to venerate a saint. In place of "Santiago" *Cymbeline* gives us Jachimo, a worldly Mediterranean villain, and in place of a pilgrim's religious motive the play gives us Imogen's earthy desire to be close to her husband Posthumus (*Cymbeline* 3.4.141–84).

We see that in all three of these plays Shakespeare specifically refers to pilgrimage (*All's Well*'s Helena's words, and Othello's) or indirectly suggests pilgrimage (Imogen's journey, and the naming of key characters after James). However, all three of the plays alter the meaning of pilgrimage from the fulfillment of religious duty to the satisfaction of wanderlust or erotic love. This alteration catered to preexisting English associations between pilgrimage and carnal pursuits. It also served the dramatic purposes of three plays in which eros, not religious faith, was a central impulse.

We recall that the Thirty-Nine Articles added to the Book of Common Prayer during Elizabeth's reign called "Worshipping and Adoration" a "Romish doctrine," "repugnant to the Word of God." Some scholars have seen this Reformed condemnation of idolatry at work in Shakespeare's characterization of the "pilgrims" of *All's Well That Ends Well, Othello,* or *Cymbeline.*[11] Indeed, all three of the plays dramatize "pilgrimages" inspired by near-idolatrous love, and in each case the pilgrim's adulation of the beloved is shown to be ill founded at best, and self-destructive at worst. Helena's description of Bertram as a "star" and herself as his "worshipper" calls attention to her callow husband's unfitness for such praise, and shows that Helena is indeed, as she confesses, "[r]eligious in . . . error" (1.1.86, 1.3.206, 205). Desdemona shows extreme reverence for Othello— she consecrates her soul to him, performs "rites" of love for him, and follows him to war-threatened Cyprus on a doting pilgrimage (1.3.254, 257–59)—and her worshipfulness contributes to her death. In contrast to (say) *The Winter's Tale*'s Hermione, who strongly challenges her husband's vicious slander (3.2.22–54), Desdemona persists in revering Othello until he is killing her. For his part, Othello's idolizing of Desdemona, whom he likens to a "perfect chrysolite" and even, perhaps to Christ, the "pearl" thrown away by Judas (5.2.145, 347), inspires his murderous disillusionment when he hears her falseness alleged, and his suicidal remorse when, dead, she is restored to his good faith.[12]

Here it may be instructive to compare Othello's jealousy with that felt by Spenser's Redcrosse Knight when, similarly persuaded of his love's infidelity by a devilish ocular deception, the knight languishes, smitten by "bitter anguish" and jealous "torment" (*FQ* 1.2.6). In Spenser's poem, in which iconoclasm coexists uneasily with reverence for Elizabeth and Una, idolatrous worship of an idealized woman is not even a partial contributor to later unmerited disgust with her. Fooled by the real devil, Archimago, rather than a devilish human, Redcrosse moves from a knowledge of Una's perfect virtue to ignorant doubt of it; his redemption from hellish jealousy involves his reclamation of Una's pristine image. He returns to his starting point, where she, no woman, appears "rocke of Diamond" (*FQ* 1.6.5). In contrast, Othello's idealization of Desdemona—his growing uneasiness with a wife who "feeds well, loves company," and "[i]s free of speech" (3.3.184–85)—helps make him susceptible to Iago's suggestions that her behavior is unseemly, and renders him tragically unable to listen to a Desdemona who is flesh and blood rather than "perfect chrysolite" or ("monumental alablaster" [5.2.5]).

Some of Shakespeare's erotic pilgrims recover from idolatry's ill effects, although Othello does not. *Cymbeline*'s Imogen, more practical than Othello or Desdemona (and certainly than the Redcrosse Knight), discards her reverence for Posthumus when, midpilgrimage, she discovers his lack of faith in *her* (3.4). Yet, although Imogen's disillusionment is comically rather than tragically resolved, it too is a means by which Shakespeare dramatizes the error of idolizing a lover, as he had done in *Othello* as well as slightly earlier in *All's Well.* Imogen's reference to Posthumus' "great fail" (3.4.64) both reminds us of her earlier view of him as inhumanly perfect, or unfallen, and of the distance between him and that ideal. "[B]lessed Milford" (3.4.59), where Imogen has come to revere her saint, is, in fact, just a place in Wales where an ordinary, fallible husband might be found.

That these three plays either gently or forcefully condemn the folly of idolatry is clear. It is less clear, however, that the exposure of the error of idolizing one's spouse had topical religious significance at the time of the plays' first performance, despite contemporary scholars' growing insistence that Shakespeare's plays played a powerful part on one side or the other of Reformation debates. The Calvinist-leaning Thirty-Nine Articles may have condemned the worship of saints, but Shakespeare's plays do not dramatize the worship of saints, but the confusion of spouses with saints, or with divinities. To be sure, Protestants would have disapproved of such extreme reverence accorded to spouses. Although English Protestant divines replaced the Catholic ascetic ideal with high respect for the conjugal relation, they were manifestly aware of the dangers of substituting spousal love for the love of God.[13] Yet this idolatry is such as Rome too would abhor (just as Rome officially abhorred "pilgrimages" inspired by mere wanderlust or an interest in exotic dalliance). The treatments of idolatry in this comedy, tragedy, and romance are thus neither Catholic nor Protestant. Instead, they show Shakespeare drawing on a wealth of imaginative material, including medieval English and contemporary Catholic reverence toward saints like Iago de Compostela, and the reputation of Compostela pilgrims as often driven by worldly interests, to fashion more general Christian dramatic comments on marital folly. Relative to the demands of each play's genre, disappointed marital idolatry is (for the characters) comically instructive, tragically fatal, or an occasion for ultimate, radical forgiveness.

Reworking the myth of Santiago—the legends that justified the Compostela pilgrimage—helped Shakespeare achieve these dramaturgical ends. Of course, to show how Shakespeare used the Santiago myth, it will first be necessary to summarize it.

The legend of Santiago de Compostela begins with the biblical account of the Great Commission, by which Christ charged his apostles to go "into all the worlde, & preache the Gospel to everie creature" (Mark 16:15). According to the myth, after Jesus's death James left Palestine to preach in Spain, arriving there by ship. After his first journey he returned to Jerusalem, where in AD 44 he was beheaded by the Roman governor Herod Agrippa and his body was thrown outside the city walls. His followers retrieved his body, reattached the head (!), and sailed with James back to Spain, where they landed on the west coast and walked northward, finally burying the apostle at the place known as Compostela, or Land's End. Beginning in the ninth century, during the *Reconquista* (the Christian encroachment on Islamic Spain), numerous legends arose among the Spanish testifying to James's appearance on horseback to inspire Christian victories against the Moors. Hence the saint acquired the name "Santiago Matamoros," or "Saint James the Moor-Killer." The association of Santiago with holy battle persisted in the Renaissance. Sancho Panza and Don Quijote discuss it,[14] and in 1589 Robert Greene mocked Spaniards' habit of seeking out "S. James of Compostella" in battle.[15] James's reputation as a warlike apostle may well have been supported by pre-Christian myths concerning Castor and Pollux, sons of Jupiter the Thunderer who came later to be associated with James and his brother John when, in the Gospel of Mark, Jesus named James and John "the sonnes of thunder" (3:17). Some Spaniards came to believe that Santiago was actually the *cause* of thunder (a datum which would have interested King Lear). Santiago's power to raise the dead was also alleged, a myth stemming partly from Mark 5, where Jesus resurrects the daughter of the synagogue ruler with the assistance of the sons of thunder (5:37–42).[16]

In the late Middle Ages, when Compostela was as popular a site of English pilgrimage as Canterbury,[17] new legends arose about the blessings of hospitality found on the road and the miracles of protection afforded to pious travelers. *El Libro de los Huéspedes*, or *The*

Book of Guests, a medieval handbook for Compostela pilgrims, stressed the importance of hospitable behavior by citing Bible stories that linked hospitality with miracles (like the account of Christ at the wedding in Cana).[18] Santiago, of course, ensured the protection of guests (as did "punishments prescribed by ecclesiastical and royal authorities for any who might molest or cheat or attack them").[19] Santiago's protection extended far from Spain to those who were beginning or ending their journeys to venerate him. A 1365 English account tells of five men of the Borough of St. James in Lincoln who, returning from a pilgrimage to Compostela, "were in great danger from a storm at sea." The men prayed for the intercession of Saint James and were delivered into "the desired haven."[20]

General resemblances between these Santiago legends and the plots of *All's Well, Othello,* and *Cymbeline* immediately suggest themselves. As I will show, as Shakespeare adapted these myths to his drama, he emphasized the *theatrical* nature of the staged miracles of romantic comedy, romantic tragedy, and tragicomic romance. Thus, as he unleashed the theatrical and erotic power of the Santiago legend, Shakespeare avoided the potential topical and particular Protestant or Catholic overtones of the representation of miracles. By presenting miracles as theatrical contrivances, Shakespeare was not attacking the beliefs of his Catholic contemporaries, but simply exploiting the theatrical possibilities of religious beliefs which Protestant England had officially categorized as fanciful.

While Protestant readings of *All's Well, Othello,* and *Cymbeline* stress the theme of idolatry, Catholic readings of *All's Well* and *Cymbeline* focus on miracles. For example, Velma Bourgeois Richmond and Peter Milward see in *Cymbeline* an expression of approval for Catholic pilgrimages to the shrines of miracle workers,[21] and David N. Beauregard, claiming that "Shakespeare was brought up by Roman Catholic parents,"[22] adduces the likelihood that the presentation of Helena's "miracle and merit" in *All's Well* affirms the existence of "post-Scriptural miracles," a doctrine accepted by Catholics but rejected by Reformed theologians.[23] Of course, Protestant readings find behind Helena's refusal to "ascribe [wondrous remedies] to heaven" (1.2.217) a more skeptical Shakespeare, who supports King James's Reformed view that "False *Miracles* and lying newes, are the foode of Superstition."[24]

Yet the "miracles" of both these plays are so qualified by dramatic exigencies that it is difficult to see how they support *or* condemn Catholic doctrine. In *All's Well*, the audience knows Helena isn't dead and so isn't surprised by her reappearance at play's end. Also, Helena's pregnancy by Bertram, who does not think he has slept with her, is amazing only to those characters who have not (as has the audience) followed the tricky role-play by which she has managed to conceive. And by leaving the final proof of Helena's miracle still gestating, Shakespeare adds to the famous conditionality of his play's "miraculous" outcome. Bertram knows that Helena is pregnant, but not that he is the father—a conspicuous change from Shakespeare's source story, wherein Helena's prototype gives birth to twins "so like" her husband that he is "astoned."[25] In Shakespeare's source all ends wonderfully well, but in his play all only "seems well" (5.3.333). Miracles are left pending.

Shakespeare similarly qualifies miracles in *Cymbeline*, where Imogen's "resurrection," amazing to her brothers, father, and husband, is not so to the play's audience, whom Shakespeare has carefully acquainted with her flight in disguise and with the fact that the potion she drinks in act 4, scene 2, is not poison but a sleeping draught (1.5.39–44). The appearance of Jupiter and the spirits of the dead Leonati in *Cymbeline*'s act 5, scene 4, are astounding events, but are also, as I will show, so obviously stage-managed that their theatricality is emphasized and their miraculousness claimed as the province of theater. More importantly still, all the "amazing" events in *Cymbeline*, like those in *All's Well*, are so wrested from the context of religious to that of erotic devotion that they clearly support the aims of comic or tragicomic romance rather than those of Catholic or Protestant theology.

In *All's Well That Ends Well*, the old nobleman Lafew is miracle's spokesman. His complaint against those who "say miracles are past" and "make modern and familiar, things supernatural and causeless" (2.3.1–2) defies both Reformed theology, which discounted miracles, and skeptical philosophy, which sought the natural causes of amazing events. Lafew's comments express his belief that Helena's surprising cure of the French king's "fistula" (1.1.34) has been the work of Providence. Helena, however, has framed the cure differently, in her earlier claim that "remedies oft in ourselves do lie, / Which we ascribe to heaven" (1.2.216–17). Her boast, made in soliloquy, of her natural ability to accomplish "miraculous" things makes her seem piously hypocritical—an actor playing at religious reverence—when later, before the King and court, she warns against the "presumption" of thinking "the help of heaven" to be merely the "act of men" (1.1.151–52). The sly second meaning of her warning is divined by the audience, who has heard her soliloquy. The remedy has not been heaven's, but her own; not the act of men, but the act of a woman.

The remedy Helena wants most to effect is, of course, the curing of her own love sickness for Bertram. But since that remedy turns out to be achieving Bertram by curing the King and thus winning her choice of husband, her early reference to earthly "remedies" does not signify saintly healing. Helena is not an apostolic doctor but an erotic one, who cures her own love longing by first raising the King. The King's raising is itself broadly sexualized (which makes the pun appropriate). Helena and the king withdraw so she can cure him in secret, leaving the audience to their own erotic imaginings about what's taking place between them. (Much is made in this play of Helena's virginity [1.3.118; 1.1.110–65; 2.1.114, 172], a fact which prompts David Haley's comparison of her king cure to the young virgin's attempt to restore the dying King David by letting her "lye in [his] bosome" [1 Kings 1:2].)[26] Earlier, leaving the King to interview Helena, Lafew—"another dirty old man," as a student of mine once called him—calls himself a pander: "I am Cressid's uncle, / That dare leave two together" (2.1.97–98). Helena markets her mysterious cure in oddly erotic terms, asking that if it doesn't work she be accused of sexual profligacy (2.1.170–73). It does work, and makes the king "*Lustick*" (2.3.41). As a reward, the lusty king gives her not only a husband but a ring, a gift associated with romantic interest, and one which parallels Helena's later gift of the same ring to Bertram in bed. The king erupts when he sees it on Bertram's finger in the play's last scene (5.3.278–84) (is he jealous?).

The erotic overtones of the king's cure and of the ring's passage from finger to finger would strip these "miracles" of Reformation-era theological significance even if the cause of one of the miracles—Bertram's possession of Helena's ring—were not plainly known, to the audience, to stem from Helena's playacting (posing as Diana in bed, she has put the ring on Bertram's finger [5.3.110]). True to her initial claim that she will create her own "remedies," Helena fosters all the play's erotic miracles, with plots and pretenses ranging from the bed trick, which issues in her pregnancy, to the false report she implicitly puts out of her death (4.4.11), which enables her pretended resurrection in the play's last scene. A passionate pilgrim, Helena disguises herself as a devotee of Saint Jaques in order to tryst with Bertram in Florence, and thus manifests Shakespeare's adaptation of exotic pilgrimage to the erotic purposes sacred to romantic comedy. As "Saint Jaques' pilgrim," "[habited]" as a palmer, Helena serves neither God nor saint but only Cupid, or "Ambitious love" (3.4.4–5 and s.d. 3.5.30).

Shakespeare drew more widely from the reputed Santiago miracles to enhance his presentation of wondrous events in Cymbeline, a romance. Although Cymbeline's heroine is like Helena in that she disguises herself to pursue her husband, fewer play "miracles" are attributable to Imogen's schemes. Still, as I have suggested, the wondrous events in Cymbeline are so obviously contrived, so "overt[ly] theatrical,"[27] that it is difficult to imagine an audience taking from them any serious validation of the Catholic belief in modern miracles. Similarly, as in All's Well That Ends Well, the frankly erotic context of many of the play's wild events secularizes Shakespeare's borrowings from the myth of Santiago.

The studied contrivance of Cymbeline's wondrous happenings begins with the play's opening dialogue, "an undisguisedly functional conversation between supernumeraries, peppered with the most improbable questions and without the slightest atmospheric buildup," to quote Marco Mincoff.[28] By means of this conversation between anonymous court gentlemen, we learn of the long-ago disappearance of King Cymbeline's two young sons, Arviragus and Guiderius. The later onstage (or just-above-stage) appearance of Jupiter the "Thunder-master" and Jupiter's prophecy regarding those boys (5.4.30, 140–43), as well as the boys' thunderous fifth-act trouncing of the Roman invaders, will bring to mind Jupiter's sons Castor and Pollux, whom both biblical and Spanish tradition connected with Saint James. (Jupiter's appearance riding an eagle will also recall the vision of Santiago on horseback. Both the god and the saint inspire military victories against invaders or armies perceived as such.) An additional event in the play tempts comparison between the royal brothers on the one hand and both Castor and Pollux and the biblical James on the other. The boys' heartbreak at the apparent death of their disguised sister, the princess Imogen, whom Arviragus calls "brother" (4.2.2–3), will evoke Pollux's grief over Castor's death, a sadness which prompted Jupiter to restore Castor to life. The boy's

attendance at the drugged princess's "funeral" (4.2) will also evoke
the biblical story of James and John at the resurrection of the synagogue ruler's daughter; like her, Imogen seems dead, but is only
sleeping. Thus echoes of Greco-Roman and biblical myth, drawn
from the syncretic tradition surrounding Santiago, will resonate in
the presentation of *Cymbeline*'s princes.

Yet, here at the play's outset, the dialogue seems designed not
only to inform the audience of these thunder-sons' existence, but
comically to foreground the fantastic nature of their amazing lives.
All the events involving them are *dramatic* wonders, which the audience is urged to accept as such. "That a king's children should be
so convey'd, / So slackly guarded, and the search so slow / That
could not trace them!" says First Gentleman. "Howsoe'er 'tis
strange / Or that the negligence may well be laugh'd at, / Yet it is
true, sir," Second Gentleman replies (1.1.63–67). This conversational strain is repeated in act five, again in connection with the glorious princes. After Postumus reports the miraculous three-man
victory of Arviragus, Guiderius, and their foster father Belarius over
the Roman army, a Lord says, "This was strange chance." "Nay, do
not wonder at it," suggests Posthumus (5.3.51, 53).

Neither the anonymous lord nor the audience should wonder at
this victory, not because it is humanly possible or, as a mark of God's
providence, theologically plausible, but because it is justified by the
extravagant conventions of romance. The appearance of thunder-
ing Jupiter, dangled above the stage by means of an awkward mechanical device;[29] the happy accident of Imogen's encounter with
her lost brothers; and the fortunate fifth-act death of Cymbeline's
wicked queen all satisfy the requirements of a genre that is, in Mincoff's words, "committed to the happy ending."[30] The happy ending of tragicomedy is distinct from that of comedy. It is not
engineered by the wit of a clever Helena, but compelled by "outra-
geous," "blatantly unrealistic" accidents.[31] Indeed, Mincoff hears in
one of Jupiter's lines Shakespeare's virtual confession that *Cymbeline*'s events are structured purely to effect comic catharsis in the audience. Jupiter tells the ghosts of the Leonati that he afflicts those he
loves in order "to make [his] gift, / The more delay'd, delighted"
(5.4.101–2). As Mincoff writes, "One may be inclined to wonder
whether [this] is not Shakespeare the dramatist rather than the
voice of providence, speaking from his knowledge that for the audience an effect of extreme happiness will best be achieved through

the contrast with suffering."[32] Thus Santiago-like miracles are cele-brated in *Cymbeline*, but only as theatrical effects.

The blatant foregrounding of illusion is also evident in Shake-speare's adaptation of elements of the Santiago myth to the Imogen plot. I have suggested that Shakespeare presents Imogen's journey to Milford Haven as an erotic "pilgrimage" which she undertakes in order to approach Posthumus, her secular saint. Once disillusioned with Posthumus, Imogen decanonizes him (so to speak), and tempo-rarily gives over the "pilgrimage." Still, she continues to have experi-ences which are evocative of the Compostela tradition. By her brothers she is granted the warm hospitality and even the medical care that were the sacred duties of hosts on the Compostela road ("You are not well. Remain here in the cave." "Brother, stay here. Are we not brothers?" [4.2.1–3]). Her encounter with the corpse of Cloten, which has been contemptuously left on the ground by his slayer, Guiderius, is a comic-erotic version of the myth of James's dis-ciples' encounter with the apostle's headless body outside the walls of Jerusalem. Those faithful disciples reattached James's head be-fore sailing with him to Spain, where, centuries later, he came back to life to assist the Goths in Christian victory. In act 4 of *Cymbeline*, Imogen, now disguised as "Fidele" (meaning "Faithful") and be-lieving Cloten's body to be Posthumus's, demonstrates not religious but marital faithfulness by "*[f]all[ing] on the body*," crying "my lord! my lord!" (4.2.332 and *s.d.*). Later, of course, she sees Posthumus's head figuratively reattached (when she discovers it was never really off).

Posthumus's initial cruel treatment of Imogen in the play's last scene seems designed not only to emphasize the theatrically con-trived nature of *Cymbeline*'s "miraculous" reunions, but to demon-strate that Posthumus is *not* a saint, and thus to emphasize the human, marital domain of the culmination of Imogen's pilgrimage. When the still-disguised Imogen calls Posthumus "my lord," he strikes her to the ground, asking, "Shall's have a play of this? Thou scornful page, / There lie thy part" (5.5.227–28). The bitter blow—uncharacteristically harsh even for angry Posthumus—creates a satis-fying contrast with the sweetness of the couple's embrace a few lines later, when Posthumus finds that it is his wife he has struck ("Hang there like fruit, my soul, / Till the tree die!" [5.5.263–64]). Thus presented, their reunion reinforces the audience's sense that in ro-mance, the motive and outcome of pilgrimages are grounded in

marital love, and that "miracles" serve lawful eros. Here again a contrast between Shakespeare's and Spenser's miracle-working characters proves revelatory. In the first book of the self-consciously
Protestant *Faerie Queene*, Redcrosse is miraculously restored by Fidelia, a female emblem of salvific faith in Christ. In *Cymbeline*, marital
reunion is effected by Fidele (the disguised Imogen), whose name
suggests not faith in God but faithfulness to a human husband. Law-
abiding eros is the source of her wonder-working power. A line from
Shakespeare's earlier comedy *The Taming of the Shrew* applies well to
Cymbeline's amazing events: "Love wrought these miracles" (*Shrew*
5.1.124).

What becomes of the figure of Santiago, in this tragicomedy that
sports with his myth? We have seen how Shakespeare comically
transposes Santiago's image with that of hanging Jupiter; with Cloten's headless corpse, which Imogen mistakenly idolizes; and with
Posthumus, the secular saint Imogen thinks the corpse to be (or
have been). Yet Shakespeare reserves Santiago's name neither for
Cloten nor Posthumus, but for Jachimo, the Mediterranean villain
who maligns Imogen's sexual chastity and prompts Posthumus's
"great fail." To illuminate Shakespeare's association of Santiago
with Jachimo, we must turn to Jachimo's rich prototype and the dra-
matization of tragic "miracle" in *Othello*.

Steve Sohmer has recently suggested that casual references to pilgrimage in *Othello*—such as Othello's use of the word "pilgrimage"
to describe his global wanderings (1.3.153)—are in fact rooted in
the play's serious consideration of issues related to Catholic pilgrimage. He points out that Venice was a common departure point for
Jerusalem-bound pilgrims, and Cyprus such travelers' "final safe
harbor"—facts that Shakespeare may likely have learned from the
popular *Informacion for Pylgrymes*, first printed by Wynteyn de Worde
in 1498.[33] Sohmer implies that, at least for Catholic members of
Shakespeare's audience, Othello's departure from Venice to Cyprus
would have borne overtones of holy journey and been associated
with "the conflict between the Catholic doctrine of works and the
Protestant dogma of election."[34] Yet in fact, as in *All's Well That Ends
Well*, the allusions to pilgrimage in *Othello* are secularized and sexualized. Jerusalem is implicitly invoked by the Cyprus journey, yet the
audience sees that *Othello*'s characters do not really sail to the place
Sohmer calls "the most exalted pilgrim destination,"[35] but to an is-

land where sexual passion will govern their actions. The name of the chief saint of Catholic pilgrimage, Iago of Compostela, is given to the protagonist, himself partly driven by lust, who inflames Othello's sexual jealousy, and the "unconsummated pilgrimage" that Othello's Cyprian journey becomes is a failed erotic journey.[36] In *Othello* as in *Cymbeline*, eros, not theology or religious practice, is the play's main concern—or, rather, the subordination of theology and religious practice *to* eros is the project of the drama.

Marco Mincoff speaks of the "atmosphere of sex lying over the whole" of *Cymbeline*,[37] present in Jachimo's lascivious excitement at the sight of sleeping Imogen (1.2.14–42), Cloten's obscene musings (1.3.14–15), and Posthumus's graphic, tortured imaginings of his wife's supposed act of adultery (2.5.15–19). *Othello*'s action, which culminates in a bedroom, is similarly suffused with sex. Iago—a creature, according to Derek Traversi, of "intense sexuality"[38]—is first to generate the play's erotic ambience, when in the opening scene he wakes Brabantio with shouted descriptions of his daughter and Othello in bed: "an old black ram / Is tupping your white ewe" (1.1.88–89); "your daughter and the Moor are [now] making the beast with two backs" (1.1.115–17). The chief source of erotic imaginings in *Othello*, Iago invokes an image of "bride and groom / Devesting" (1.3.180–81), pictures Othello making "wanton the night" with Desdemona (2.3.16), and speaks of Desdemona "lying naked with [a] friend in bed" (4.1.3). Further, it is Iago who incites Othello's imagination until Othello speaks in the same vein ("she can turn, and turn; and yet go on / And turn again" [4.1.253–54]).

It may be granted that many of Iago's, and subsequently Othello's, sexual imaginings are ignoble and ugly. Brabantio calls Iago's shouted comments "profane" (1.1.114), and there is no hint of wholesome eros in Iago's comment that lovers might be "as prime as goats, as hot as monkeys" (3.3.403), or in Othello's comparison between a violated marriage bed and "a cestern" in which "foul toads . . . knot and gender" (4.2.61–62). Still, as is not often noted, both Iago's and Othello's poetic lines and gestures frequently turn audience attention to the grace of sexual interaction and the frightening power of erotic attraction. They do so even when Othello bends to kiss the woman he is about to kill ("One more, one more" [5.2.18]) and even when animals are the vehicles of sexual metaphor, as when Iago warns Brabantio, "you'll have your daughter cover'd with a Barbary horse" (1.1.111–12). The Barbary horse image is nearly mythic in its evocation of a human union with a beautiful, strong, exotic beast. It brings to mind Leda and the Swan, or Europa with Jupiter disguised as a bull. (Indeed, Iago will later call Desdemona "sport for Jove" [2.3.17].) Iago's horse metaphor also suggests to us the numerous instances throughout Shakespeare's plays, from Bottom's ass transformation to Cleopatra's fond nickname, "serpent of old Nile" (*Antony and Cleopatra* 1.5.25), when beastliness is linked to human sexual power.[39]

It is notable that in *Othello*, Shakespeare transformed the iconic image of Santiago on his charger, battling the Moors, to another such startling erotic metaphor, in which a Moor is literally (or literarily) repositioned as the potent horse. No less notable is Shakespeare's transformation of Santiago Matamoros, the Moor-killer, to the erotically minded and sexually jealous Iago. I would argue that both these alterations of Santiago's myth served Shakespeare's dramaturgical purpose. That purpose was to adapt stories of religious wonder to a romantic tragedy, where the plot was impelled by sexual jealousy.

That Shakespeare intended a link between Iago and Santiago Matamoros has been noted by Peter Moore and Eric Griffin. Griffin further notes that both Shakespeare and his audience thought of Venice as a cosmopolitan city where people "of all nations" might be found (*Merchant of Venice* 3.3.31).[40] Iago, with his Spanish name, might readily have been thought a displaced Spaniard, and indeed Griffin cites a 1625 English ballad about Shakespeare's *Othello* which calls Iago a "false Spaniard." Of course, Jacobean anti-Spanish feeling could only have assisted the reception of "Spanish" Iago as villain, as Griffin also notes.[41]

Yet, while Shakespeare capitalized on anti-Spanish prejudices in the naming of villainous Iago, in *Othello* he avoids making anti-*Catholic* suggestions (and thus shows that English Renaissance anti-Hispanicism and anti-Catholicism were not always one and the same). In *Othello*, as in *All's Well That Ends Well* and *Cymbeline*, Shakespeare shows less interest in Reformation controversies than in exotic myths. In this play as in the earlier two he used elements of the Santiago legend to dramatize the power—here the tragic power—of uncontrolled erotic passion.

In *Othello*, miracles, affirmed by the Santiago myth and by Catholic tradition, are not called into question, but changed to erotic marvels. Othello's utter transformation by sexual jealousy is, to Lodov-ico, a wonder. "[T]his would not be believed in Venice. . . . Is this the nature / Whom passion could not shake?" (4.1.242, 265–66). Once Desdemona is gone, Othello likens her to the "pearl" that was Christ (5.2.347) and to an "entire and perfect chrysolite" (5.2.145), lines John Donne may have remembered when he imagined a de-ceased lover in "The Relic": "All measure and all language I should pass, / Should I tell what a miracle she was" (ll. 32–33).[42] Both Shakespeare and Donne adapt a Catholic language of religious won-der to the glorification of a lost love.

Since Iago is intensely sexualized (to adapt Traversi's phrase), the diabolical "miracles" he works also proceed from erotic excess. In-deed, in making Othello a Christian rather than the pagan he is in *Othello*'s source story,[43] Shakespeare prevents the audience from im-puting religious hatred to Iago. Unsaint-ed (or "desacralized")[44] Iago would destroy only one Moor, and *his* reason is sexual rather than holy. He not only resents Othello for promoting Cassio, he suspects that Othello has cuckolded him (1.3.387–88, 2.1.295–96, 4.2.147) and desires Desdemona ("Now I do love her too" [2.1.291]). Thus even his apparently miraculous influence over the storm in act 2 lacks religious resonance, despite its religious associations. The storm, which destroys the Turkish fleet and leaves Iago's ship un-touched, evokes both the Christian victory over the Turks at Lepanto in 1571 and England's defeat of the Catholic Spanish Armada in 1588, as Griffin has noted.[45] Iago seems to control the storm: "Tem-pests themselves, high seas, and howling winds" let Desdemona's ship go by, says Cassio (2.1.68–73), but her ship is also Iago's ship, and so its deliverance might also have reminded audiences of the English pilgrims' safe return to Lincoln after praying to Santiago, a legend I recounted earlier. Yet, unlike the legendary or historical sea miracles, the sea deliverance in *Othello* harbors neither an anti-Islamic or an anti-Catholic warning. After all, when Desdemona lands in Cyprus, she is greeted in terms which evoke the image of Mary: Cassio's "Hail to thee, lady! And the grace of heaven, / Be-fore, behind thee, and on every hand, / Enwheel thee round!" (2.1.85–87) is hardly a Protestant effusion. Nor are Muslims demon-ized in *Othello* as they are in the Santiago Matamoros myth, for in *Othello* it is not pagans but Christians who "[turn] Turks" and run amok (2.3.170). What causes their madness is not religious error, but the jealous passion that is tragic eros.

Beyond the attraction of Santiago's miracles—beyond his fame as the wondrous vanquisher of Moors—what would lead Shakespeare to give his name to the sexually jealous deceiver of *Othello*? What made Iago's name so suggestive of subterfuge and erotic passion that Shakespeare would revive it, in Italian, for *Cymbeline*'s lustful villain, Jachimo?

At this point readers will be either relieved or disappointed to discover that I am not going to talk about King James. Instead, I will turn to the biblical book of James, whose lessons Renaissance playgoers would most readily have associated with the apostle.

The introduction to the book of James in the Geneva Bible stresses that James "wrote [his] Epistle to the Jewes which were converted to Christ, but dispersed throughout divers countries," warning them not to "boast" and to "bridel the tongue" and "rule the affections." Shakespeare first invoked the name of James of Compostela in *All's Well That Ends Well*, a work in which boastful, slanderous tongues were prominent trouble causers. *Othello* shows Shakespeare's continued interest in James's lessons regarding the danger of unbridled tongues and unruly affections.

James devotes almost a whole chapter to the tongue, which he calls a "fire" and an "unrulie evil, ful of deadelie poyson" (3:6, 8). He accuses the tongue of inflaming destructive passions, such as "bitter envying and strife in . . . hearts" (3:14), and mentions envy again in 3:15. Chapter 4 specifically characterizes the envy incited by the disorderly tongue as *sexual* envy: "From whence are warres and contentions among you? Are they not hence, even of your lustes . . . ? Ye luste, and have not: ye envie, and have indignation" (4:1–2). Chapter 4 also warns against slander ("Speake not evil of one another" [v. 11]), and counsels Christians to "resist the devil" (v. 7). Indeed, James's first chapter frames the later instruction to resist slander and envy as a call to maintain faith in the face of the devil's temptations. "Blessed is the man, that endureth tentation," and whose faith does not falter, like that of a "wavering minded man" (1:12, 8). The strong man keeps faith in God and his brethren and does not submit to the impulse to slander or credit slander. For "[t]here is one Law giver, which is able to save, and to destroye. Who art thou that judgest another . . . ?" (4:12).

James's counsel underlies *Othello*'s plot and much of its language. Iago, a "demi-devil" (5.2.301), slanders Desdemona out of his own envy; this slander is "poison" (3.3.325) that "burn[s] like the mines of sulphur" (3.3.325, 329). "[C]hanged by [the] poison" (3.3.325), Othello becomes the faithless, "wavering minded man" described by the apostle (James 1:8): "I think my wife be honest, and think she is not; / I think [Iago] just, and think [he is] not" (3.3.384–85). D. Douglas Waters argues that Othello's "double conflict of thinking his wife honest and dishonest" distinguishes him from Shakespeare's single-minded tragic heroes: Othello's tragedy is deepened by the fact that he kills what he still loves.[46] Agreeing, I would argue that that destructive inner doubleness is what the apostle James calls "wavering" and associates with unbridled slander and uncontrolled carnal passion. That jealous passion, which culminates in a markedly erotic murderousness, leads Othello to assume the right James reserves for God, the "one Law giver" (James 4:12). In *Othello*'s last scene, declaring that Desdemona "must die, else she'll betray more men" (5.2.6), Othello arrogates the role of divine judge ("Who art thou that judgest another . . . ?," James warned [v. 12]). (Here Othello proves also ignorant of James's warning that "he that said, Thou shalt not commit adulterie, said also, Thou shalt not kill" [James 2:11].) Othello repeats his error when he evades Venetian justice and punishes himself in the same manner in which, he brags, he smote a Turk who "traduc'd the [Venetian] state" (5.2.354). With his final speech and action he claims God's proper power both "to save, and to destroye" (James 4:12).

The jealous passion that culminates in Othello's last actions originates, of course, in Iago, the double man who swears by two-faced Janus (1.2.33) and says "I am not what I am" (1.1.65). Those early references to doubleness signify Iago's deceptiveness, but also mark him as the kind of man Othello, goaded by him, will become: one inwardly riven by painful erotic fantasies. "I do suspect the lusty Moor / Hath leap'd into my seat; the thought whereof / Doth (like a poisonous mineral) gnaw my inwards," Iago tells the audience (2.1.295–97). As Mark Van Doren has suggested, Iago is the thing that Hamlet praises Horatio for *not* being, namely "passion's slave" (*Hamlet* 3.2.72).[47] A. C. Bradley was wrong to say Iago's desires were "moderate" and that he was not "habitually burning with envy,"[48] despite the coldness of the flame with which envy burns in Iago. For Iago, before Othello, is the envy-tossed man whom the apostle James describes. He "luste[s], and ha[s] not"; he "envie[s], and ha[s] indignation" (James 4:2). Thus by Shakespeare's curious process, James the apostle, who preaches against slander, lust, and unbridled passion, lends his name to Iago, who embodies all three of those vices.

This imaginative inversion is dependent on the apostle James's parallel existence as the Santiago Matamoros of Iberian myth, and on Shakespeare's familiarity with Santiago's legend. Not only was Santiago famous for his hostility to Moors, he had by the seventeenth century become intimately associated with Spain, and was thus available for the provoking of English anti-Hispanic prejudices. I have mentioned (and Eric Griffin has demonstrated) that Shakespeare's Hispanicizing of *Othello*'s villain would have been supported by the anti-Spanish feeling of Jacobean audiences. Their prejudices included the notion that Spaniards were "unfaithfull, ravenous, and insatiable" (*A Comparison of the English and Spanish Nation* [1589]), that the Spaniard engages in "pretences" (Thomas Scott, *Vox Populi* [1620])[49] and "mangleth, and massacreeth . . . the Gospell" (*A Fig for the Spaniard* [1591]),[50] and that Spanish men were susceptible to murderous lust and vengefulness ("Italianate" plays featuring Spanish avengers, like Kyd's *Spanish Tragedy* [1592] and Middleton's and Rowley's *Changeling* [1624], attest to this last). In the characterization of Iago, Shakespeare may also have capitalized on the anti-Semitism that targeted the numerous European Sephardic Jews of Spanish origin. Seventeenth-century English men and women did not automatically associate Spanishness with Jewishness, but they had good reason to associate Jewishness with Spanishness. (As James Shapiro has verified, early-modern European Jews were more likely to speak Spanish than Hebrew.)[51] In Iago, English anti-Spanish and anti-Jewish prejudices combine. Peter Milward has suggested that Iago's two references to his "tribe" (1.3.356, 3.3.175) would have prompted Shakespeare's audience to think Iago a member of "the tribe of Judah,"[52] a theory supported not only by Iago's Spanish name but by his association with the author of James, who addresses himself to "the twelve Tribes" (James 1:1), and who was, of course, a Jew. Hints that Iago is a Spanish *converso*, or "Christianized" Jew, help explain his bond with Othello, another convert and alien. They also deepen the dramatic fitness of Othello's absorption of Iago's "double," shifting mind, which is unstable in ways James warned against ("a wavering minded man is unstable in all his wayes" [James 1:8]).

Indeed, Peter Berek's description of the Renaissance *Marrano*— the Jew pretending to live as a Christian—brings Iago to mind. Speaking of the *Marrano*'s "experience of self-division,"[53] Berek writes that "Jews claiming to be converted to Christianity, are plausible representations of the idea that identity is not stable. . . . The Jew who insists on preserving at all cost his identity as a Jew does so by transforming identity into a succession of useful fictions." Berek suggests that this "condition" was "the most important quality of Jewishness in Elizabethan England" in the eyes of "the Christians amongst whom [Jews] lived. A 'Jew' was likely to be a . . . person who advanced in the world by his own ingenuity." Therefore, from the English perspective, "you would never know to what extent he really was what he gave every appearance of being."[54] Thus, when he offers hints that Iago is *Marrano*, Shakespeare is exploiting the English fear of the hidden Jew to enhance his audience's sense of Iago as a diabolical player, a fiendish improviser, a malevolent masker of his inward villainy. "I am not what I am," says "honest" Iago (*Othello* 1.1.65). Of course, by representing Iago's doubleness through an overtly theatrical technique—by dividing his stage discourse between self-revealing soliloquy and deceitful conversation—Shakespeare also reminded his audiences of the artificiality of *Othello*'s plot as a whole.

If the English idea of the covert Jew was anti-Semitic, it was culturally rather than religiously so. Iago's "Jewishness" makes no claims against Judaism, any more than his "Spanishness" maligns Catholicism. In *Othello* Shakespeare subordinates ethnic prejudices, the biblical warnings of James, *and* the exotic myth of Matamoros to his dramaturgical intent. That intent, as I have suggested, was the representation of the spectacular psychic and physical destruction born of slander and unbridled eros. This was the stuff of romantic tragedy.

So, just as the Henry plays root Shakespeare's fascination with sacred kingship in that doctrine's theatrical power, *All's Well That Ends Well*, *Cymbeline*, and *Othello* show his interest in Santiago de Compostela to have been dramaturgical, as surely most of his interests were in the end. Like his contemporary Cervantes, who used the Santiago myth to craft comic chat between Don Quijote and his squire, Shakespeare exploited the legend's appeal to fantasy. He did so in ways that fulfilled comic, romance, and tragic conventions, variously adapting Santiago's story to the plans of a witty comic heroine, the miraculous wonders of a romance plot, and the chilling violence required by romantic tragedy. While plot structures in comedy, romance, and romantic (or domestic or marital) tragedy differ, the genres are alike in that in each, characters' key motives are erotic.

Thus in each of the three plays Shakespeare shifted the Santiago myth from a religious to an erotic context, and thereby drained the myth of topical religious significance. He did likewise with the words of the biblical James, the first-century apostle whom myth would transform to Santiago.

When I say that Shakespeare drained references to the book of James of topical religious import, I do not claim that his use of James is devoid of Christian moralizing. Indeed, I have shown that Othello and Iago are destroyed by the very vices against which the Christian apostle James preaches. The degradation of Othello's mind spills forth in his speech; he calls Desdemona "the fountain from . . . which my current runs," now "a cestern for foul toads" (4.2.59, 61), while James, warning against such slanderous speech, says that the mouth's fountain cannot "send forthe at one place swete water and bytter" (James 3:11). Othello's decline justifies the warnings of the Christian apostle. Yet, as I have earlier suggested, the "Jamesian" vices Shakespeare thematizes here and, later, in *Cymbeline* —vices such as erotic idolatry and soul-destroying slander—were repugnant to Jacobean Catholics and Protestants alike. The use of James in these plays shows neither a Protestant nor a Catholic Shakespeare, but an author whose Christianity is more universal than such denominational labels suggest.

Likewise, Shakespeare's adaptations of the miraculous myth of Santiago, while they cater to anti-Mediterranean and anti-Semitic prejudices, constitute neither Catholic affirmations nor Reformed refutations of the doctrine of saints and miracles. After all, the formal work of such refutation had long been concluded in England. Why should Shakespeare proselytize, or do anything with saints, pilgrimages, and miracles but employ them dramatically, now that Protestantism had put them in play? Thus *All's Well*'s and *Cymbeline*'s heroines' "saints" are their husbands, and all three of the "Iago" plays' blatantly stage-managed miracles serve purposes so erotic that neither Catholic nor Protestant audience members would likely have linked them with apostolic wonders. Or, more accurately, playgoers who found religious suggestions in these miracles imposed such meanings on them, like those who found in the history plays either affirmations or denials of sacred kingship, and like zealous modern scholars who find in Shakespeare evidence of the playwright's Catholic or Protestant sympathies. For what serious theological comment can there be in Helena's use of her healing power to secure the husband of her obsession? Or in the transformation of the beheaded apostle to the corpse of clownish Cloten, for Imogen's caress; or in Iago's seeming control of both the storm and Othello's mind?

These questions return us to Stephen Greenblatt's claim that representations of the miraculous in Shakespeare demonstrate the "evacuated" status of religious superstition in Reformed England,[55] where "displaced . . . Catholic beliefs," newly stamped "illusion," found a home on the stage.[56] That secularized miracles, saints, and pilgrimages were found on the early-modern stage is undeniable, and has here been shown. Yet in his histories and his "Santiago" plays, Shakespeare so transformed those traditions that their representations were no longer Roman Catholic, or religious at all. In the Henry plays, as we have seen, saints, miracles, and sacred journeys are exposures of the theatrical workings of king worship and imperial pilgrimage. In *All's Well That Ends Well, Cymbeline,* and *Othello,* they are such stuff as erotic dreams—and nightmares—are made on.

5

The Passionate Pilgrim:
From Sacramental Eros to the Mapped Body in
the Poems of John Donne

> . . . in my idolatry
> I said to all my profane mistresses,
> Beauty, of pity, foulness only is
> A sign of rigour. . . .
>
> —"Holy Sonnet 13," ll. 9–12[1]

> To see God only, I go out of sight
> —"A Hymn to Christ, at the Author's
> last going into Germany," l. 30[2]

In my last chapter I suggested that Shakespeare's use of pilgrimage tropes on the popular English stage did much to strip such tropes of traditional religious significance. In adapting the language of pilgrimage to plots involving not just national expansion, but amorous encounter, Shakespeare mined the rich theatrical possibilities of holy adventuring, but did so, paradoxically, in a secular vein. He thus made the language of Catholic pilgrimage available for wider play in English erotic poetry.

English writers, of course, were not the first to liken their amorous poetic speakers to worshipful pilgrims. In my first chapter I discussed Petrarch's Sonnet 16, wherein the poet, seeking the beloved's "blessed image," compares himself to a penitent journeying to the holy city of Rome. Yet, as I then showed, that poem draws a contrast between the two journeys, stressing the idolatrous nature of the erotic pilgrimage and the genuine piety of the religious one.

When we turn from such a sonnet to the love poems of John Donne, we see references to Catholic pilgrimage employed quite differently. A Protestant poet, Donne often uses reference to Catholic practices and rituals, including pilgrimage, to describe a lover's falseness, or, at times, an aspiring courtier's superficiality. In so doing he displays the conventional English suspicion, seen in Spenser, of the deceptive shows of Catholicism—the Protestant disdain for garish images that mislead—yet turns that suspicion from a grave Spenserian theological use to a playful satiric one. Slain by a woman's scorn, Donne's dead poet wears a wreath of her hairs which "might breed idolatry, / If into others' hands" the "relics came" ("The Funeral"). [3] At other times, in love poems that describe not rejected but reciprocal passion, Donne subsumes the language of reverential pilgrimage, as well as language borrowed from transubstantial eucharistic celebration, to a religious celebration of eros. In poems like "The Canonization" and "The Ecstasy," the flesh-and-spirit union of two lovers' minds and bodies seems a sacred thing.

But this is play. Donne's poems that present faithful lovers as saints, whose shrines and relics merit veneration, redeem Catholic pilgrimage for profane ends by placing it in an amorous poetic context. Such "idolatry" suits the address of "profane mistresses," to quote Donne's Holy Sonnet 13. Thus such poems' sport with the idea of holy journey will form a key portion of this chapter's argument. Yet some discussion of the vexed question of Donne's own religious faith, as well as of his poetic play with other banned Catholic beliefs and rituals, will clarify his treatment of erotic pilgrimage, so with this I will begin.

Although Donne was raised as a Protestant, he was born into a Catholic family, and much has been written of the effect on his poetry of his early exposure to Catholic beliefs and traditions.[4] Most scholars have stressed the relative tolerance of Catholic thought that Donne—as compared, for example, with Spenser—shows, and have championed him as the consummate poet of the *via media*, the English Church's "middle way" between Geneva and Rome. Speaking of Donne's sacred verse as well as his sermons, Robert Whalen writes that Donne's "gestures toward the middle road that the church sought to pave and maintain represent a significant attempt to fuse the ceremonial and sacramental impulses of the Old Religion with the introspective, word-centered, and predestinarian pieties of English Calvinism."[5] Going further, Richard Strier sees Donne as a radical who, so far from embracing an official Protestant theology,

asserts his "independence from *any* established religious position."[6]
Without denying either of these claims, we may yet strive for what
Mary Arshagouni Papazian calls "a deeper understanding of Donne's indebtedness to the Reformation,"[7] and discern in Donne's
poems a Protestant fascination with the sometimes dangerous *material* element of Catholic practices: what Paul White has referred to as
Catholicism's paradoxical merging of the sacred with the profane.[8]
Relics of hair and bone, rosary beads, saints' images, and even the
Catholic Eucharist enter into Donne's erotic verse, not as avenues
to God, but as signs of destructive or, at times, creative sensuality. It
is as though Donne found Catholicism itself, in its lush carnality, its
sacramental merging of spirit and matter, particularly apt for the poetic exploration of erotic love, since for Donne that love, in its best
aspect, fuses spirit and intellect with sense. (We may recall T. S. Eliot's famous comments that Donne could realize the "feel" of an
idea and that his poems were in the habit of "sensualising
thought."[9]) Indeed, the traditional use of the word "metaphysical"
to describe Donne's application of unusual material signs to spiritual experiences has sacramental overtones. But in Donne's love
poems, the sacrament that is either thwarted or gloriously arrived at
is *erotic* sacrament. These poems celebrate the union of lovers, not
the sinner's reclamation by God.

Donne's sacred verse is something else again. There, as I will ultimately show, flesh is no sacrament, but a thing that, in its decay,
preaches its own insufficiency. In Donne's devotional poems the no-
longer-Catholic "pilgrim" forsakes the body and moves inward, into
the private, invisible soul ("Of the Progress of the Soul," l. 398),[10]
to figure his spiritual struggle by means of hard, vivid images: nails,
wood, the flesh and blood of Christ. But these are mere images, and,
further—like the crosses and beads of Spenser's *The Faerie Queene*—
they are verbal, or text. Outward physical things do not incarnate
grace in the devotional poems. Rather, physical things are transubstantiated into words which both figure and work an inner spiritual
purification.[11] Thus the sacred poems turn sacramental process inside out. Indeed, in Donne's late sacred verse, the poet's body is not
a vehicle for and participant in redemption, but a mere map of the
sacred, one which identifies the contours of a holy landscape, but
also signifies that landscape's distance from what can be spiritually
approached and known.

In contrast, in Donne's erotic poems bodies are not just maps or signs, but holy lands themselves. Such poems employ images of love-making bodies to convey a sense of union that, while spiritual, remains carnal, apprehensible by the senses. In the love poems the language of forbidden Catholic beliefs, rituals, and practices, including pilgrimage, is used to convey the worthlessness of the mistress who disdains to be party to such sacramental eros, or, more happily, it is used to celebrate erotic reciprocity.

Thus terms drawn from Catholic beliefs and practices are staples in Donne's erotic lexicon (as they are in his satires on the court, called a "purgatory" or "Mass in jest" ["Satire 4," ll. 3, 9]).[12] Indeed, Donne frequently inserts references to theological disputes between the Protestant churches and Rome in his secular, often erotic verse, where the light courteous, socially satirical, or frankly amorous context of these references drains them of doctrinal seriousness. That saints, whose worship for Protestants was sacrilege, might by Donne's time be playfully invoked is evident not only in "The Canonization," wherein Donne and his lover become erotic saints, but in a verse letter Donne wrote to Lady Carey from French-Catholic Amiens, which begins,

> Madame,
> Here, where by all, all saints invoked are
> T'were too much schism to be singular,
> And 'gainst a practice general to war;
>
> Yet, turning to saints, should my humility
> To other saint, than you, directed be,
> That were to make my schism a heresy.[13]

Here saints are, if not frankly eroticized, reduced to images of kind female friends, or of a particular friend. (Similarly, to the Countess of Bedford Donne writes, "I study you first in your Saints, / Those friends, whom your election glorifies" [ll. 9–10];[14] the dead Elizabeth Drury was both "saint" and "pilgrim," in a line that blurs the religious valence of both terms.)[15] The heresy of saint worship is more explicitly carnal in "The Relic," a second poem in which Donne imagines that a bracelet of his mistress's hair "about [his] bone" might prompt idolatry, were his grave to be dug up "in a time, or land, / Where mis-devotion doth command" (ll. 12–13).[16] In "The Will," Donne sports with the Reformation divide between the relative salvific values of faith and works, secularizing Catholic

and radical Protestant positions by including both in a running satirical list of purely social evils. "My faith I give to Roman Catholics; /
All my good works unto the schismatics / Of Amsterdam; my best
civility / And courtship, to an university. . . . / Thou Love taught'st
me, by making me / Love her that holds my love disparity, / Only
to give to those that count my gifts indignity" (ll. 19–27).[17] Similarly
irreverent is "To Sir Henry Wotton," another satirical poem in
which religious differences are presented as evils set, to religion's
detriment, against the virtues of a good friend. Wotton is "free from
German schisms . . . and fair Italy's faithlessness" (ll. 65–66).[18]

   Such light treatment of grave Reformation disputes has, to be
sure, the serious ecumenical purpose of condemning the fractured
state of Christendom, and, as Richard Strier has argued, of declaring
Donne's independence from divisive, exclusionary religious teachings. Still, Donne has a distinctly Protestant manner of belittling Reformation disputes. By this I mean that, as I have suggested, Donne
is drawn to make Catholic heresies the vehicles for his celebration
of both thwarted and triumphant eros. Like the later Richard Lovelace, for whom Lucasta's breast is a "nunnery,"[19] Donne finds an
"hermitage" in his lover's body ("The Canonization," l. 38).[20] In
"Love's Exchange," a mistress's face corrects Catholic mistakes: it
could "change the idolatry of any land," "call vowed men from
cloisters" (ll. 30, 32).[21] When lovers are dishonest or disdainful,
their falseness is realized in unconventional poetic terms which yet
invoke conventional Protestant (and Neoplatonic) suspicion of
Catholic ocular deceptions and idolatries, by which icons and relics
make invalid substitutes for living presences. In "Sappho to Phi-
lenis," the poet fears his own loyalty to his mistress will fade since
"Only thine image, in my heart, doth sit, / But that is wax, and fires
environ it" (ll. 9–10).[22] In "Witchcraft by a Picture," Donne fears
that his mistress will take possession of his image reflected in her eye
and, by "drown[ing]" it "in a transparent tear," kill him with the
sorcery associated by Protestants with devilish Catholic priests.[23] The
wreath of woman's hair with which the poet is interred in "The Funeral" would, as a relic, "breed idolatry" if left unburied, because
the woman is not worthy of worship. Cruel, she would "save none
of" the poet (l. 24), for whom veneration of the wreath and, by implication, reverence of the woman have also been idolatry. Thus the
poet is "Love's martyr" (l. 19) only in a jesting sense.[24] The wreath,
a "sign," is a "subtle . . . mystery" (ll. 2–3) only because he can't

fathom why she gave it to him; it promised bliss, but yielded only
"pain" (l. 15). Thus, "[w]hate'er she meant by it," he says bitterly,
"bury it with me" (l. 17).

A Protestant skepticism regarding the value of such physical symbols of piety—even erotic piety—as the wreath of hair is also seen in
"A Jet Ring Sent," wherein a dark, "brittle" ring (l. 2) sent by an
unfaithful mistress is fit only to represent the negative qualities of
the lovers' relation. "[N]othing sooner broke. . . . / I am cheap, and
naught but fashion, fling me away" (ll. 4, 8).[25] The same skepticism
pervades "The Token," wherein the poet begins by beseeching his
love to "[s]end him some token, that [his] hope may live," but goes
on to reject all the conventional love gifts that might serve.

> I beg no riband wrought with thine own hands,
>   To knit our loves in the fantastic strain
> Of new-touched youth; nor ring to show the stands
>   Of our affection, that as that's round and plain,
> So should our loves meet in simplicity;
>   No, nor the corals which thy wrist enfold,
> Laced up together in congruity,
>   To show our thoughts should rest in the same hold;
> No, nor thy picture, though most gracious,
>   And most desired, because best like the best.
>   (ll. 9–14)[26]

The woven "riband" would falsely invoke the giddy, self-involved
fantasies of youth, while the circular band, though "round and
plain," would yet (as the Puritans held) be too showy an announce-
ment of a simple pledged troth.[27] Laced corals or a picture would
seem but not be the shared thoughts and body they represented.
Thus the only acceptable token of the woman's love is no token at
all, but rather her acceptance of the poet's love for *her*. "Send me
nor this, nor that, to increase my store, / But swear thou think'st I
love thee, and no more" (ll. 17–18).

As the last line of "The Token" suggests, the impulse that redeems romantic love from Romish idolatry is reciprocity. In Donne's
poems that celebrate amorous connection, references to transubstantial Communion, relics, images, hermitages, saints, and, finally,
pilgrimage, transported from a context of Reformation debate to
one of love's argument, figure the sacramental character of
achieved eros. In Holy Sonnet 13 Donne recalls his youthful argu-

ment to mistresses: that their "pity," in prompting them to return his love, would turn the "foulness" of "rigour" into "Beauty" (ll. 11–12). In the erotic poems themselves we see that that "rigour," or unrequited eros, makes the poet's passion "spider love, which transubstantiates all, / And can convert manna to gall" ("Twicknam Garden," ll. 6–7)[28]—that is, whose mystical operations are destructive rather than salvific. Love in isolation does not infuse the elements with the god. Love's "drink was counterfeit, as was his meat," Donne writes, in a poem describing his lover's false tears ("Love's Diet," l. 17).[29] But shared physical love, in contrast, is life-giving, redemptive, and holy.

Donne describes such sacramental eros in "The Ecstasy," wherein "love . . . interanimates two souls" through two bodies' physical conjointure (ll. 41–42).[30] Holding hands, the lovers produce a sweat that is "balm" and unites them (l. 6); meeting each other's eyes, they knit their two gazes "upon one double string" (l. 8). In this poem their images in each other's eyes, because mutually reflected, are not destructible icons, as in "Witchcraft by a Picture," but, as T. Anthony Perry has noted, living children:[31] "pictures in our eyes to get/ Was all our propagation" (ll. 11–12). Though the poem begins with the lovers themselves in stasis, frozen with locked glances and hands, it ends in a celebration of necessary sexual consummation. "So must pure lovers' souls descend / T'affections, and to faculties, / Which sense may reach and apprehend, / Else a great prince in prison lies. / To our bodies turn we then" (ll. 65–69). Sex is erotic transubstantiation and liberation of love, "a great prince." It renders love physical and available to a communion of two. Such communion does not offer the "Mass in jest" of superficial court life, nor the "counterfeit . . . meat" of the false mistress, but a genuinely transformational erotic sacrament. Of course, it is because Protestant Donne can refer to the Catholic Mass "in jest" that he is free to apply its symbolism to his serious poetic treatment of reciprocal eros.

Relics, like the Catholic Eucharist, are available to Donne for the description of shared erotic love, and are rendered true secular relics by their particular history. The poet's "ragged bony" name scratched in his lover's window is a Christly promise, telling her he, "Being still with [her], / . . . will come again" ("A Valediction: Of My Name in the Window," ll. 23, 28–30).[32] In "The Funeral" the woman's wreath of hair was a meaningless symbol of a false promise;

it needed burial so as not to prompt idolatry. But in "The Relic" the "bracelet of bright hair about the bone" is the real thing, since it signals the commingling of two lovers' remains and suggests their mutual fidelity in life. While in "The Funeral" he who "comes to shroud" Donne will find his corpse alone, crowned, pathetically, with the "wreath of hair" (ll. 1, 3), the sexton of "The Relic" uncovering the braceleted bone, will, Donne hopes, "let *us* alone" (l. 7, my emphasis).[33] Like "The Funeral," the second stanza of "The Relic" expresses concern that the hair-bracelet will inspire Catholic idolatry: "If [the exhumation] fall in a time, or land, / Where mis-devotion doth command / Then, he that digs us up, will bring / Us, to the Bishop, and the King / To make us relics. . . ." (ll. 12–16). Yet while "The Funeral" maintains its skeptical tone about the bracelet throughout its three stanzas—"Whate'er she meant by it, bury it with me"—"The Relic" proceeds to justify the sexton's errors and to turn "mis-devotion" to warranted reverence, as though Donne decided midpoem that he and his love *were* worship worthy. "All women shall adore us, and some men," he writes, "And since at such time, miracles are sought, / I would have that age by this paper taught / What miracles we harmless lovers wrought" (ll. 19–22). In "The Relic," the third stanza records what were "love's miracles" (to adapt Shakespeare's phrase),[34] stressing, as is usual for Donne, the paradoxical unity achieved by the two. "Difference of sex no more we knew, / Than our guardian angels do" (ll. 25–26). Important to the figuring of the lovers' sainthood is the poem itself, written on "paper" that explains the mystery of the bracelet. This recorded poem resembles an alchemist's secret writings more than holy scripture in its riddling account of love's miracles ("we loved well . . . / Yet knew not what we loved" [ll. 23–24]). In Donne's poems which compare or link lovers to books, this is generally so. "Love's mysteries in souls do grow, / But yet the body is his book," concludes the poet in "The Ecstasy" (ll. 71–72); of these lines Stanley Stewart writes, "the mystery of love is in the *alchemy* of blending two souls into one" (my emphasis).[35] In "A Valediction: of the Book" Donne's and his lover's letters are like ancient written guides to "sciences, spheres music" (l. 27).[36] In "Elegy 19. To His Mistress, Going to Bed," women are "mystic books" (l. 41).[37] The magical books that figure lovers suggest hermetic philosophy but also, again, the dark arts Protestants associated with the Roman Catholic Mass.

Yet such sinister transformational magic is sportively redeemed by its use to describe loving bodies that incarnate and fulfill erotic desire.

Faithful erotic reciprocity between lovers, then, accomplishes the mystical joining that renders them worthy of sainthood—of "Catholic" worship, including pilgrimage to their shrines. They are erotic saints indeed. In "The Relic" the remains of the lovers' bodies, joined in death, render them "a Mary Magdalen" and a "something else" (one of her lovers, and a studied refusal to name "Jesus Christ," which, as Christopher Ricks notes, is the phrase's metrical equivalent).[38] Those "women . . . and some men" who "adore" them (l. 19) will presumably journey to honor their relics, which Donne twice describes as "us": as the lovers themselves. Unlike the falsely sweet "pilgrimage" described in "Song," a fruitless quest for a faithful woman,[39] those who journey to honor "Mary Magdalen" and "something else" will revere faithful lovers.

The most prominent example of Donne's fanciful doctrine that (in Eugene Cunnar's words) "human love has its saints"[40] is, of course, "The Canonization." In this poem, as in "The Relic," Donne seems to give himself ideas as he writes, spinning ever-more extravagant hypotheses of the ways and reasons why he and his mistress might be venerated. By constructing images of their sacred mystery in the poem's last three stanzas, he liberates himself from the implicit criticism of his male listener, whose loathed presence and mundane interests are implied by the irritated retort comprised by Donne's first two verses: "For God's sake hold your tongue, and let me love / . . . Take you a course, get you a place, / Observe his Honour, or his Grace" (ll. 1, 5–6).[41] The listener's concerns, Donne implies, are the worldly ones; he and his love's erotic union, by contrast, is a mystery that transforms the conventionally profane to the sacred. While in stanza 3 Donne likens their holy mystery to self-burning tapers, the resurrected phoenix, and the life-preserving hymn of the poem, he reaches a satisfying climax in his final, enthusiastic conceit, realized in stanza 4, that they shall be saints visited by erotic pilgrims.[42] As Pierre Legouis has noted, the lack of a period between the fourth and fifth stanzas communicates the excitement with which Donne's canonization of himself and his lover overruns the male auditor's presumed objection.[43] Donne writes,

> And by these hymns, all shall approve
> Us canonized for love:

And thus invoke us; "You whom reverend love
   Made one another's hermitage:
You, to whom love was peace, that now is rage;
   Who did the whole world's soul contract, and drove
      Into the glasses of your eyes
      (So made such mirrors and such spies,
That they did all to you epitomize,)
     Countries, towns, courts: beg from above
     A pattern of your love!

                                       (ll. 35–45)

In Legouis' words, "The new-made saints are already 'invoked' by lovers who come after them; their intercession is prayed for in the most approved papistical style; the repetition of the words 'You whom,' 'You to whom . . . , who . . . ' suggests a litany."[44] Yet the "papistical style" itself, by virtue of being papistical, strips the religious language of serious devotional purpose, and prevents the description of the predicted "worship" from being blasphemous or heretical. For Donne's Protestant readers, traditional saints' veneration is heresy. Playful transformation of saints to lovers or lovers to saints, is, on the other hand, a recuperation of discarded religious terms for fanciful play. That Donne's canonized lovers are not privy to God's real secrets but (like Lear and Cordelia)[45] privy to the world's is suggested by lines 41 through 44, which credit the pair's eyes with concentrating, distilling, and transforming not God's grace, but "the whole world's soul," or "Countries, towns, courts." Thus these lovers are empowered to mediate not for sinners' salvation but only for a divine "pattern of [erotic] love." Said another way, poems like "The Canonization" do not concern "Jesus Christ," but "something else."

Donne, then, finds it possible lawfully to exalt eros only in traditional Catholic, not Protestant, religious terms. While his use of any religious language to glorify physical love might be said to show a Protestant scorn for celibacy, and a glorification of the marriage bed, I do not say that. While many of Donne's love poems were doubtless written for his wife, the poems themselves celebrate an erotic communion between lovers who may not be formally married—indeed, whose communion exceeds formal marriage bonds. And as C. S. Lewis has noted, while Renaissance English Puritans as compared to Roman Catholics were "the indulgent party" with regard to the marriage bed, they—and earlier Protestants—were not similarly indulgent with regard to extra- or premarital sex.[46] In fact, as I have argued, English Protestants regarded Catholic pilgrims as being so. Thus Donne's use of religious terminology to celebrate achieved eros cannot be a Protestant celebration of godly marriage. His poetic eros is Protestant in less direct ways. It suspects the ocular deceptiveness of mere images and relics, and prefers conjoined minds and bodies as the true sign and presence of love. Further, it displays a Protestant tendency to associate erotic pursuit and fulfillment with saint worship and pilgrimage.

Accordingly, what I call (among other things) Donne's erotic redemption of Catholic pilgrimage displays some of the other features of Protestant redirection of pilgrimage to secular ends that I discussed in this book's first chapter. In his professional existence, Donne showed an interest in colonization and foreign trade; he invested, for example, in the Virginia Company's 1609 expedition.[47] Yet Donne's wholly or partly satirical poems, like Shakespeare's *Love's Labor's Lost, As You Like It*, and *Measure for Measure*, contain passages that mock the Reformed Englishman's tendency to indulge his travel lust by commercial pilgrimage or mere secular tourism. "[A]ll which go to Rome, do not thereby / Esteem religions, and hold fast the best, / But serve discourse, and curiosity," Donne writes to the Countess of Bedford, and jests that in praising her in this poem, he'll imitate such touring pilgrims, who revere God's houses rather than God. "So in this pilgrimage, I would behold / You as you are virtue's temple, not as she" (ll. 37–44).[48] When the English choose to "roam / Giddily, and be everywhere, but at home, / Such freedom doth a banishment become" ("To Mr Roland Woodward," ll. 28–30).[49] From such "giddy" travels, exhaustion and not refinement of the soul results. In "Upon Mr Thomas Coryat's Crudities" Donne ridicules Coryat's eternal geographical search for "Venice' vast lake" and "some vaster thing" (ll. 3–4), as well as his use of his picaresque experiences to write a very bad book. The *Crudities*, consecrated to vainglorious bragging about what the author has seen abroad, is an invalid "mystical" tome, "And rather than read all" of it, Donne "would read none" (ll. 75–76).[50] Whatever his private financial interests, in his poetry Donne also devalued New World exploration, linking it to the laughable attempt to map the cosmos. In a verse letter to the Countess of Bedford, Donne suggests that a willingness to die would better serve Christians than would all the new discoveries available through travel or astronomy. "We have added to the world Virginia, and sent / Two new stars lately to the firmament; / Why grudge we us (not heaven) the dignity / T'increase with ours, those fair souls company?" (ll. 67–70).[51]

Donne also attacks vain errands to court, which he presents as the English domestic equivalent of frivolous global travel or of warmongering, both of which he had experienced and, by 1613, had enough of. (He fought in Cadiz under Essex in 1596 and traveled for various diplomatic purposes between 1600 and 1612.)[52] "Idios" (Idiot) of the 1613 "Eclogue" thinks himself "fantastic" since he has "a part / In the East-Indian fleet" (ll. 56, 57), and busies himself traveling giddily to court, where (in papist style) he lays "burnt incense" on such notables as are his "altars" (ll. 229, 235).[53] In "To Sir Henry Wotton," Donne says of the court, "Here's no more news, than virtue, I may as well / Tell you Cadiz' or Saint Michael's tale for news, as tell / That vice doth here habitually dwell" (ll. 1–3). After likening petty court battles to those among the English, Spanish, and Indians, Donne bids his friend a fashionable farewell, "*At Court*, though from Court, were the better style" (l. 27). For Donne, traveling is a Romish vanity that still smacks of frivolous pilgrimage. In "The Bracelet," Donne singles out Spanish coins as ubiquitously "still travelling," thus "become as Catholic as their king" (ll. 29–39).

Yet, as in "The Canonization," "Catholic" travel achieves Donne's secular blessing when it is done in the service of true eros. "Such a pilgrimage were sweet"—and no longer frivolous—if its object was a true lover (unhappily, not found in "Song"). Thus "Love's Progress," after presenting a sustained comparison between Donne's lover's body and foreign geographies ("her fair Atlantic navel" [l. 65]), ends by comparing his own kisses to a pilgrim's successful arrival at a papal audience in Rome. "[T]he kiss / Which at the face begun, transplanted is / Since to the hand, since to the imperial knee, / Now at the papal foot," where the poet "delights to be" (ll. 81–84). Like this pilgrimage to an eroticized Rome, early-modern modes of travel, used metaphorically in other poems, are sanctified and celebrated by their paradoxical absorption by reclining lovers, who hardly go anywhere. In "The Canonization," the saintly lovers accommodate and reduce the world's geographies into their own shared gaze, which makes their bed "[t]he world" (to borrow a phrase from "The Sun Rising").[54] In "The Sun Rising," "both th'Indias of spice and mine/ . . . lie" with the poet (ll.17–18). The naked mistress in "Elegy 19" is Donne's "America," his "new found land" (l. 27). Only when foreign excursions are made metaphorical expressions of such happy erotic contact or, more rarely, of inward virtue ("virtue's an India" ["To Mr. R. W.," l. 32]),[55] are they acceptable. Unlike the glorious French wars happily remembered in Shakespeare's Henry plays, foreign wars in Donne's poems are stupid. "In Flanders, who can tell / Whether the master press, or men rebel? / Only we know, that which all idiots say, / They bear most blows that come to part the fray" ("Love's War," ll. 5–8).[56] Therefore, "Here let me war; in these arms let me lie" ("Love's War," l. 29). Holy travel is not military service or commercial or diplomatic expeditions, but an embrace, or the movement of amorous hands. That Donne describes such erotic journeyings by an indiscriminate mix of references to Catholic pilgrimage, English war campaigns, and commercial voyaging shows that for him, all those forms of travel were equally secular. Being profane, they were available for the metaphorical expression of profane love. Cleanth Brooks wrote that Donne took "both love and religion seriously,"[57] and he was right. But it did not follow that this English Protestant poet took love religiously. In fact—as his investment of eros in the tropes of relics, saints, pilgrimage, and secular travel show—he did not.

We may more plainly see the distinction Donne drew between erotic and sacred domains in poetry, and the language appropriate to each, when we turn to his devotional poems. While Donne's erotic verse playfully glorifies saints and their shrines and relics, involving all these in descriptions of fulfilled lovers, both his sacred poems and his satires whose subject is religion are straightforward and even conventional in their condemnation of place or shrine pilgrimage and saints' idolatry. A fool, wanting "true religion," "Seeks her at Rome, . . . because he doth know / That she was there a thousand years ago" (ll. 43, 45–46).[58] While Luther's fracturing of the Church is "Lament[ed]" in Holy Sonnet 18, still, the Roman Church is witheringly described as "she, which on the other shore / Goes richly painted" (ll. 4, 2–3).[59] Donne's Protestant iconoclasm is heard in lines from "A Litany" which regret times "When plenty, God's image, and seal / Makes us idolatrous, / And love it, not him, whom it should reveal" (ll. 185–87).[60]

   Yet the deeper influence of Reformed thought on Donne's sacred
poems is seen in these poems' reconfiguration of holy pilgrimage as
a "journey" toward God. I qualify "journey" because, like Spenser,
Donne expresses Luther's (and Calvin's) conviction that the sinner's redemption is achieved "not according to [his] . . . running."[61]
As in *The Faerie Queene*, salvation in Donne's holy poems is submission to a grace extended by God through Christ. Vain even is the
sinner's struggle to achieve the faith, humility, and penitence pre-
requisite to the receipt of grace, since these qualities are also God's
gift. Calvin writes that saving grace is prompted by an initiating
grace that renders the sinner open to salvation, asserting, "All those
things in [man] which are said to have pleased God he received
from God's grace—so far is he from preparing himself to receive
grace . . . through his own effort."[62] Donne's Calvinist view that even
initiating (prevenient) grace was bestowed, not earned, and that salvation was thus not to be achieved through personal works—even
the internal work of spiritual pilgrimage—is evident in the question
he raises in Holy Sonnet 4: "grace, if thou repent, thou canst not
lack, / But who shall give thee that grace to begin?" (ll. 9–10).[63]
   Thus the internal spiritual "journey" toward which Donne works
in his sacred verse is not a journey at all. To the contrary, it is an
assumed position of humble acquiescence. These poems continually
reiterate Donne's prayer to be—like Spenser's Redcrosse Knight—
corrected in his wanderings, and brought home to God. Spenser,
of course, compromises that vision of holy homecoming by setting
against it the competing ideal of the earthly Cleopolis, the seat of
Queen Elizabeth's power, a place which seems finally to usurp Redcrosse's reverence and claim authority over his travels. Donne's vision of God's claim on his soul is simpler (however complex the
conceits with which he describes it). Earthly travels of any sort—
even those done in the service of the Protestant state—take him
from and not to God. Of a westward ride done at the behest of Sir
Edward Herbert in 1613, he writes to God, "I am carried toward the
west, / . . . when my soul's form bends toward the east" (ll. 9–10).[64]
In Holy Sonnets 4 and 6 Donne uses the words "pilgrim" and "pilgrimage" to describe not the progress of his soul toward God, but
profane physical journeys which have distracted him from God's expectations of him.[65] "Oh my black soul!" he says in Sonnet 4, "Thou
art like a pilgrim, which abroad hath done/ Treason, and durst not
turn to whence he is fled" (ll. 1–4). The treasonous soul is like a

traveler to (most likely) Compostela, who has made his specious holy journey an occasion to traffic with the Spanish enemy, and whose return to England—analogous to Heaven—is now imperiled. Sonnet 6 describes an ailing Donne's imminent departure from his profane body as his "pilgrimage's last mile": the "last pace" of a "race / Idly . . . run," quite distinct from the "flight" his soul will now take toward God (ll. 2–3, 9). Here it may be instructive to compare Donne's use of the idea of pilgrimage with that of his greatest Spanish contemporary, the Catholic poet Quevedo. Although the melancholy Quevedo evinces a "Protestant" skepticism regarding the value of journeys to Rome—"Buscas en Roma a Roma, ¡oh peregrino!, / y en Roma misma a Roma no lo hallas" [Look in Rome to Rome, oh pilgrim!/ and in Rome herself you won't find her] (ll. 1–2)[66]—still, he is drawn to imagine progress toward God as a pilgrimage. "Yo . . . haré que peregrino y abrasado,/ en busca vuestra por los aires vaya" [I . . . will become a pilgrim, lit with fire, / in search of your fires, through the air I go] (ll. 63–64).[67] Death itself is not, as in Donne's Sonnet 4, a sudden "summon[ing]" (l. 1) of the errant pilgrim to an immediate encounter with God, but a purgatorial phase in the pilgrim's journey heavenward. "[E]l cuerpo en tierra está peregrinando" [The body in earth does pilgrimage], Quevedo writes ("Madrigal," l. 10).[68] Unlike Catholic Quevedo, Protestant Donne feels he must morally qualify references to such "holy" travel in his devotional poetry. Thus he quakes at the thought of God's judgment on his idle or treasonous earthly pilgrimage.

Further, though "fear . . . shakes [Donne's] every joint" as he thinks of meeting God (Holy Sonnet 6, l. 8), this characteristic Donnean anxiety regarding his prospects of salvation does not suggest spiritual work he thinks he must to do to effect his redemption. There is none, beyond the necessary Protestant labor of thoughtful Bible reading, an action that is, paradoxically, *worked* within the sinner by God. (In other words, receipt of salvation through scripture is work to which God compels the elect Christian.) The treasonous pilgrim of Holy Sonnet 4 considers two possible self-initiated modes of achieving salvation—"make thyself with holy mourning black, / And red with blushing, as thou art with sin" (ll. 11–12)—but then seems to reject both in favor of the only true means of redemption, the submission to purification by means of Christ's blood, here fused with the image of scripture: "Or wash thee in Christ's blood, which hath this might / That being red [read], it dyes red souls to white" (ll. 13–14). Here we may recall my second chapter's discussion of the Protestant paradox at work in Spenser's book 1 of *The Faerie Queene*. There I noted that while Calvin writes that "no one can embrace the grace of the gospel without . . . applying his whole effort to the practice of repentance," still, this repentance "has its foundation in the gospel" and is precipitated by the gospel, through which God only works. Accordingly, in the House of Holiness, scriptural salvation is administered to the Redcrosse Knight by means of guides like Fidelia and Una who school and feed him. Like Redcrosse's, Donne's profane physical and spiritual travels have been a backsliding through which only gospel-bestowed repentance can redeem him. However, as Paul Cefalu has recently shown, fear and anxiety regarding such backsliding, so far from suggesting that Donne has not been sufficiently engaged in the work of salvation, indicate that he has been. "God . . . knows best" Donne's "true grief, for he put it in [his] breast" (Holy Sonnet 8, ll. 13–14).[69] Grief is the healing antidote for poisonous pride. Cefalu discusses the Calvinist warnings against the traps of pride preached and written by early-seventeenth-century pastors like Jeremiah Lewis, and, of course, Donne himself.[70] Calvin himself entitles a chapter in his *Institutes*, "Boasting About the Merits of Works Destroys Our Praise of God for Having Bestowed Righteousness, as Well as Our Assurance of Salvation."[71] If overconfidence in one's redemption is a sign of reprobation, then, as Cefalu suggests, the salvation anxiety Donne shows in his sacred verse suggests he is "well on his way to regeneration and glorification according to Pauline soteriology"[72] (the doctrine set forth in Second Corinthians 7:10 that "godly grief produces a repentance that leads to salvation"). Well might Donne say, then, "Those are my best days, when I shake with fear" (Holy Sonnet 19, l. 14).[73] Donne's first holy sonnet clearly presents him as the appropriately anxious sinner who, rather than engage in arduous practices of penitence—in "running," to recall Luther's word—must simply wait for God "like adamant" to "draw [his] iron heart" (l. 14), as Christ says in the Gospel of John ("No one can come to me unless the Father . . . draws him" [John 6:44]).

Pilgrimage to saints for salvific intercession, then, is replaced in Donne with descriptions of anxious waiting—the anxiety, again, suggesting that he *has* been saved (since it would be dangerous to enjoy it)—or with hopeful imaginings of being gently or, sometimes, violently rescued. "I, like an usurped town, to another due, / Labour to admit you, but oh, to no end," Donne laments in Holy Sonnet 14 (ll. 5–6).[74] "Take me to you" (l. 12). "[F]or thine own work fight," the poet urges God in Holy Sonnet 2 (l. 11).[75] "I sail towards home," he writes in "The Progress of the Soul," yet home is not a far region but, as for Spenser's Redcrosse, a place "not farre away" (*The Faerie Queene* 1.10.3). It is the place where Donne "began" ("The Progress of the Soul," l. 57). Donne's attitude toward the moral progress offered by physical or spiritual travel is as skeptical in his devotional as in his erotic verse. In the love poem "A Valediction: Forbidding Mourning," travel does not compromise Donne's affection for his mistress or wife, which, unlike "Dull sublunary lovers' love," can "admit / Absence" (ll. 13–15), but it is an unwelcome and incorrect obligation. He "must . . . obliquely run" until finally redeemed by her constant fidelity and his predicted return to her ("Thy firmness . . . / . . . makes me end, where I begun" (ll. 34–36).[76] Donne's sacred verses replace the image of the beloved woman with that of God, who is likewise to draw him home, "like adamant" (though the penitent sinner accedes to being drawn with far more fear and trembling than the homebound lover). Journeying is travel from rather than to Heaven. God stays present to the Christian by recalling him spiritually, so that the Christian spiritually recalls (in the sense of "remembers") him. As Donne rides westward in "Good Friday, 1613," God is "from [his] eye," but "present yet unto [his] memory" (ll. 33–34). In this poem Donne makes his westward journey acceptable by imaginatively reconfiguring it as no journey at all, but a simple turning of the body to receive morally purgative corrections while standing or kneeling. "I turn my back to thee, but to receive / Corrections" (ll. 37–38). "Good Friday, 1613" describes the God-sinner bond which we also find in George Herbert's "The Collar," wherein God's relation to the Christian surpasses and overwhelms his designs to travel "abroad" (ll. 2).[77]

Thus, while the God who brings Donne home is more formidable than the beloved women of Donne's erotic verse (and than Herbert's gently chiding Lord), and Donne's encounter with him more painful than pleasurable, still, Donne imagines the God-sinner relationship in conceits which parallel those he uses to depict "holy" lovers. In both kinds of poem, the geographical field of travel and earthly activity is profane, and what is sacred is the close and immediate contact between lover and loved one, which figuratively annihilates space. In "Good Friday, 1613," as in love poems like "The Sun Rising" and "Elegy 19. To His Mistress, Going to Bed," Donne verbally transforms distance to presence and far-flung travel to a close physical encounter between two. We recall that "both th'Indias of spice and mine, / . . . lie . . . with" the poet in the person of his mistress in "The Sun Rising" (ll. 17–18), and that in "Elegy 19" the woman Donne caresses is his "America," his "new found land" (l. 27). It should thus not surprise us that Donne's passionate imagination, ever drawn, as Eugene Cunnar writes, "to accommodate . . . the sexual and the sacred,"[78] would sometimes figure the sacred as sexual, as it does in "Sonnet 14," when the poet begs God to "ravish" him (l. 14). For Donne, thoughts of erotic and heavenly love are both bound to the sense of or longing for extreme closeness, and with the impulse to cross separating distances.

Hence the world itself is reduced to a map or "anatomy" in one of Donne's most famous elegies.[79] In this poem, the memory of Elizabeth Drury, who is now in heaven, turns the world into an abstract or mirror of her virtues, much like the "glasses of [Donne's and his lover's] eyes" in "The Canonization," which "epitomize . . . countries, towns, courts." Drury is "She to whom this world must itself refer, / As suburbs, or the microcosm of her" (ll. 236–37); like the mistress of "Elegy 19," she absorbs "that rich Indy," since India's gold "Is but as single money, coined from her" (ll. 233–34). Yet, unlike that mistress and the erotic saints of "The Canonization," "Drury is dead; she's dead" (l. 38)—not with us and capable of mediation, as a Catholic saint, if believed in, would be. The Drury elegy is religious, not profane, verse. As such it concedes that the only person who has died and yet can contract and span spiritual distances, to the salvation of the treasonous, wandering pilgrim, is Christ, who overcame death.

Hence Donne describes Christ's dying sacrifice in ways which express continuing wonder at the Crucifixion's eradication of space. Christ's Cross is the picture of geographies confounded, although— as does Spenser where he narrativizes Redcrosse's shield—Donne redeems that picture from iconolatry by realizing its mystery through elaborate verbal conceits.[80] Donne dare not "th'image of [Christ's] Cross deny" ("The Cross," l. 2),[81] but to him its image is verbal. The Cross in language destroys space, as well as time. In "The Progress of the Soul," Donne collapses various holy places

into the central significant area where Christ died. The "low . . .
room" in which Jesus was born was

> . . . no low room, nor than the greatest, less,
> If (as devout and sharp men fitly guess)
> That Cross, our joy, and grief, where nails did tie
> That all, which always was all, everywhere,
> Which could not sin. . . .
> Stood in the self same room in Calvary,
> Where first grew the forbidden learned tree,
> For on that tree hung in security
>   This soul, made by the Maker's will. . . .
>
> (ll. 70–80)

The Cross absorbs the separate places of Bethlehem, Golgotha, and
Eden, then returns us to Golgotha, the all-important site that dispensed with differences of place (as well, again, as time). In the
phrase "where nails did tie / That all . . . everywhere," Donne employs a technique the Argentinian poet Jorge Luis Borges, speaking
specifically of its use in Jacobean literature, called "oximoron": the
"deliberate alternat[ion]" of "two registers" of meaning.[82] The
nails in Christ's hands and feet do not sever flesh or split bone, but,
like a cord, "tie all . . . [things] everywhere" tightly together, joining
all sites at the site of his sacrifice. No earthly place matters—no
ground or shrine is holy and conveys special blessings—for all places
are absorbed into the Cross.

Again and again Donne turns to the Cross as the nullifier of all
geographies, an action that most importantly figures the eradication
of distance between the Christian and God. "[B]e thou nailed unto
my heart / And crucified again," Donne beseeches God; "Part not
from it, though it from thee would part" ("A Litany," ll. 14–16).[83]
In "The Cross," Donne closes the physical gap between himself and
the God on the Cross by imagining himself as a Cross, then transforming that Cross to a swimmer who is both Donne and his reader,
and who traverses vast watery distances. Finally the Cross becomes
everything that swimmer sees and the whole universe which encom-
passes him.

> Who can deny me power, and liberty
> To stretch mine arms, and mine own cross to be?

Swim, and at every stroke, thou art thy cross,
The mast and yard make one, where seas do toss.
Look down, thou spiest out crosses in small things;
Look up, thou seest birds raised on crossed wings;
All the globe's frame and sphere's, is nothing else
But the meridians crossing parallels.

(ll. 17–25)

The Christ-bearing Cross is properly realized in poetry as all things and all places. The image of Christ as the World was not original with Donne; the thirteenth-century German Ebstorf Map, for example, pictured the known and named points of the world as parts of the body of Christ, whose head topped the map.[84] What Donne has done is to eliminate detailed geographies and confute maps in a poem which not only turns image to text, but dispenses with earthly topographies, conflating them with each other and the Cross in fourteen words ("All the globe's frame and sphere's, is nothing else / But the meridians crossing parallels"). In the Ebstorf Map, Christ's head is next to the presumed site of Eden and the center of his body is Jerusalem.[85] "The Cross," in contrast, denies the existence of specific sites wherefrom to draw especially close to God. Donne's poem does not glorify holy spaces, but subsumes space in its description of Christ's sacrifice. Something similar is done in "Good Friday, 1613." That poem, as befits its title, is an extended meditation on the Crucifixion, which "made [God's] own lieutenant Nature shrink": "made his footstool"—the earth—"crack" (ll. 19–20). Christ's hands stretched apart on the Cross "span the poles"; his form contains the "endless height which is / Zenith to us, and t'our antipodes" (ll. 21, 23–24). It is Christ's concentration of man's universe into one broken body that makes possible the poem's final conceit, wherein Donne's journey westward becomes a stationary stance of humility, as the poet stays to receive "corrections" from the God behind him. Physical removal from Christ is not possible when Christ contains "all . . . everywhere" ("The Progress of the Soul," l. 73).[86] Christ "fills all place, yet none holds him" ("Nativity," l. 10).[87]

I think it is because Donne sees Christ as the annihilator of geographies, and travel as something God halts in order to unite himself to the sinner, that his sacred poems more often present the Christian as a stationary city than as an errant pilgrim. As a city, the beleaguered Christian stays put, waiting for God to come to him. In "Obsequies to the Lord Harrington," Donne poetically transforms the holy city of Jerusalem, traditional site of pilgrimage, to English churches: "churchyards are our cities, . . . / There are the holy suburbs, and from thence / Begins God's city, New Jerusalem," he writes.[88] But the image of the church or temple habitually prompts Donne's association of the building and the body, "a temple of the Holy Spirit" (1 Cor. 6:19). Thus images of church and city merge with that of the body in Holy Sonnets 2 and 14, both of which poems beseech God to rescue the sinner from the devil's usurpation. In Sonnet 2, "My self, a temple of thy Spirit divine," asks, "Why doth the devil then usurp on me?" (ll. 8–9),[89] while in Sonnet 14, the sinner is "an usurped town, to another due," who awaits the city's capture by the battering ram of the "three-personed God" (ll. 5, 1). Donne's interest in Bible translation was not pronounced, but he chose to translate from the Vulgate and Tremellius the Lamentations of Jeremiah, an Old Testament book in which the prophet speaks in the voice of the suffering city. "Because I have rebelled so much, as fast / The sword without, as death within, doth waste" (ll. 79–80).[90] In Lamentations the city comes to stand for the sinful community, while in Donne's version, heard alongside the intensely personal laments of his whole body of sacred verse, the city's voice seems to sound from the poet's own private depths. Jerusalem, like all earthly places, is not proposed as a place to journey to, but employed as a verbal image of the poet's inner world. In Donne's erotic verse, that world is blessed by the presence of the poet's lover. In his sacred verse, the poet awaits the lover's arrival.

Thus in these divine poems we see, exalted to a devotional register, the same disdain for travel and place differences that animate many of Donne's love poems, as well as his satires. Love, be it erotic or divine, makes all places one. (In "To Sir Henry Wotton, at his going Ambassador to Venice," Donne asserts, "God is as near me here" [l. 40].)[91] Paradoxical language is the medium by which the poet and his reader can apprehend this mystery. In his sermon on Matthew 4:18–20, which recounts Christ's call to Peter and Andrew to become "fishers of men" (Matt. 4:19), Donne asserted that "Eloquence is not our net; . . . onely the Gospel is." But Donne's sacred poems seem to argue otherwise. Providing artful meditations on the biblical accounts of Christ's sacrifice—indeed, in the translation of Lamentations, merging with an authentic biblical longing for that sacrifice—they imply their status as what Jeffrey Fruen, speaking of Spenser's poems, called "complementary scripture."[92] By these poems, as by the gospel, Christ's blood may be "red" (Holy Sonnet 4).

Attention to Donne's metaphor of his verse as a map—an image he never uses to describe the Bible—may dispel the apparent contradiction between his employment of verse to salvific ends and his claim that "Eloquence is not our net; . . . onely the Gospel is." Donne's "verse, the strict map of [his] misery," is "as a picture" of the Word (to adapt lines from his dedicatory poem "To Mr T. W.").[93] It is not (excepting the Lamentations) the thing itself—not, finally, sacramental—but consubstantial, a Protestant verbal emblem of and pointer to the redemptive sacrifice it repeatedly requests and describes. (In a less sublime register, Donne describes himself, a poet, as a "map . . . of" the virtues of the Countess of Bedford.)[94] The importance of the body, also described in the sacred verse as a map, is likewise reduced by the conceit. When Donne represents his body as a city or temple, he is calling it something distinctly other than the thing it houses (as where, writing to the Countess of Bedford, Donne says he beholds her as "virtue's temple, not as she"). When Donne calls his verse or his body a map, he is distinguishing between verse and body on the one hand, and the place toward which both point, on the other.[95]

We have seen the comic stress Donne lays on the distinction between map and represented territory in his nonsacred verse. In Satire 4, he calls hell a mere "scant map" of the horrid court, where he has just been [l. 4], and in a letter to the Countess of Bedford he mocks the arrogance of English claims to have "added to the world Virginia" as though that region has suddenly been called into being by cartographers' inclusion of it on a globe. When we view his satires alongside his sacred verse which employs similar images, we see that map, temple, verse, and body are analogous terms for Donne. Donne's divine poetry proposes that these things be seen in contrast to a spiritual reality that surpasses them. None is God, for each is a thing that houses or points to God.

How does the body, specifically, so direct the Christian? Donne turns body to navigational chart through mediating the flesh in verse which, unlike his poems of idolatrous eros, divests that flesh of sacramental value. For the love poet Donne, as we saw, the body incarnates erotic love. It is no contradiction for him or for us to say

that it cannot incarnate heavenly love. The body can only, in its with-
ering, figure that love's absence, and thus point to divine love's presence elsewhere. In treating the dying body as a map, Donne stresses
its absolute separateness from God. The profane—the world of
Catholic saints, shrine pilgrimage, and eros—is not infused with the
sacred; not "charged with the grandeur of God," as the twentieth-
century poet and Jesuit Gerard Manley Hopkins would one day
write.[96] In the words of Edward Wheeler, Donne's divine poems do
not "preserv[e] a . . . sentimental belief in human physical incor-
ruptibility."[97] In "Hymn to God my God, in my Sickness," Donne's
approach to "that holy room" that is God's presence chamber is
made possible only by his soul's discarding of the map that graphs
his journey towards death, the room's entranceway.

> . . . my physicians . . . are grown
>   Cosmographers, and I their map, who lie
> Flat on this bed, that by them may be shown
>   That this is my south-west discovery
>   *Per fretum febris*, by these straits to die,
>
> I joy, that in these straits, I see my west;
>   For, though their currents yield return to none,
> What shall my west hurt me?
>
>   (ll. 6–13)[98]

"Be this my text," Donne says of his verse (l. 29), combining the
images of body, map, and poem. All three things are finally reduced
to terms describing, but not rendering, union with God.

   Yet God is no great distance—indeed, no physical distance at all—
from the dying Christian. Donne stands "here at the door" of the
"holy room" (ll. 4, 1). His soul's utter flight from his body, enabled
by that body-map's diminishment, delivers the longed-for reunion.
More simply said, death does so. Thus for Donne's redeemed Christian, death is the simple substitute for all physical or spiritual journeys. As Donne's contemporary George Herbert wrote in "The
Pilgrimage," death is "but a chair"—a term which, in M. H. Abrams's words, "implies rest and immobility, but also . . . convey-
ance."[99] As Nabil Matar suggests, in Donne's "Hymn to God my
God," death is a gracious removal of a separating wall.[100] Death gives
easy access to the ultimate lover, who is ready at hand. "*Salvation to*

all that will is nigh," Donne wrote in "La Corona" (1, l. 14)[101]—that is, near not only in time, but in space. The dying Donne would have agreed with Spenser's claim that for the questing Christian, Heaven is no distant goal of an arduous pilgrimage, but a homely region that is "not farre away."[102]

6

Milton and the Pilgrim Reader

In former times saints made many pilgrimages to Rome, Jerusalem, and Compostella in order to make satisfaction for sins. Now, however, we can go on pilgrimages in faith, namely, when we diligently read the psalms, prophets, gospels, etc. Rather than walk about holy places we can thus pause at our thoughts, examine our heart, and visit the real promised land and paradise of eternal life.

—Martin Luther, *Table Talk*[1]

He that can apprehend and consider vice with all her baits and seeming pleasures, and yet abstain, and yet distinguish, and yet prefer that which is truly better, he is the true wayfaring Christian.

—John Milton, *Areopagitica*[2]

WE HAVE SEEN THAT JOHN DONNE'S RELIGIOUS VERSE, DESPITE ITS SOME-times amorous language, forsakes the glorification of the actual flesh to which his erotic verse was consecrate. In Donne's poetry as in Shakespeare's plays of romance, pilgrimage, like other Roman Catholic practices, is appropriated—in the sense of "made appropriate"—by eros. But only by eros. When holy charity is Donne's subject, the pilgrim appears in his poems as an errant wanderer, whose departing back must be scourged to purify him for his recall by Christ. The Christian's travels mire his flesh in this world, but Christ opens the door that his soul may enter the next. The body is finally no more than a decaying map of the death that overwhelms it. It will be discarded once death, which is also God's doorway, is granted to the sufferer's imprisoned spirit. Donne's fallen sinner is Calvin's "sad ruin," its "flesh panting for every subterfuge by which it thinks that the blame for its own evils may . . . be diverted from itself to another,"[3] its soul "something essential, separate from the body," but itself "so corrupted that whatever remains is frightful de-

134

formity," such that even the "beginning of our recovery of salvation" is provided "through Christ."[4] As for that soul's reliance on the intervention of saints and the purgative value of pilgrimage to their shrines, we may recall that Calvin called belief in those things "stupidity."[5]

It is intriguing that Donne, whose erotic verse glorified the body, and who lamented the Church's fractured state and abhorred theological dispute, expressed in his sacred verse such a Calvinist rejection of Catholics' sacramental outlook. That is, we do not initially expect Donne to repudiate the Catholic view, not just (or primarily) of the transubstantiated Eucharist, but of the human body's ability volitionally to approach God through works of pilgrimage, as well as the soul's capacity to do so.

Conversely, we do not expect John Milton, a far more radical or "advanced"[6] seventeenth-century Protestant than Donne, to celebrate the flesh *or* the powers of the human spirit: to argue on behalf of either bodies' or spirits' ability to approach Heaven through any sort of pilgrimage at all. We do not, that is, expect a radical Puritan to be *less* Calvinist than John Donne, Dean of Saint Paul's and champion of the Anglican *via media*.

Yet so it is. Milton does, like Donne (and drawing from the Bible),[7] use images of physical travel predominantly to figure flight from, not approach to, God. Yet unlike Donne, Milton finds little evocative emotional power in the Gospel verse which attributes to God all power to bring the erring Christian home ("No one can come to me unless the Father who sent me draws him" [John 6:44]). Not only does Milton reject Calvin's doctrine of predestination, he attributes some self-saving ability to the Christian himself. Most surprisingly, Milton also redeems the flesh in a way some scholars have linked to the Catholic doctrine of transubstantiation. Unlike Donne, who, despite his transcendent celebrations of sacramental eros, finally found the body wholly separate from the redeemed spirit, Milton embraced a Neoplatonism that led him to see the body itself as a thing connected to the soul. Milton suggests that though that connected body and soul is corrupt, both elements may be transformed, and, according to the sinner's choice, may draw the Christian upward into the heavenly life.

Herein lies our paradox. Milton was not only virulently anti-Catholic but an enemy of the episcopacy in the Reformed England of the mid-to-late-seventeenth century, a despiser of the church mid-

dle way with which Donne has become associated, and an avid participant in the type of religious debate that Donne thought
anathema to Christendom. Yet it is Milton, not Donne, who rejects
Calvin's position on the abject corruption of the soul and the final
irrelevance of the flesh, and also Milton whose work accords a measure of salvific ability to the Christian's own intellect, or reason. Of
course Milton, like Calvin and like Luther before Calvin, gives original credit for man's reasoning capacity to the Creator, and holds (as
do all Christians, Catholics included) that it is God who ultimately
permits salvation. Yet more than other Protestant writers Milton lays
stress on human freedom to act in accord with that permission, to
become damned or saved. Specifically, in *Paradise Lost*, while glorify-
ing the body, Milton explores the intellectual choices by which man
may maintain, acquire, or reject the gift of Heaven. Thus while Milton rejects the traditional Catholic works—such as the Mass, cloistered prayer, and pilgrimage to saints' shrines—by which, in the
terms of an older English Christianity, the sinner might approach a
state of grace, he yet supplies a doctrine of mental work, done by
humans, that precedes salvation. Such work brings the Christian
into a position to choose, and thus receive, his or her own redemption.

   This intellectual labor involves the fallen man's or woman's journey of intellectual discernment through the digestion of *language*.
In *Paradise Lost* (1667) and the prose essay *Areopagitica* (1644), the
works on which I will chiefly focus in this chapter, Milton sets forth
the task of the pilgrim reader.

   In *Paradise Lost*, the endangered soul begins in intellectual darkness,
or darkened-ness. As though Satan and his demonic retinue were
human and potential recipients of salvation, Milton employs them
to dramatize how sin clouds the intellect, by representing sin's effect
on these fallen angels. To express sin's results he employs images of
physical travel. Here, like Spenser and Donne before him, Milton
portrays travel not as Godward pilgrimage but as fruitless action that
bodies forth sinfulness and then confusion in the sinner's mind.
"Going somewhere" in *Paradise Lost* is going nowhere, or someplace
worse. Satan and his fellow travelers first undergo a forced physical
separation from God that confirms a chosen (predominantly) spiritual separation, and then various chosen physical journeys that
further that spiritual separation. In all cases, journeying is accompa-

nied by a mental darkness that, in turn, redounds on the journey, confirming its mazy, wandering, errant nature. Thus physical journey in the epic figures both separation from God and the chaos of fallen thought.

In describing the "nine days'" Hellward falling of the disobedient angels (5.871), Milton merges time with space to convey the scope of their physical distance from God. Yet the bad angels' moral collapse is also figured by an account of their prior spatial separation from their Creator. When telling Adam of the war on God, the angel Raphael recounts its beginning in Lucifer's decision, out of anger at Christ's anointing by God, to withdraw from God's throne to "the quarters of the north" in Heaven itself (5.689), where he and his confederates plan their attack. The hurling of the rebels from Heaven upon their defeat thus reiterates and elaborates their initial self-removal from God. Milton thenceforth associates travel with confusion and becoming progressively more lost. Hell is "darkness visible" (1.63), an arena of ignorance where, for all their rhetorical purposefulness, the bad angels move in ways Milton repeatedly describes as "wandering." After Beëlzebub suggests that they fly above Hell to attack Eden, Satan reframes the projected assault as a sort of meandering voyage, asking, "Who shall tempt with wand'ring feet / The dark unbottomed infinite abyss . . . ?" (2.404–13). Once he himself is launched on the journey and traveling through the realm of Chaos, Satan—apparently truthfully—tells the embodied spirits of Rumor, Chance, Tumult, Confusion, and Discord whom he meets there that he is "Wand'ring" their "darksome desert," "half lost" (2.973, 975). In Eden as well his movements are famously circuitous; they are serpentine; "oblique," "sidelong," and "mazy" (9.510, 512, 161). The other devils disband after the infernal council to go "wand'ring, each his several way" through Hell, as "inclination or sad choice / Leads [them] perplexed" (2.524–25). Milton here projects a future of continued and more extended wandering for the devils, once Adam's and Eve's fall—which, when it happens, dooms the fallen humans to "wand'ring steps" (12.648)—shall enlarge the demons' territory. "[W]and'ring o'er the earth," the devils will acquire new names and "by falsities and lies" continue to corrupt mankind (1.365, 367–68).

Milton's account of these devils' mazy wanderings implies his skepticism regarding both the traditional heroic values of the war campaign and the energies many early-modern English expended in global exploration and conquest.[8] The angels' armed revolt in Heaven is, of course, devilish. They are presented as the inventors of firearms (6.504, 584–95), and the "gamesome mood" in which they discharge them lowers the ludic metaphor with which Shakespeare celebrated war travel in *Henry V* to a diabolical register (*PL* 6.620). In Shakespeare, imperial pilgrimage was something to cheer for, if only in the playhouse. In *Paradise Lost*, imperial aggression is malign. "What think'st thou of our empire now?" Sin asks Death and Satan once Adam and Eve have sinned, and Hell has annexed Earth (10.592)[9]. In Hell, the devils explore their "dismal world" in "squadrons," "On bold adventure to discover wide," but travel chiefly to distract themselves from the pain of their own damnation. "Roving on / In cónfused march forlorn," these "advent'rous bands" find no exotic treasures, but a "universe of death," and "no rest" (1.570–73, 614–15, 622, 618). The explorers in *Paradise Lost* all inhabit or come from Hell. We may recall that for Richard Hakluyt, recorder of early-modern navigations, the global adventurer was a hero who might "work many great and unlooked for effects, increase [England's] dominions, enrich her coffers, and reduce many pagans to the faith of Christ."[10] Milton takes a different view. For him the Hell-bound explorers are pathetic devils, and the "great adventurer" who goes in "search / Of foreign worlds" is Satan himself (*PL* 10.441–42). Satan's own person and habiliments are linked to earthly exploration, an association which discredits the activity. Making his own voyage of discovery through Hell, the soaring fiend resembles "a fleet descried" hanging

> on the clouds, by equinoctial winds
> Close sailing from Bengala, or the isles
> Of Ternate and Tidore, whence merchants bring
> Their spicy drugs: they on the trading flood
> Through the wide Ethiopian to the Cape
> Ply stemming nightly toward the pool. So seemed
> Far off the flying Fiend. . . .

> (2.636–42)

His flight upward from Hell to Eden will take him "abroad / Through all the coasts of dark destruction" (2.463–64). In book 4, Milton likens the last stages of Satan's malevolent journey to the voyage of men "who sail / Beyond the Cape of Hope" and, approaching their goal, "slack their course" (4.159–60, 164). Again the metaphor of water travel is deployed in Milton's description of Satan-as-serpent's winding crawl toward Eve: "As when a ship by skillful steersman wrought / Nigh river's mouth or foreland, where the wind / Veers oft, as oft so steers, and shifts her sail; / So varied he" (9.513–16). While he is still in Hell, Satan's shield is linked to the "optic glass" through which Galileo "descr[ies] new lands, / Rivers or mountains" in the moon's "spotty globe" (1.284–91), a simile that links early-modern exploratory voyaging with feats of astronomical discovery, and, Donne-like, calls both sorts of "travel" into question.[11] In book 11's account, when tempted by Satan, Jesus will be notably resistant to the glories of empire, to which Milton adds "Rich Mexico the seat of Motezume" and "El Dorado" (11.384, 407, 411).

Milton's epic contempt for voyages of exploration is rooted in his skepticism regarding seventeenth-century England's fusion of Protestant evangelism, exploration, and commerce. Steven Pincus has recently shown that Milton's prose writings criticize his country's new "self-conscious commercial society" that prides itself on the vigor of its far-flung trading ventures. In *Areopagitica*, Pincus notes, Milton proposes that such a society encourages its members to consider even their religious faith a commodity, or "dividual movable," and to find "religion to be a traffic so entangled, and of so many piddling accounts, that . . . [they] cannot skill to keep a stock going upon that trade."[12] Milton, as Pincus writes, was "no defender of the new commercial society";[13] nor was he a defender of the global roving through which that society declared its identity and in which it invested its faith. His own three years' travel in Europe was consecrated to study, to intellectual commerce with writers he thought great, and to the perfection of languages, a skill which he found vital for the literary pilgrimages he underwent and fostered after his happy return to England, his earthly version of the Promised Land.[14] Travel for mere adventure, sensational tourism, or profit he disdained.

It stands to reason, then, that travel in *Paradise Lost* should be tainted by this disdain, and mostly be hellish. Adam and Eve do not embark on it until they are fallen. When they must go from Eden, they are, of course, happier journeyers than the demons, having "Providence" as "their guide" and the prospect of an ultimate "place of rest" (12.647). Still, their travel outward from the garden manifests their sinful state, and the fallen world spread "all before them" for their journeyings (12.646) is no compensatory blessing, but a feature of their punishment.

The moral reduction of travel in *Paradise Lost* as a whole is linked to a horror of vastness, of unmapped and unbounded space. As Adam will say, the unfallen world is "[m]easured," but "beyond is all abyss" (12.554–55). The realm of Chaos through which Satan flies is, frighteningly, "a vast vacuity" (2.931), "Illimitable ocean without bound, / Without dimension, where length, breadth, and highth, / And time and space are lost" (2.892–95). Its boundlessness is opposed to the heavenly realms, where God made "order from disorder" and "vast infinitude confined" (3.713, 711), using "golden compasses" to "circumscribe / This universe" (7.225–26).[15] Working (to quote *Macbeth*'s Malcolm) in "measure, time, and place" (5.9.39), God fixes boundaries and limits travels, as do unfallen Adam and Eve as they curb the else-wayward growth of their garden. Satan, of course, is partly characterized by his refusal to be confined within these geographical "narrow limits" (4.384). He leaves Hell, the "bounds prescribed / To [his] transgressions" (4.879–80), and "overleap[s] all bound / Of hill or highest wall" to enter the Garden of Eden. Against the circumscribed Eden, a world of "smallest magnitude" (2.1053), is set not only Satan's will to travel freely, but the ghastly size of the universe in which he may do it. That universe's regions include the Catholic Limbo in which Satan briefly pauses before coming to Eden. In *Paradise Lost* Limbo is Hell's annex, a "spacious field" where "the Fiend" walks "at large," as will one day walk human "pilgrims," who "strayed so far to seek / In Golgotha him dead, who lives in heav'n" (3.430, 476–77). Here Milton fuzzily merges Satan's time in Limbo with that of the deluded and punished Catholic pilgrims, to propose a likeness between his and their journeys. He first uses the past tense to describe what for Satan would be a future event (pilgrims not yet born have already "strayed"), and then moves entirely into the present tense, as though the just-alighted Satan and the damned pilgrims were in Limbo at the same time, now ("All who have their reward on earth, the fruits / Of painful superstition and blind zeal, / . . . here find / Fit retribution" [3.451–454]). Thus traditional religious pilgrimage is made to appear satanic. We may here recall devil's advocate Duessa's recollection, in *The Faerie Queene*, of her claim to have performed such pilgrimages as have led Milton's Catholics to this vast "Paradise of Fools" (*PL* 3.496). Like Milton's Holy Land pilgrims, who have sought "In Golgotha him dead / Who lives in heav'n," Duessa has fruitlessly "throughout the world . . . straid" to find Christ's "woefull corse" rather than the living God (*FQ* 1.2.24). By placing such travelers as Spenser's Duessa in a wide fool's paradise, where they continue to "roam" (3.475), and by juxtaposing them with Satan's journey through Chaos, Milton underscores the horror of all such errant pilgrimage through "antres vast and deserts idle," to borrow Shakespeare's Othello's phrase (*Othello* 1.3.140). "Long were to tell / What I have done, what suffered, with what pain / Voyag'd th'unreal, vast, unbounded deep / Of horrible confusion," Satan tells the devils on his return from his mission, in a perverse parody of Othello's "dilat[ion]" of his exotic global "pilgrimage" (*Othello* 1.3.153)—the "travel's history" with which he has won Desdemona (*Othello* 1.3.139). Milton associates such journeys and their recollections with Hell. The rovings that in Shakespeare are secular and erotic are in *Paradise Lost* Catholic and diabolical.

Wandering is hellish, of course, because it figures the errancy of the mind as sinners choose damnable spiritual pathways. Physical wandering manifests errant thoughts that themselves restlessly "wander through eternity" (1.148). Wandering thoughts are not blissful. At worst they are torture, at best, "perplexing" (8.183). They ensue when the unreasonable mind wilfully seeks not useful truths but vain "intricacies"; "Seek[s] them with wandering thoughts, and notions vain," as unfallen Adam tells his tutor Raphael. Such purposeless wondering is like unbounded wandering, and as harmful: though "apt the mind or fancy is to rove / Unchecked," "of her roving is no end; / Till warned" (8.188–89). Intellectual pride is at the root of this restlessness, and is seen in the choice of sinners to live guideless, trusting themselves to be arbiters of best action. Even in Hell, already damned, Satan shows his pride in his specious request for counsel regarding the spirit who should attack Eden, which masks his prior conclusion that it should be he. Having proclaimed that he will go, he rises to "preven[t] all reply" (2.467). He goes alone, and tells the denizens of Chaos that he travels "without guide" (2.975), thus bodying forth in his travels the independence that has precipitated his fall.

Superficially Satan's independence seems to express the freedom Milton had championed twenty years before in his famous defense of wide reading and a free press, *Areopagitica*, where he exulted that God had given his creatures "minds that can wander beyond all limit and satiety."[16] Yet Satan's behavior actually refuses the wide reading, or consulting of other minds, that Milton advocated in that prose work, which does not call for rigorous defense of one's chosen intellectual position, but attacks the limits imposed by imperfect censors on the literary advice one might seek. "[H]ow should the licencers [censors] themselves be confided in, unless we can confer upon them, or they assume to themselves above all others in the land, the grace of infallibility, and uncorruptedness?"[17] Satan is not only a rotten judge, but the cause that rot is in other judges (to adapt Falstaff's self-description). This is so chiefly because he operates without the wisdom of Christ, later the Word whose gospel will prove Christians' chief guide—and, in Milton's terms as in those of the Gospel of John (1:1), already the "Word" even prior to his human incarnation (God calls him this in 3.170). Satan, indeed, has sinned originally by refusing to honor that Word. In so doing he has fashioned for himself the kind of "fixed mind" (1.97), closed to all question, that Milton abhors and likens to "a muddy pool" in *Areopagitica*.[18] His set single purpose makes inevitable the mistakenness embodied in his "sidelong" travels (9.512), and sets him against the unfallen Adam, who questions Raphael, his moral and intellectual guide, about spiritual truth in book 5. Conversely, Satan's self-chosen guidelessness likens him to Eve and then Adam when they themselves refuse guides or unreasonably choose them. Eve's decision to embark on her own without Adam's superior reason to guide her precipitates what Kent Lehnof calls her "aural" seduction by Satan,[19] and what Adam calls her moral "wandering" (9.1146). After the fall, Christ chastens Adam for having made Eve his "guide" by inclining to her voice before God's (10.145–46). Christ seems (oddly) inaccurate here, for book 9 makes clear that Adam eats of the apple undeceived by Eve's verbal "guidance" and fully aware that her trespass is "fatal" (9.204). His decision to join her in disobedience constitutes a surrender not to her judgment, but to his own unassisted conclusion, which, in defiance of God's superior wisdom, is that a life without her would be eternally painful ("loss of thee / Would never from my heart" [9.912–13]). Set on Eve, Adam's thoughts constitute a "dismissal of wisdom," in Vincent Di Benedetto's phrase.[20] Here Adam's "fixed mind," like Satan's, results— paradoxically—in erroneous spiritual wandering.

Paradise Lost repeatedly makes physical travel accompany and embody the spiritual travel precipitated by the mind uncurbed by a reasonably chosen guide. Eve departs from Adam and morally errs. Adam, departing from God's instructions, leaves Eden alongside Eve. Satan flies upward in an attempt to regain his celestial seat, but his physical progress is spiritually retrograde. He proclaims that the decision of the infernal synod to attack Heaven will "from the lowest deep / . . . once more lift [them] up" (2.392–93), but the reverse is of course true; his journey upward to Eden is accompanied by his own descent into mental and spiritual darkness and confusion.

The self-torturing circular reasoning that will characterize him when he first regards Eden is predicted in the experience of Sin, gatekeeper of Hell, allegorically presented in book 2. Sin is literally self-absorbed. She alternately eats and is eaten by her young, who either gnaw her internally or "with conscious terrors vex [her] round" (2.801), and is obvious literary kin to the monstrous mother Error in book 1 of Spenser's *Faerie Queene.*[21] Both monsters figure the spiritual jail to which error confines the sinner. Yet the difference between the monsters is profound. Spenser's Error represents the misleading of Christians by others; she vomits ungodly "books and papers" that, read, lead souls astray. In contrast, Milton's Sin, no less mired in error, issues from Satan's refusal to "read" the judgments of others—to look outside himself for guidance to truth. Sin is Satan's daughter and paramour, born of his solipsistic spiritual intercourse with himself, a more perverse intimacy even than incest. "Out of [Satan's] head," Athena-like, Sin has "sprung" (2.758); Death emerges from her intercourse with Satan, who self-generated her; and repeated carnal knowledge among the diabolical trinity leads to sins who continually return to her womb, in an antithesis of progress and a continuing expression of self-mired error. This vivid image of prideful self eternally consulting itself is, to quote (again) Thomas Kyd, "no life, but lively form of death." It is also the antithesis of progressive pilgrimage toward God.

The caught, reticular reasoning of the solipsistic thinker is embodied in the oblique movements of Satan in Paradise, but is best expressed in his tortured soliloquies and, later, in those of the fallen Eve and Adam. Seeing Eden, Satan's body, attempting to reach it, retracts and fails like his aspiring mind.

> . . . [H]is dire attempt . . .
> . . . boils in his tumultous breast,
> And like a devilish engine back recoils

> Upon himself; horror and doubt distract
> His troubled thoughts. . . .
>
> (4.17–20)

Speaking to himself, as will be his increasing habit, his thoughts and
words are "much revolving" (4.31). The beauty of Eden inspires
him only to engage in prolonged stationary lament, wherein he
stops still, considers a possible groveling return to God, literally
questions himself as though he were two people ("Hadst thou the
same free will and power to stand?" [4.66]), reasons at length in
one direction, and then turns back in the original one ("But say I
could repent . . . / . . . [H]ow soon would highth recall high
thoughts" [4.93–95]). Book 9 repeats this pattern of lengthy, iso-
lated, self-questioning and nonprogressive discourse: "O earth, how
like to heav'n, if not preferred / More justly . . . . / But neither here
seek I, no nor in heav'n / To dwell" (9.99–125). Such "relentless
thoughts" (9.130), expressed in soliloquy, are indeed the "notes . . .
tragic" (9.6) which express the entrapment of the fallen in the antipilgrimage of mazy intellectual wandering.[22] As Anthony Low writes,
"the Fall brings . . . the obsessive habit of anguished soliloquizing,
and an inward, spiraling fall into ever-expanding depths of terror,
loss, and loneliness"[23]—though "ever-constricting" rather than
"ever-expanding" would be my expression.

Such soliloquizing is the immediate result in Eve of her mere entertainment of Satan's suggestion that she eat the fatal fruit. She addresses not Satan but herself, inquiring whether "if death / Bind us
with after-bands, what profits then our inward freedom?" and continuing at length. Her self-consultation, a parody of guided delibera-
tion, culminates in sin. Adam too degenerates into soliloquy once
he has transgressed, lamenting his fall in almost two hundred lines
which variously self-question, propound, and show his entrapped
thought twisting backward, Hamlet-like, on itself. "How gladly
would I meet / Mortality my sentence. . . . / Yet one doubt / Pursues
me still, lest all I cannot die. . . ." and so on (10.775–83ff.). As Beverley Sherry writes, in book 9 "duologue gives place to monologue, a
characteristically fallen mode of utterance in *Paradise Lost*."[24]

Yet there are also fallen dialogues in the epic: conversations between two or more that are as circular and nonprogressive as the
fallen soliloquies. After eating the forbidden fruit, Adam and Eve
spend "fruitless hours" in "mutual accusation," "neither self-con-

demning," and "of their vain contést appears no end" (9.1187–89). In Hell itself, in book 1, some spirits sit and debate "providence, foreknowledge, will, and fate, / Fixed fate, free will, foreknowledge absolute, / And f[i]nd no end, in wand'ring mazes lost" (1.559–61). The near-chiasmus of this passage's first two lines expresses the circular entrapment of the lost angels' discussions.

Milton's prose writings—notably *De Doctrina Christiana* (1640s) and *The Reason of Church Government* (1642)—are ample evidence that he did not, as did Donne, abhor theological argument of the kind in which the fallen spirits here engage. Why, then, does *Paradise Lost* present such debate as a hellish activity? Again, the missing element in their debate is that whose lack has clouded the reason of Satan: Christ, God's "Word" and "wisdom" (3.170). In book 5 Milton makes the spirits' self-separation from God stem directly from their rejection of Christ, who alone makes God's truth visible to lesser spirits. The vain debate of the fallen spirits repeats the stalemated combat between the fallen and unfallen angels in Heaven (though that is described later, in books 5 and 6). Each conversation is an "endless," "perpetual fight" (5.694, 693) which can only be brought to final issue by the intervention of Christ, who settles the matter. "[N]one but thou / Can end it," God tells the Son, "thy power above compare" since "[thou art] worthiest to be heir" (5.703–7). Richard Strier's mystification regarding the nature of the special virtue by which Christ may win the war (or, by extension, might turn the fallen spirits' aimless debate toward truth) arises from his insufficient attention to the symbolic value of Christ's identification as Word. "[I]t is hard to see what 'worthiest' can mean here [when applied by God to Christ] except most powerful," Strier says,[25] but it is only hard when we fail to interpret Christ's warfare as an assault of reasoned truth against the false logic with which Satan has seduced his followers. In his prose works Milton is also drawn to identify combat with aggressive, truthful language, as Thomas Corns has noted: in the *Second Defense of the English People* Milton claims himself to have met an opponent "in single combat and plunged into his reviling throat this pen."[26] "Like the Son," Corns says, Milton "is the godly champion in the great duel."[27] This identification of warring Christ with God's articulated truth is urged not only by God in *Paradise Lost*, but by Milton in *Areopagitica*, where he writes, "Truth indeed came once into the world with her Divine Master." Absence from or lack of alliance with the Truth that accompanies

Christ dooms those who argue about truth to reticular, endless error, as they fail to engage in the search for wisdom that Milton describes as an authentic spiritual pilgrimage. "Suffer not these licensing prohibitions to stand at every place of opportunity, forbidding and disturbing them that continue seeking, that continue to do our obsequies to the torn body of our martyred saint" (Truth), he writes.[28] Since the texts to whose censoring *Areopagitica* objects are not the Gospels, Milton's association of the perusal of them with and the search for the martyred saint, Christ's Truth, is radical. It identifies Christ not as a personal divinity manifested in scripture but as a spirit of truth available in a variety of inspired writings, of which—why not?—Milton's own might be some. Seeing that both *Areopagitica* and *Paradise Lost* identify Christ with a divine and truthful Word not embodied in one particular scripture enables us to distinguish between the authentic spiritual pilgrims, who, like unfallen Adam, seek knowledge of God, and the inauthentic ones: the fallen humans and debating demons who argue only for the sake of self-aggrandizement. "Vain wisdom all, and false philosophy, indeed" (1.565).

Paradise Lost suggests that fruitless intellectual travel of the sort enacted by the quarreling Adam and Eve, by the falsely philosophical demons, and by the bitterly soliloquizing Satan culminates in idolatry. In *Paradise Lost,* misdirected worship is the action of a mind weakened by its lack of interest in truth or in anything beyond itself. Thus self-seeking Satan is half-worshipful toward Eve because of her physical rather than her intellectual beauty, finding her "divinely fair" (9.489), and Adam, allowing himself to be swayed into sin by his own argument concerning his need for her, proves "weak / Against the charm of beauty's powerful glance" (8.532–33). These descriptions of the dangers of Eve's beauty demonstrate an iconoclasm more resolved than that of Spenser, whose *Faerie Queene,* we recall, was divided between distrust of images' seductive power and studied celebration of the visual glory of Queen Elizabeth's court.[29] (Indeed, Albert Labriola finds a retrospective criticism of the cult of Elizabeth in Milton's condemnation of Eve worship.)[30] Eve's own submission to the serpent results not just from her unguided acceptance of his fraudulent argument that she should rebel against God, which appeals to her vanity (Eve should not obey, but "be obeyed" [9.570]), but from her amazement at his physical beauty.[31] "[C]arbuncle his eyes; / With burnished neck of verdant gold, erect /

Amidst his circling spires, . . . / Pleasing was his shape" (9.500–03). The unguided Eve's inclination to overvalue visual beauty has been made evident by Milton's earlier account of the preference she accords her own reflection over Adam, "less fair, / . . . Than that smooth wat'ry image," until Adam teaches her of the superior beauty of his "wisdom" (4.478–91). Maverick Protestant though he is, Milton's iconoclastic skepticism is by now familiar enough. It suggests to us that in *Paradise Lost*, as in other devout Protestant poetry, the only recommended quest for God—or, in Milton's terms, Truth—is a word-centered, inward pilgrimage, away from the distractions of the seen world.

However, distinctions obtain between Miltonic iconoclasm and that displayed by Spenser and the finally flesh-hating Donne. While both Spenser and Donne saw scripture as armor against the soul attacks of the misleading images and idols of the physical world, Milton perceives scripture as only one defense, or at least has a broader view of what scripture may be. Milton finds compensation for his own blindness in the fact that, walling him from the attractive visible world of "nature's works," sightlessness "shut[s] out" the inferior knowledge that world offers and opens his mind to a brighter "celestial Light" that will "purge" his invisible thoughts (3.49–54). This light will fit him to assist his readers' pilgrimage back to God by "justify[ing] the ways of God to men" (1.26)—that is, by not only explaining God's actions, but also straightening and making traversible the pathways between humans and their Creator. Read this way, Milton's famous line not only suggests that Christ's justifying work is incomplete, but proposes that there are several routes to and from Heaven. Christ says, "I am the way, the truth and the life, no man cometh unto the Father but by me" (John 14:6). Milton begs to differ.

It may be useful here to reflect on the means of redemption proposed not just in the Bible but in the religious poetry of Spenser and Donne, further to illuminate Milton's departure from it. Both Spenser's *Faerie Queene* and Donne's sacred verse stress, in Calvinist fashion, the sinner's inability to restore his lost understanding or even to precipitate personal repentance. The process of Redcrosse's salvation in the House of Holiness requires his passivity and the intervention of holy guides like Fidelia (Faith), who is not summoned by but sent to him, and who spoon-feeds him with scripture. Similarly, Donne's sacred verse repeatedly stresses the sinner's desperate state without God's rescue. It is only "by [God's] leave" that he can "rise again" (Holy Sonnet 1);[32] "Except [G]od enthral" him, he "never shall be free" (Holy Sonnet 14); a doomed pilgrim, he wonders "who shall give [him] that grace"—Calvin's initiating or prevenient grace—"to begin" to repent (Holy Sonnet 4). Further, since, for both Spenser and Donne, God must "draw" the sinner's "iron heart,"[33] repentance, like all Godward movements, is itself the product and evidence rather than the guarantor of salvation. In other words, God even supplies the penitence. Finally, in both Spenser and Donne, though Christian poetry may point to the Bible, the Bible itself is the sole means by which God makes salvation available. The scripture Fidelia reads to Redcrosse mysteriously is "Christ crucified" (1 Cor. 1:23). "Being red"—read—"it dyes red souls to white" (Donne, Holy Sonnet 4).[34]

Milton departs from Spenser's and Donne's Calvinist "pilgrimage" in two important ways. The first is constituted by his repeated stress on human (as well as angelic) choice, not just to fall, but to seek redemption. In *Paradise Lost*, as Barbara Lewalski writes, "God himself den[ies] predestination."[35] In book 3—in an apparently Calvinist formulation, to whose meaning I will return—God tells Christ that though he has "chosen of peculiar grace" some "Elect above the rest." Still, Milton qualifies this apparent Calvinism immediately, having God add the Arminian proposition, "The rest shall hear me call, and oft be warned" and "offered grace" (3.182–87). The Old Testament God may "harden heart[s]" (Exod. 4:21), but Milton's doesn't. In *Paradise Lost* God vows to "soften stony hearts / To pray, repent" (3.189–90), yet God's heart-softening is not the "drawing" of the heart to which Donne and the Gospel of Mark allude. Milton's God vows to place heart-working conscience in humans only as a "guide" (3.194) to which they may listen or not. "[I]f they will hear" it, "Light after light well used they shall attain, / And to the end persisting, safe arrive" (3.195–97). "They who neglect and scorn" God will "hard be hardened, blind be blinded" by their own turn from the light of God's truth (3.1.200). In other words, sinners choose whether or not to accomplish the spiritual journey to God. They are not drawn Godward like steel to adamant. "God left free the will," Adam warns Eve, in a statement that departs not only from Calvin's views but also from Luther's.[36] "[F]or what obeys / Reason is free, and reason he made right," Adam adds (9.351–52). "[R]eason also is choice," God says (3.108). "Reason is but choosing," Milton writes in *Areopagitica*.[37] Reason, then, is allied with conscience as the inner light by which the pilgrim may travel. That power of reason is broadly associated with God's word, which the Psalmist calls the "lamp unto [the Christian's] feet" (Ps. 119:105) For Milton reason is the pilgrim's walking staff. With it the Christian accomplishes his redemptive journey, which is one of intellectual work.

In this regard—that which proposes that the Christian's obligation is to "take an active part in reading and interpreting" what is written of God, to quote Su Fang Ng[38]—Milton's thought continues a Protestant tradition of lexical labor that began with the Lollards and continued with Tyndale. Yet a comparison of Milton to earlier Reformers reveals to us the second crucial way in which Milton's Protestantism is maverick, and a departure from theological principles fundamental to both Calvin and Luther (as well as to Wycliffe, before Luther; and to Tyndale, before Calvin). For all these Protestants and proto-Protestants, it was the Bible alone which laid legitimate claim to the Christian's interpretive efforts. As Ng says, Christian "literacy was focused on the reading of the translated scripture," "the ultimate authority and representive of God."[39] Martin Luther saw Bible reading as the only appropriate Christian "pilgrimage," saying, "[i]n former times saints made many pilgrimages to Rome, Jerusalem, and Compostella in order to make satisfaction for sins. Now, however, we can go on true pilgrimages in faith, namely, when we diligently read the psalms, prophets, gospels, etc. Rather than walk about holy places we can thus pause at our thoughts, examine our hearts, and visit the real promised land and paradise of eternal life." For Luther, such a Bible pilgrimage, while diligent, was the natural work of a Christian whom faith, working through scripture, had already saved. Milton's variant view is not just that the inward pilgrimage progresses toward, not out of, salvation, but that the Bible is only one text—albeit the greatest of them— within which the pilgrim may walk.[40] In *Areopagitica* he reduces the importance of scripture in the Christian's education, arguing that "[t]he Christian faith . . . is not unknown to have spread all over Asia, ere any Gospel or Epistle was seen in writing."[41] Thus the Christian's virtue is appropriately tried and whetted by his exposure not only to scripture but to a variety of writings, even foolish or evil ones, so as to exercise virtue not only by learning from the best thought, but by distinguishing between good thought and bad. "He that can apprehend and consider vice with all her baits and seeming pleasures, and yet abstain, and yet distinguish, and yet prefer that which is truly better, he is the true wayfaring Christian." For this reason "the approaching Reformation" depends on Christians "fast reading, trying all things."[42] Salvation—for an individual or a people—is not a humble acceptance of the gift of love that is Christ's sacrifice, mystically rendered to sinners by means of its scripture. It is instead a work of reason that embraces wisdom—a wisdom found in scripture, but in other places as well, including the mind itself, which builds its own wisdom by reading and rejecting wrong arguments. Milton does not hold, as did Donne in a sermon, that "onely the Gospel" is the "net" which catches sinful fish.[43]

What might other redemptive "nets" be? They are textual nets, books and essays where are articulated "new notions, . . . much writing, many opinions" both good and ill, as well as moral poetry. Spenser's own *Faerie Queene* stressed the unique value of scripture to the sinner's salvation. In Milton's account, "the sage and serious poet Spenser" is not only "a better teacher than Scotus, or Aquinas," but, it appears, as good as the Bible, since Christian faith may spread—has spread—in the absence of scripture.[44] Indeed, for Milton Christ-the-Word is not Truth, but Truth's most perfect possessor. "Truth indeed came into this world once with her divine Master." Since Christ's time on earth, Truth has been "hewd" and "scatter'd . . . to the four winds"—this despite Milton's seventeenth-century readers' possession of the full Bible in the vernacular—and Truth's pieces must still be sought. "We have not yet found them all."[45] Milton's habit in *Areopagitica* of inserting references to scripture in lists of nonsacred writings—for example, "the judgment of Aristotle . . . of Salomon, and of our Savior"[46]—has the effect of stripping the Bible of uniquely sacred status. His transformations of Genesis in *Paradise Lost* (e.g., his having Christ, not God the Father, confront the fallen humans [10:103ff.]) show that he felt his own work might in parts not just complement but rival the Bible. Thus both Milton's prose and his great epic poem demonstrate how, in Donald Guss's words, "when the Word is no longer [perceived as] divine, a revolutionary, Protestant hermeneutic serves . . . to valorize human praxis, human interpretation, human freedom."[47] It seems contradictory to associate a "Protestant hermeneutic" with a loss of belief in the sanctity of scripture, but in Milton's particular case it is appropriate. For Milton, in the human realm, only reason is sacred. After all, "a

wise man will make better use of an idle pamphlet, than a fool will
do of sacred Scripture."[48]

Milton's desire to present reason as the Christian's tool—the pilgrim's walking staff—accounts for the emphasis he places in *Paradise
Lost* on Christ as Word, the articulation of divine wisdom, rather
than as Love.[49] "My word, my wisdom," God calls the Son in book 3
(3.170). Milton pays lip service here to Christ's love, in God's statement that in Christ "Love hath abounded" (3.312) and in God's
characterization of the Son's impending self-sacrifice as "charity . . .
dear" (3.216). Yet Christ's sacrificial nature is undercut by his own
shrewd prediction that God won't, after all, let him be dead long:
"[O]n me let Death wreck all his rage; / Under his gloomy power I
shall not long / Lie vanquished; thou hast giv'n me to possess / Life
in myself forever" (3.241–43). The emphasis here is on Christ's perfect, prescient wisdom and, in fact, his logic. How much colder is
this Christ than the doubting, suffering man of Gethsemane, who
fears Crucifixion but agrees to it anyway! And yet he is a fuller expression of the reasoning faculty in which Milton placed his faith. In
Milton Christ on the Cross is not, as in Donne, the central salvific
wonder, alone equipped to "ravish" the sinner, to batter down the
walls of the besieged city (Sonnet 14). When Milton imagines "a City
besieg'd," he sees it not assaulted by sin, but "blockt about" by
error; not helpless without divine rape, but well on the road to redemption through its inhabitants' "disputing, reasoning, reading,
inventing, discoursing" so as to defeat its encircling foes by superior
knowledge.[50] The Christians of this city do not passively await
Christ's deliverance, but get busy, forging their own intellectual
path to Heaven.

Milton's emphasis, in *Paradise Lost* and elsewhere, on the Christian's ability to "stand" only superficially contradicts this ideal of intellectual busyness. God creates Adam "Sufficient to have stood,
though free to fall," and says "Freely [the angels] stood who stood"
(3.99, 102). "They also serve who only stand and wait," writes Milton
in his sonnet on his blindness.[51] While "stood" and "stand" invoke
passivity, to Milton, standing for God is in fact an activity, distinct
from the prone subservience granted Satan by the devils (2.40). In
Nicholas Jones's words, in *Paradise Lost* "images of posture continually figure forth . . . crucial moral decisions."[52] The standing posture
is, as Richard Strier implies, superior to flying around on "pointless
errands," as do the angels in *Paradise Lost*[53] (in Milton's sonnet,

these angels "at [God's] bidding speed / And post o'er land and ocean without rest"[54]—an activity that sounds less heavenly than punishing). When Milton's God asserts that the sinner shall one day "stand / On even ground against his mortal foe" he is describing a battlefield stance, an active posture of defense and even assault against an enemy (3.178–79). This idea of militant standing is borne out in *The Reason of Church Government,* wherein, as Carol Barton says, Milton "exhorts his readers"—as he himself did in his tireless fight for the cause of revolution—"to respond stoically to adversity"—to, in his words, "stande . . . firmly" with "stedfaste resolution to establish the truth, though it were through a lane of sects and heresies on each side."[55]

Described thus—to "stande . . . through"— standing is going. Its vigorous activity is emphasized in *Paradise Lost* through Milton's radical association of the intellectual and spiritual faculties of created beings with their physical natures: all need energy, or fuel, to do their work. Raphael tells Adam that "whatever was created, needs / To be sustained and fed; of elements / The grosser feeds the purer," and calls this process "transubstantiat[ion]" (5.414–16, 438). The "thirst after knowledge" to which Milton refers in *Areopagitica*[56] (the metaphor is repeated by lunching Adam [*PL* 8.8]) is thus a more literal appetite than that conventional phrase seems to imply. The body that eats converts food to the energy with which the mind thinks and craves intellectual sustenance. When that intellectual sustenance is absent, the dearth brings "a famine upon . . . minds." Conversely, in the "dyeting and repasting of . . . minds," "[b]ooks are as meats and viands are," and virtuous minds can "qualifie and prepare these working minerals" (*Areopagitica,* 559, 513, 512, 521). Both words and food are transmutable into higher thought. Miltonic transubstantiation departs from the clear distinction between flesh and spirit, sacred and profane, made in Donne's holy poems, though it is nothing like the bread becoming God in the Eucharist of Catholic faith (is indeed, among other things, a "satirical attack on the Roman-rite Mass," as John King argues).[57] As Bruce Boehrer writes, unlike the ritual of Eucharist, Miltonic transubstantiation is a means by which creatures may "engage in various sorts of dramatic personal transformation"[58]—that is, may adapt earthly material to the "alimental" purpose of raising themselves to celestial heights (3.424).[59]

This is the intellectual pilgrimage toward which Milton urges readers in *Areopagitica*. He exhorts them to undertake a lexical journey, to read widely among texts both good and ill, in order to exercise reason through choice of good *over* ill. (For this reason Brian Hampton speaks of Milton's "pilgrim reader's hermeneutical journey.")[60] This lexical work is a Christian task better suited to a fallen than to an unfallen world, as Milton himself suggests, when he says in *Areopagitica*, "perhaps this is that doom which Adam fell into of knowing good and evil, that is to say of knowing good by evil. . . . As therefore the state of man now is, what wisdom can there be to choose, what continence to forbear, without the knowledge of evil?"[61] This statement renders illogical Milton's later description, in this same text, of Adam's original fall as an instance of such "choosing" between good and evil, since in Heaven and the unfallen world evil was not a presence to be distinguished from good. Thus Strier is right to argue that Milton's requirement that humans and angels constantly manifest their goodness by choosing obedience makes no sense. Unfallen beings inhabit a world where disobedience is not, for them, knowable—"a realm of experience wider and perhaps richer than that of self-conscious and deliberate moral choice."[62] Postlapsarian Eden and seventeenth-century England are something else again. Those places are fallen battlefields of words, in which what is needed is deliberate moral choice—the choosing of the best words and thoughts, all of which regulate spiritual states and prompt just action.

Milton emphasizes the lexical character of the human pilgrimage, describing the Godward journey as an ingestion rather than a transmission of truth: a pilgrimage composed more of reading than of writing. This is paradoxical, for one would expect Milton, an author with a profound sense of spiritual mission, to show more interest in the act of writing as a means of approaching personal salvation. Yet when in *Paradise Lost* Milton prays for inward light by which to steer his thoughts and language, the end goal of that prayer is not his own salvation—which he seems to assume—but the salvific instruction of his readers. "[T]he mind through all her powers / Irradiate," he prays, "that I may see and tell / Of things invisible to mortal sight" (3.52–55). Milton saw his own writing as food to be ingested by less enlightened wayfarers; as an evangelical work for the salvation and continuing reform of the community—chiefly the English nation—rather than for his own spiritual rescue. (As J. Martin Evans writes in his discussion of Milton's Nativity ode, Milton is concerned with "the *reader's* conversion.")[63] Milton is one of those who is "chosen of peculiar grace," as God says in *Paradise Lost*—not, or not primarily, that they may be specially saved, but that their "published labors [may] advance the good of mankind" (*Areopagitica*).[64]

Thus in *Areopagitica* he addresses his exhortations regarding wide reading and disputing to "a Nation not slow and dull, but of a quick, ingenious, and piercing spirit, acute to invent, subtle and sinewy to discourse, not beneath the reach of any point the highest that human capacity can soar to."[65] He is a member of this nation, but one who, by special dispensation, speaks from the place of intellectual salvation to which other pilgrims must travel. In Steven Fallon's words, Milton is "the specially gifted spokesperson of God."[66] The opening of *Paradise Lost* frames Milton's plea to be directly instructed by the Holy Spirit, to be illuminated so as "to justify the ways of God to men"—that is, to make possible that journey of understanding among readers, like a new Moses,[67] or to illuminate their minds with perfect truth, like a second Christ (as Milton construes Christ). Milton's *Areopagitica* speaks, we recall, of a time when the pieces "yet wanting to the body of Truth," the torn and martyred saint, will be refitted together, and says that these pieces will not all be found until Truth's "Master's second coming."[68] In so doing, Milton echoed the thought of Tyndale, who wrote of scriptural translation, "In tyme to come (yf God have apoynted as there unto) we will geve [the Bible] his full shape: and putt out yf ought be added superfluuity: and adde to yff ought be oversene thorowe negligence."[69] Yet in suggesting, in 1642, that additions might still be made to the truth revealed in the established, Englished Bible, Milton asserted an instructional prerogative far beyond the one Tyndale had claimed over a century before. Twenty years after he wrote of Truth's "Master's second coming" in *Areopagitica*, Milton's own suppliance to the Bible of Truth's missing pieces implied his radical presumption of a likeness between himself and God's son, perfect transmitter of the Word. In the introduction to *Paradise Lost*, Milton asserts a Christlike poetic function of facilitating the lexical pilgrim's way.

What are some of the characteristics of a God-justifying poetic geography—one through which "the true wayfaring Christian," the godly reader, may fruitfully travel?

One quality to which Milton accords a kind of sacredness is a matter of technical style. In an early sonnet, "How Soon Hath Time,"

Milton prophesies that the great work for which his "great Taskmaster" has fitted him will be "in strictest measure even."[70] That strict evenness of poetic measure is a dominant quality of *Paradise Lost*'s poetry, which André Verbart calls "distinctive by its extremely strict adherence to the norm of ten syllables per line," adding, "the percentage of hypermetrical lines, lines with a feminine ending, is much lower than in [Milton's] other blank verse."[71] Milton avoids "wandering feet" in his iambics. His rare hypermetricality occurs at moments when divine order is disrupted (as Verbart also notes),[72] and when irregular rhythms occur. We hear such metrical disruptions when Eve has persuaded Adam to taste the apple: "she embraced him, and for joy / Tenderly wept, much won that he his love / Had so ennobled, as of choice to incur / Divine displeasure for her sake" (9.990–93). The evenness of measure with which these moments of moral rupture so forcefully contrasts incarnates the universal order which Milton attributes to God's physical creation and plan for humankind, an order which I earlier discussed. In perfectly ordering his narrative, Milton regulates his transmission of truth, safeguarding the reader against a chaos of poetic sensation, "[w]ithout dimension, where length, breadth, and highth / And time and place are lost" (2.893–94). For Milton, justifying God's ways is literally ordering divine pathways, which in *Paradise Lost* are lines of verse.

Also integral to the divinely inspired poet's task is the transformation—or transubstantiation—of pagan myth to Christian story. Milton, of course, performs this priestly work everywhere in both his verse and his prose. An example most relevant to our discussion is his comparison in *Areopagitica* of the Egyptian god Osiris to the Truth that came into the world with Christ: "as that story goes of the Egyptian Typhon with his conspirators, how they dealt with the good Osiris, [deceivers] took the virgin Truth, hewed her lovely form into a thousand pieces, and scattered them to the four winds."[73] Examples of the Christianization of Egyptian and classical myth in *Paradise Lost* are nearly countless, and these examples have been much noted;[74] Milton associates the fallen spirits not only with idols spoken of in the Old Testament but with Roman gods like Mulciber, calls on Urania to be his Muse in book 7, and implicitly compares Athena's birth to that of Sin, who springs "a goddess armed / Out of [Satan's] head" (2.777–78). In the adaption of classical myth to Christian history, what is most revelatory of Milton's sense of himself as poetic justifier is his self-conscious and explicit correction of the earlier myths, as he places them in their proper historiographical context. Of one of Satan's chief lieutenants, he writes,

> Men called him Mulciber; and how he fell
> From heav'n, they fabled, thrown by angry Jove
> Sheer o'er the crystal battlements: from morn
> to noon he fell . . .
>
> . . . .
>
> On Lemnos th' Aégean isle: thus they relate,
> Erring; for he with this rebellious rout
> Fell long before. . . .

(1.740–47)

When he calls on the muse Urania he similarly corrects readers' understanding of her provenance.

> Descend from heav'n Urania, by that name
> If rightly thou art called . . .
>
> . . . .
>
> The meaning, not the name I call: for thou
> Nor of the muses nine, nor on the top
> Of old Olympus dwell'st, but heav'nly born. . . .

(7.1–7)[75]

Such instructive passages allow Milton to maintain the myths of his beloved classical world even as he redirects them to the service of Christian readers' understanding and to the improvement of those readers' classical understanding. This treatment of pagan myth in explicit relation to Christianity is a hallmark of the mature Milton. In his Nativity ode, composed in 1629, Christ's birth silences the pagan gods.[76] In *Paradise Lost*, Milton restores to his readers the gods' corrected voices.

Nor does Milton confine himself to the rewriting of *pagan* myth in *Paradise Lost*. I have discussed Milton's alteration of Genesis to comport with his sense that Christ's mission was and is to be the perfect enactment of God's Word, so that Christ, rather than God, visits the fallen humans in Eden to confront them with God's knowledge of their trespass. Throughout the epic, Milton continues his Old Testament corrections and enhancements,[77] recounting in detail a war in Heaven, distinguishing between the motives of Eve's and of Adam's disobedience, and inventing a detailed relation between Satan and the snake which he justifies (or tries to justify) in book 10 (ll. 165–68). In book 12, Milton provides (to adapt Tyndale's earlier phrase) the "full shape" of the New Testament as well, seamlessly grafting onto Michael's account of Christ's human life and the acts of the apostles the history of the decline of the church up to the modern moment: "[The apostles] die; but in their room, as they forewarn, / Wolves shall succeed for teachers, grievous wolves, / Who all the sacred mysteries of heav'n / To their own vile advantages shall turn / Of lucre and ambition" (12:508–11). This "scripture," which echoes Milton's harsh condemnations of seventeenth-century English prelates in other poems and prose,[78] re-presents the church-outed Milton as inspired speaker of God's Word, who offers the sustenance of latter-day truth to the hungry, wayfaring reader.

What are the necessary lexical actions of this pilgrim reader, charged to participate in the transubstantial lexical process? First, this reader must not emotionally be carried away by Milton's poetic justification of Heaven's behavior. Instead, he must assimilate Milton's just lessons by vigorous intellectual labor.[79] Such a reader will not succumb, as do Eve in book 9 and some devils in book 2, to "words clothed in reason's garb" (2.226), which counsel illogical transgression or "peaceful sloth" (2.227). God infuses his creations with reason—he "clear[s] their senses dark" (*PL* 3.188)—but it is up to those creations themselves to see that "light after light"— truthful lesson after truthful lesson—is "well used." "[T]o the end persisting," they will "safe arrive" at their salvation (3.196–97). Truth as light is a metaphor Milton has also used in *Areopagitica*, where a nation that has seen reason is like an eagle "kindling her undazzled eyes at the full midday beam; purging and unscaling her long abused sight at the fountain . . . of heavenly radiance."[80] The word "undazzled" is significant, for in *Areopagitica* as in *Paradise Lost* the right reaction of reasoning humans to truth's light is participatory intellectual understanding rather than stunned amazement.[81] It is the lesser birds of inferior understanding who "flutter about," "amazed" at what the strong eagle "means"[82]—that is, not understanding what she means. In *Paradise Lost*, struck with Eve's dangerous beauty, the amazed Satan is momentarily "stupidly good" (9.465). That is not very good, and the events that soon follow prove it is not. Stupid amazement is distinct from the "new-waked" "wonder" that humans' proper intellectual model, the unfallen Adam, expresses at Raphael's lesson on the working of the cosmos (8.4, 11). Through Raphael's discourse Adam "read[s God's] wondrous works, and learn[s]" them (8.58–59). Adam, of course, ingests knowledge through listening rather than actual reading, which suggests the interest of Milton—who, blind at the time of *Paradise Lost*'s composition, would himself have "read" by listening—in homiletic as well as lexical lessons, and thus in a word-sorting pilgrimage done through hearing as well as through reading. Bryan Hampton has astutely argued Milton's own writings' influence by Protestant homiletic tradition.[83] Yet reading, for Milton, was the safest means of ingesting knowledge, as the word confined to print protected pilgrims from the danger of mind-stopping auditory dazzlement posed by what Bryan Crockett calls the dramatically voiced "verbal pyrotechnics" and "dizzying biblical paradoxes" invoked by preachers like Thomas Playfere and even John Donne. Such pastors, Crockett notes, carried their audiences to emotional heights and moved them to tears.[84] For Milton, salvation is not achieved through such sudden emotional ravishment by beautiful-sounding words. A churchgoer must be ever-vigilant against the temptation to "believe things only because his pastor says so."[85] Thus the reasoning Christian must resist such oratorical blandishments as rich vocality and riddles, and thus Raphael answers Adam's questions in voice "mild" (5.371), though Satan speaks to Eve "all impassioned,"and so "amaze[s]" her (9.678, 552).[86] And thus, rather than dizzying Donnean paradoxes of salvation, Milton offers straightforward narrative enriched by grand epic similes; and by writing instead of preaching ensures that the pilgrim reader may make his passage without distraction in the quiet conducive to the operations of thought. Not, to be sure, that reason must proceed without vocal discussion and argument. Raphael and Adam speak, and we recall that in *Areopagitica* Milton urges "discoursing" as a means to truth's rediscovery. But self-engagement in such conversation is distinct from rapt submission to the "glozing" voice of another—like Eve's submission to the voice of Satan (3.93, 9.733ff.).

Thus, reading and pondering, and conversing and pondering, "not surpassing human measure" of understanding (7.640), the intellectual pilgrim can gradually be "raise[d] . . . to what highth [God] will[s]" (8.430), "disciplined," platonically, to move "[f]rom shadowy types to truth" (12.302–3). Though fallen, man will see his reasoning ability restored through the exemplary action of Christ, who will not only die for mankind's sins but incarnate perfect reason in the world. As M. H. Abrams notes, Christ as embodiment of right reason is suggested by the Jesus of *Paradise Regained*, who is impelled less by the promptings of love than by "hard intellectual struggle through which [he] comes to understand himself and his mission and defeats Satan by renouncing the whole panoply of false or faulty versions of the good life and of his kingdom."[87] Such is the task of the pilgrim readers who follow him.

Not (yet?) being Christ, of course, these fallen pilgrims must seek the wisdom of more elevated guides, among which the Bible figures importantly but, as discussed, does not stand alone. Throughout *Paradise Lost*, as through *Areopagitica*, Milton stresses the importance of pilgrims' quest for instruction. We recall that Satan's damnableness is manifest in his decision to journey "without guide" through the cosmos (2.975), and that Eve's sin is directly related to her choice to forsake Adam's guiding companionship the morning Satan tempts her. Eve's argument for so doing—"[W]hat is faith, love, virtue unassayed / Alone, without exterior help sustained?" (9.335–36)—brings to mind Milton's defense of free choice in *Areopagitica*, where he rejects a "cloistered virtue, unexercised and unbreathed, that never sallies out and sees her adversary."[88] But the arguments' resemblance is superficial. *Areopagitica*'s whole proposal is in fact that the pilgrim actively seek the intellectual guidance available in texts. Readers are never counseled to expose themselves solely to bad argument, as does Eve. Instead they are instructed to weigh good arguments against bad ones, "to cull out, and sort [good and evil arguments] asunder,"[89] which Eve, by depriving herself of the presence of Adam—her good argument—weakens her power to do. Paradoxically, the fallen pilgrim reader must prove wiser than "yet sinless" Eve (9.559). He must school his own reason by ingesting invalid argument only along with its valid counterpart and retaining the worthier thought. "[A] wise man like a good refiner can gather gold out of the drossiest volume"[90]—but only if the gold is there. The properly motivated Christian reader goes in quest of the gold which is wisdom, and this wisdom enables him to discard the folly, or dross.

Milton's insistence on the pilgrim reader's self-sought guidance, and his ostentatious presentation of himself as his own readers' guide in *Paradise Lost*, brings us to the last crucial feature of pilgrim readership. Many Protestant authors present spiritual pilgrimage as a private journey, in which the sinner travels alone toward God. For example, George Herbert's "The Pilgrimage" describes a near-empty landscape through which the traveler walks away from the sole other person in the poem, a voice that warns him *against* the journey.[91] Milton, in contrast, urges communal salvation. To "wand[er], each his several way," "as inclination or sad choice" leads, is what the fallen spirits do in Hell (2.523–25). Heaven is characterized by "concord" (l. 371). "[D]isputing, reasoning, reading, inventing, discoursing" are, we recall, the proper activities of *Areopagitica*'s wayfaring Christians in the city besieged by error; among these five actions, two at best are private. As Thomas Festa writes, for Milton spiritual education is a "collective endeavor," involving "the intersection of several minds."[92] Milton's poem "At a Solemn Music" looks forward to a time when, in response to some celestial question, God's creatures "may rightly answer" "with undiscording voice."[93] Thus in *Areopagitica* Milton stresses the value of "convincement" in the building of "a knowing people."[94]

That the first of these people will be English does not go without saying, and so Milton says it frequently, if not in *Paradise Lost*, then decisively in *Areopagitica*. Miltonic pilgrimage is finally less concerned with moving the Christian out of this world than with reforming the world in which English Christians live in, and letting the example of these most Reformed serve all of Christendom. The reasoning eagle, undazzled by the sun of reason, that Milton sees "shaking her invincible locks" is England, a "nation chosen before any other, that out of her as out of Sion should be proclaimed and sounded forth the first tidings and trumpet of Reformation to all Europe."[95] Through the labor of Milton and others of the intellectual elect, "God shakes a kingdom with strong and healthful commotions to general reforming."[96]

What, then, is the final destination of the English lexical pilgrimage? For Milton, the goal of note is not the celestial Jerusalem from which Spenser's knight, drawn by the glories of Elizabeth's city, turns, for this life, away. Nor is it that close and more private "heavenly room" into which the dying Donne steps. Instead it is the refined and restored cosmos predicted in Revelation, "new heav'ns, new earth" (*PL* 12.549). For Adam and Eve, the earth is newly broken, and its renewal is historically distant. It may not be so for contemporary Europeans, Milton's *Areopagitica* suggests. "We reckon more than five months yet to harvest," Milton writes. "[T]here need not be five weeks; had we but eyes to lift up, the fields are white already."[97] In this great prose tract Milton's excited urgings of industrious lexical work suggest his hope that moral enlightenment, presently known by a few, may be rapidly disseminated through the West following the abolishment of restrictions on allowed discourse. In my last chapter, I observed that for both Donne and Spenser, Heaven was not far away. Milton's redeemed Europe is not the Heaven of either earlier poet, just as his reasoning pilgrimage is not the total submission to Bible-nurtured faith prescribed by *The Faerie Queene*'s Fidelia and by Donne's sacred verse. Yet no less for the hopeful Milton, the destination of wayfarers—once all are granted free intellectual travel—is close at hand.

7

Coda:
The Pilgrim's Progress in
English Renaissance Literature

[T]hey will take my meaning in these lines
Far better than his lies in silver shrines.
—John Bunyan, *The Pilgrim's Progress*[1]

IF ANYTHING COLLECTIVE CAN BE SAID ABOUT THE PILGRIMAGES PRO-
posed in the work of Renaissance English authors, it is that these
adventures' radical variance shows the liberty Reformed authors enjoyed with respect to the holy journey's depictions. The dismantling
of the shrines and official condemnation of pilgrimages under
Henry VIII freed poets, playwrights, and other authors to imagine
geographical pilgrimages that were no longer holy at all, and to
stress—or, like Shakespeare in his Henry plays, to hint playfully—
that they weren't. In early-modern English literature as in early-modern English life, pilgrimages were military campaigns, erotic quests,
commercial expeditions, ventures of geographical exploration, or
plain vagabondage. Of course, Shakespeare's, Hakluyt's, Jonson's,
and others' descriptions of them as such were partly rooted in earlier English representations of "religious" pilgrimages as carnal
pleasure trips. After all, the Reformation by which England transformed its relation to traditional Christian practices was long, or, to
use Milton's phrase, "slow-moving."[2]

Paradoxically, the very gradualness of England's changing religious practices—as distinct from the rapidity of shrine dismantling
when, in the 1530s, the law banning them was instituted—ensured
some continuity in the way pilgrimages were regarded. I mean not
just that representations of pilgrimage on stage and page retained
an old association between "holy" journeys and carnal delight, but
also that the word "pilgrimage" could not wholly be severed from

the idea of an approach to sanctity, in the minds of the more religious Protestant writers. What occurred, then, was those authors' literary transformations of pilgrimage in ways that expressed their views on how sanctity was to be gained. Book 1 of Spenser's *The Faerie Queene* shows its author divided between a reverent, iconophilic approach to an earthly Jerusalem— London, the seat of the Protestant monarch's power—and an inward spiritual pilgrimage whereby faith, administered through scripture, calls home the wandering Christian knight. Shakespeare, less explicitly religious in his concerns than Spenser, shows the humorous folly and, in *Othello*'s tragic register, the spiritual dangers of a pilgrimage honoring an earthly lover who is not and cannot be divine. Donne consecrates descriptions of traditional Catholic pilgrimage to erotic verse that celebrates the transubstantial union of lovers, while in his sacred verse he presents the pilgrim's earthly wanderings as fruitless revolt from the God who draws him home. Less Calvinist, finally, than Donne, Milton derides in *Paradise Lost* the secular, pride-and-custom-inspired journeyings which early-modern travel worshippers like Richard Hakluyt had associated with the progress of Christian evangelism. For Milton, true religious progress is distinct from a voyage of geographical discovery, but also from the submission to God's backward recall that Calvinist poets like Donne and Herbert so powerfully dramatized in their devotional verse. As *Paradise Lost* and Milton's prose tract *Areopagitica*—as well as the record of Milton's sustained service to the "Good Old" revolutionary cause—make clear, Milton saw proper Christian pilgrimage as an arduous civic effort to uncover and proclaim spiritual truth, by the exercise of reason. In his epoch this meant, most importantly, a shared pilgrimage of deliberative reading, which was to ensue in virtuous work in the world.

That work was necessarily evangelical. Milton would have himself and other English thinkers enlighten and extend the rest of Christendom. In this respect Milton shares (though he broadens) the biblical apostolic imperative crucial to notions of Protestant pilgrimage since Wycliffe. While the Heaven- (or Purgatory-) bound Catholic pilgrim approached God through the virtuous work of hard travel to saints' shrines and the earth's holy places, the Protestant pilgrim, redeemed at the outset by Christ's rescue of him or her, journeyed forth to convert other sinners. The New England Pilgrims, Separatists who accompanied William Bradford to North America, traveled to escape English restrictions on their worship—or perhaps, as a Dutch-American colleague of mine would have it, to escape Dutch religious freedom. In either case, they left already saved, by their lights, and God came with them on their ships. They did not see America as a holy land which might further sanctify them on their arrival. Rather, the holiness of their Christ-renewed hearts would sanctify America, and would serve as an evangelical beacon to its "succeeding plantations," to recall John Winthrop's words on the deck of the westbound ship Arbella. These pilgrims themselves were and would be the new Jerusalem, a "city upon a hill" providing light for the spiritual betterment of others.

The Pilgrims were radical—or "advanced"—Protestants, and yet their view that their pilgrimage ensued from and did not create their proximity to God displayed a basic Protestant idea, seen expressed in the works of more moderately Reformed thinkers than John Winthrop. Protestant Christians' view of themselves as already saved transformed their pilgrimages to, in part, a journey to redeem the rest of the world. We recall the travel author Hakluyt's exhortation to English youth not to improve their own spiritual condition by New World travel but to improve that of the pagans they colonized, whom they might "reduce . . . to the faith of Christ." Walter Ralegh, we also recall, mingled descriptions of Indian gold with professions of concern for Indian souls in his account of his voyage to Guiana. The work of Spenser, Ralegh's and Hakluyt's contemporary, expresses in darker allegorical terms the Protestant enthusiasm for harvesting both foreign souls and foreign kingdoms. Spenser's Redcrosse spends all of *The Faerie Queene*'s first book avoiding and then, at the end, embracing redemption himself, and so has little time for evangelical pilgrimage. Yet the final charge given him to conquer, for Elizabeth, pagan lands (including, by implication, unwilling Catholic nations like Ireland) demonstrates that Spenser, like Hakluyt and Ralegh, applied the Protestant evangelical imperative to secular nationalism. Sacred and profane ambitions are confused in *The Faerie Queene*, but the confusion was common to English Protestant writers.

Common, but not universal. Donne derides global expeditions, evangelical or otherwise. He weaves his apostolic net solely from devotional writings, sermons, and sacred poems which urge salvation as antipilgrimage: in other words, as Calvinist submission to the backward-drawing love of the rescuing Christ. Milton, as noted, shows disdain in both his epic and his prose for the mixture of religion and commercial voyaging urged (if not by the Pilgrims) by

Hakluyt and Ralegh. As *Areopagitica* makes clear, Milton's Protestant evangelism was largely a matter of the lending and borrowing of books, whose communal reading was to inspire brotherly debates about the value of what was written therein. Lexical and dialogic pilgrimage was to be practiced on a wide range of ancient, later, and contemporary writings, including but not limited to the Bible. The ensuing English consensus or "harmony" of thought[3] was to spread evangelically to less enlightened people, so that all would be raised into a final and complete reformation of belief, church and civic governance, and human manners (thus Milton looks for "the glory of reforming all our neighbours").[4] The English intellectual pilgrim, having achieved, in concert with other English folk, the salvation of his or her reason, is to help shine the collective light outward, assisting the rest of the world on a journey which is also, presumably, lexical, spiritual, and intellectual. The end result, Milton hopes, will not be arrival at an otherworldly Heaven, but a cultural renewal emanating from transubstantiated minds, a restored human world refitted to hang from Heaven by a "golden chain" (*Paradise Lost* 2.1051).

All these Spenserian, Shakespearean, Donnean, and Miltonic themes are reprised, faintly, loudly, or with significant alteration, in *The Pilgrim's Progress* (1678). John Bunyan's narrative of Christian's salvation is a Restoration work which, in its intense concern with sinners' relation to Christ, and with the power of ingested text to improve that relation, seems more properly (like Milton's *Paradise Lost*) to belong to the Renaissance. Yet it is in some ways a work that could not have been written without the influence of its literary predecessors, for in it we see the studied reflections of prior treatments of Protestant pilgrimage.

The book that most deeply informs *The Pilgrim's Progess* is the Bible. But apart from his clear and heavily annotated scriptural references, Bunyan's most obvious literary borrowings are from Spenser, from whom he took not only the allegorical form of a Christian's journey, through personified spiritual dangers, toward a heavenly city, but also the very language with which Spenser described *The Faerie Queene*'s structure in the letter to Ralegh he appended to his work. Like Spenser, who called his epic an "allegory, or dark conceit,"[5] Bunyan defends in his prologue his use of "Dark Figures, Allegories."[6] More Puritan than Spenser, Bunyan looks exclusively to the Bible, not to "excellent poets" like Homer and Virgil,[7] to defend his method, asking, "[W]as not Gods Laws / His

Gospel-laws in olden time held forth / By Types, Shadows, and Meta-phors?"[8] The influence of a century of growing Puritan skepticism regarding the value of pagan myth—a skepticism which Milton nota-bly defied—can be seen in Bunyan's insistence that his book "contains / Nothing but sound and honest Gospel-strains."[9] Yet some of his metaphors, or "types" and "shadows," though they (like Spenser's) draw heavily on scripture for their significations, are modeled as well on Spenserian tropes. Like the Redcrosse Knight, Bunyan's Christian finds himself in the province of Despair, meets Ignorance, is imprisoned by a giant (though Spenser's giant is Pride while Bunyan's personifies Despair), and is inspired by the vision of a heavenly city. Like Spenser's, Bunyan's spiritual landscape dis-places the spatial realm; truth, inwardly discerned, replaces the con-crete shrines of saints to which traditional pilgrims traveled. "[T]hey will take my meaning in these lines / Far better than [Sa-tan's] lies in silver shrines," Bunyan writes in his preface, associating his detractors with idolatrous Catholic worshippers.

Yet significantly absent from Bunyan's account of pilgrimage is the reverence toward earthly monarchy rendered by both *The Faerie Queene* and, more ambiguously, by Shakespeare's dramatic represen-tations of imperial pilgrimage. In *The Pilgrim's Progress* the name of the road leading to the Celestial City, the "King's Highway," invokes none of the secondary awe for Charles II that references to the Fa-erie Queene in Cleopolis, the earthly Jerusalem, did for Elizabeth. Christian is not armored, like the knight, nor does he fight En-gland's enemies at the behest of his earthly ruler. In Bunyan's post-war, post-Interregnum, post-Milton work the allegory of Christian salvation is fully divorced from that of the subject's duty to the mon-arch, or indeed to all earthly magistrates, who here are impediments to spiritual progress. The governors of earthly society in Bunyan's tale are the shortsighted officials of Vanity Fair, like Lord Hategood, the judge who tries Christian and orders the death of Faithful. Their ultimate allegiance is to a "Prince" who is Satan.[10]

What moral earthly powers replace the discredited magistrates and princes? In place of Gloriana, Bunyan offers the companionship and exhortation of fellow Christians. In the dungeon of Despair, Christian's companion Hopeful "did moderate the mind of his brother."[11] On the King's Highway, Christian shares Bible lessons with Mr. By-ends and Mr. Hold-the-World, and urges them toward faith and reliance on scripture. Here Bunyan is in one way distant from Milton, who puts forward his account of Genesis as a "justification" of God's story implicitly superior to the one scripture offers. Bunyan has Christian diminish his own gospel glosses by referring Hold-the-World directly to the Bible, a superior text: he breaks off his tale of Dinah and Jacob with "Read the whole story, Gen. 34.20, 21, 22, 23." However, the emphasis here and throughout *The Pilgrim's Progress* on the evangelical necessity of minds' intersection, through fruitful dialogue, owes something to the stress Milton laid on intellectual community, as well as to an older *debat* tradition seen in English literature as early as the staged arguments among Heywood's "Four Ps." (In *The Pilgrim's Progress*, only Ignorance walks alone.) Christian's brotherly conversational interventions attack the spiritual deadness born of custom; we first saw this attack figured in the paralysis imposed by Spenser's monstrous, man-eating Error in her cave, and later found it expressed in Milton's ridicule of those of "implicit faith" (a faith unlived because not understood, though the words pertaining to it, derived from "some divine of note," are parroted by the thoughtless.)[12] Bunyan's representative of such fools is Talkative, who will "talk of things heavenly or things earthly; things moral, or things evangelical," though in his life is "neither prayer, nor sign of repentance for sin."[13] Christian's and Faithful's mockery of Talkative's religious hypocrisy has roots in the early dissension of Luther from the Catholic Church, which is evident in Luther's scorn for Erasmus, who was not Reformer enough for him. "See how he [Erasmus] blabbers about the psalm, 'Blessed is the man who fears the Lord,' etc. [PS. 112:1] . . . . He mentions Christ . . . but he doesn't care," for "The godless papists only imitate our words."[14] By the 1640s Milton had shown that "there be . . . Protestants . . . who live and die in as arrant an implicit faith as any lay papist of Loretto."[15] By the late seventeenth century, godly Protestants no longer saw papists as the wolf at their Church's door. (In *The Pilgrim's Progress*, the pope is not the fire-breathing dragon of Spenser's *Faerie Queene*, but a crazy old man who sits "grinning at pilgrims as they go by, and biting his nails, because he cannot come at them.")[16] The threats to a godly church were now complacent English Christians themselves.

Yet such is the Protestant evangelical imperative that these false Christians are not fled from, but preached to. Just as in *Areopagitica* Milton urged the prodding of sluggard intellects into real thought and belief, in *The Pigrim's Progress* Bunyan's true pilgrims challenge

Talkative, trying to save him, and end content, despite their lack of apparent success, with the faith that he "will think of [their discourse] again."[17] Bunyan claims disingenuously in his preface that he wrote *Pilgrim's Progress* his "own self to gratify," but his entire apology, which justifies and explains the work in light of scripture, and the large portions of the tale devoted to similar soteriological explanation, argue otherwise. No less than Milton's reasoned elect, Bunyan's pilgrims and Bunyan himself seek communal salvation, partners in pilgrimage.

Yet that pilgrimage, less than for Milton's lexical travelers, is—in a traditionally Protestant way—already achieved by the true travelers very early in their expedition. That is to say that for Bunyan's Christian, redemption is not a result of but a prior condition of the celestial walk, which is now a journey of proselytizing as much as it is one of spiritual growth. In this, again, Bunyan narrativizes the doctrine of salvation through faith that distinguished Luther and Calvin from Catholic thinkers. Christian and the other truly saved pilgrims, Faithful and Hopeful, enter early through the "wicket gate" that symbolizes Christ, and are distinguished from the false pilgrims who, like the thieves and robbers Christ condemns (John 10:7–9), "came not in by the door."[18] Since they have already arrived at salvation, their journey has two narrative purposes: to demonstrate, like the first cantos of *The Faerie Queene*, the many traps of error into which sinners may regressively or damnably slide, and to body forth the Protestant evangelical imperative.

All Protestant pilgrims begin the true celestial journey "already there," redeemed a priori by God. Thus Redcrosse's travels constitute an antipilgrimage before he is spiritually salvaged, late in his story, in the House of Holiness and set on the largely secular and fully nationalist evangelical path of quelling England's enemies (beginning with the Catholic dragon). Shakespeare's Henry V's imperial pilgrimage *begins* with his own conversion from worldly prince to Christian king. Milton sensed that his own spiritual election, or restored intellect, was what qualified his setting forth the geographical territory to be traversed by reader-pilgrims. For Donne, an antipilgrim, dread of his "black soul's" earthly wanderings (Holy Sonnet 4) marks his own resistance to damnable complacency, and shows the humility Calvin thought a sign of salvation, as we have seen.

Thus Christian, though such an "arrived" pilgrim, still walks, both helping others find the way and finding aids to his humility (and Bunyan means to stress humility's value) in the many spiritual trials of his journey. His task is to preserve his own awareness of his salvation, yet to do so humbly. The good works he performs are the fruit of that salvation rather than the means to obtain it, as he makes clear in his evangelical discourse with Talkative, wherein he stresses "the insufficiency of our works."[19] Though the impediments to travel which Christian encounters present evangelical opportunities, in the main they are byways *from* the highway rather than stages of it; Christian struggles to resume "the way" by escaping them.[20] Obstacles include the giant Despair's dungeon, the deep pit of vain confidence, and the carnal delights of Vanity Fair (against which the "English Nation, with some [Protestant] others," who lack merchandise booths, are specially armed).[21] From all of these traps Christian is rescued by grace—his friend Faithful is martyred in Vanity Fair, but "he that over-rules all things . . . wrought it about, that Christian for that time escaped them, and went his way"[22]—and responds with appropriate disclaimers of his part in his own redemption. "([T]hrough the goodness of him that is best) I am as you see alive: yet I cannot boast of my manhood," Christian says after his escape from robbers on the King's Highway. He and other Christians who have entered by the true gate find "their King . . . at their whistle, he is never out of hearing; and if at any time they be put to the worst, he . . . comes in to help them." Christian, Faithful, and Hopeful do not journey toward the divine, but with the divine. As promised in Psalm 23, Christ accompanies Christian through the Valley of the Shadow of Death, and makes one of the pilgrims' "convoy." "[Y]ea," observes Christian, "he will go with us himself."[23]

If God is with and has already redeemed Christian, toward what does he journey?

The answer, finally, is death. The martyred Faithful is blessed in finding early access to the city, for life, *The Pilgrim's Progress* suggests, offers no incremental approach to Heaven, but only distractions from it: barriers that must be circumvented. Bunyan's work does not show its pilgrims moving steadily toward Paradise, like the penitents in Dante's *Purgatorio*, or like palmers who in their earthly journeys approach saints, holy places, Purgatory, and Heaven. Instead, they fall off the road and are graciously returned to it by God, who has already rescued them. Death, in the form of access to the Celestial City, provides the visible proof of their accomplished salvation. The city is the culmination of and final deliverance from the Christian antipilgrimage, from the series of earthly traps that distract sinners from its straight approach. It is Spenser's "new Hierusalem" and Donne's small, music-filled heavenly room.

All Protestant literary visions of celestial arrival are visions of return. The Redcrosse Knight longs for Cleopolis, the place where his journey began. Donne wishes to "end / where [he has] begun," not, finally, in the arms of a waiting wife or mistress, but in the "holy room" of Heaven from which he was sent forth. The Reformation rhetoric of Luther, Calvin, Foxe, and others stressed its authors' search for the gospel-based principles of what Foxe called the "primitive" church[24]—even Milton spoke against "new forms of government for our Church"[25]—and for the scriptures' original language. The search for biblical return was manifested in the mastery of Hebrew and Greek and the labors of translation performed by Wycliffe and Tyndale, and, much later, by Milton; as well as in Spenser's, Shakespeare's, Donne's, and Milton's reliance on Tyndale's text, which was absorbed by the Geneva, and, later, by the King James Bible.[26] The work of Christian reform was an attempt to recover moral truth, a desire expressed by Milton's urging of the search for Truth's "mangled body" and by his later attempt to recollect mankind's original history, at the moment of creation.

In a homelier vein, Bunyan's Christian's entry into the Celestial City represents Christian's homecoming, a final triumph over the wanderings that separated him from a place whose vision he remembers throughout his travels. Part 2 of *The Pilgrim's Progress* restores him to his original home by reuniting him with his family. For George Herbert, the "heart in pilgrimage" is "Prayer . . ., / God's breath in man returning to his birth."[27] Even the pilgrimage plays of Shakespeare, a less explicitly religious Protestant than Spenser, Donne, Milton, or Bunyan, show this yearning for return. *Henry V*'s tired soldiers exult in the prospect of their voyage back to England, "where ne'er from France, / Arrived more happy men" (4.9.126). Lovers' travels circle back to their places of origin—to Rousillon or *Cymbeline*'s Romanized English court—or are tragically interrupted, as in *Othello*, by murderous jealousy, so the homeward journey belongs to others who will tell their tale. Russell Fraser has said that the *Quem quaeritis* trope's reunion between Mary Magdalen and the resurrected Christ prefigured the great homecoming embraces to come on Shakespeare's stage.[28] I would add that Shakespeare's travel-ending reunions—such as that between Posthumus and Imogen—recall us, and recalled their audiences, to the even greater scenes of biblical recognition and reunion that originate in scripture. In all, the goal of journeying is shown to be the return to, and true recognition of, the wayfarer's starting point.

Thus the "pilgrimage" works of Spenser, Shakespeare, Donne, Milton, and Bunyan express an impulse pervasive in English Protestant literary versions of the holy journey: the wanderer's paradoxical, Odyssean longing not to travel, but to go home.

Notes

CHAPTER 1. THE PROTESTANT PILGRIMAGE

1. Article 22, *Articles of Religion of the English Church*, in *Creeds of the Churches: A Reader in Christian Doctrine from the Bible to the Present*, 3rd ed., ed. John Leith (Atlanta: John Knox, 1982), 274.

2. John Heywood, *The Play Called the Four PP*, in *Medieval and Tudor Drama*, ed. John Gassner (New York: Bantam Books, 1963).

3. In 1522, just prior to the English Reformation, Robert Langton of Salisbury published a book about his numerous pilgrimages in Europe in which he dwelt on descriptions of saints' shrines. For descriptions of English pilgrimages to both Canterbury and Compostela during the late Middle Ages, see G. Scott Thomson, *Medieval Pilgrimages* (London: Longman, 1962), and Robert Plötz, "La proyección del culto jacobeo en Europa," *Las Peregrinaciones a Santiago de Compostela y San Salvador de Oviedo en la Edad Media. Actas del Congreso Internacional celebrado en Oviedo del 3 al 7 de diciembre de 1990*, coord. Juan Ignacio Ruiz de la Peña (Oviedo: Servicio Publicaciones, 1993), 57–72.

4. See A. Jessopp, *Visitations of the Diocese of Norwich*, cited in A. G. Dickens, *The English Reformation* (New York: Schocken Books, 1964), 5.

5. Jean Froissart, *Chronicles*, 1395, translated into English by Lord Berners 1523, excerpted in D. W. Robertson, Jr., *The Literature of Medieval England* (New York: McGraw-Hill, 1970), 340.

6. Dante Alighieri, *The Purgatorio*, trans. John Ciardi (New York: Signet, 1961).

7. Geoffrey Chaucer, *The Canterbury Tales*, in *Chaucer's Poetry*, 2nd ed., ed. E. T. Donaldson (Glenview, IL: Scott, Foresman, 1975), Prologue, ll. 1, 13, 16. Snatches of the Walsingham ballad appear in Francis Beaumont's *The Knight of the Burning Pestle* 2.503–6, in *Drama of the English Renaissance*, ed. Russell A. Fraser and Norman Rabkin, 2 vols. (New York: Macmillan, 1976), 2:517–48.

8. For one excellent discussion of Catholic interpretations of life as a spiritual pilgrimage, see Samuel C. Chew's *The Pilgrimage of Life* (New Haven, CT: Yale University Press, 1962).

9. William Langland, *Piers Plowman: The B Version*, ed. George Kane and E. Talbot Donaldson (London: Athlone Press, 1975).

10. *The Book of Margery Kempe*, ed. Sanford Brown Meech, Early English Text Society (EETS), no. 212 (New York: Oxford University Press, 1961), 69.

11. Norman Cantor, *In the Wake of the Plague: The Black Death and the World It Made* (New York: Free Press, 2001), 85.

12. Erasmus, *Ten Colloquies*, trans. Craig R. Thompson (New York: Liberal Arts Press, 1957), 81.

13. Ibid., 81–82, 86.

14. Carol Piper Heming, *Protestants and the Cult of the Saints in German-Speaking Europe, 1517–1531* (Kirksville, MO: Truman State University Press, 2003), 471.

15. Eamon Duffy, *The Stripping of the Altars: Traditional Religion in England 1400–1580* (New Haven, CT: Yale University Press, 1992), 155–205.

16. Dickens, *English Reformation*, 5.

17. Stanford E. Lehmberg, *The Reformation of Cathedrals in English Society, 1485–1603* (Princeton, NJ: Princeton University Press, 1988), 53.

18. *A Description or Breife Declaration of all the Ancient Monuments, Rites, and Customes belonginge or beinge within the Monastical Church of Durham before the Suppression*, quoted in ibid., 51.

19. Lehmberg, *Reformation of Cathedrals*, 53.

20. Jacques de Vitry, quoted in Jonathan Sumption, *Pilgrimage: An Image of Medieval Religion* (London: Faber and Faber, 1975), 257.

21. Sumption, *Pilgrimage*, 257.

22. *A Description or Breife Declaration of all the Ancient Monuments . . . within the Monastical Church of Durham*, quoted in Lehmberg, *Reformation of Cathedrals*, 50–51.

23. Lehmberg, *Reformation of Cathedrals*, 43. See also R. A. L. Smith, *Canterbury Cathedral Priory* (Cambridge: Cambridge University Press, 1943), 52.

24. Martin Bucer, quoted in Heming, *Protestants and the Cult of the Saints*, 45.

25. Martin Luther, quoted in Heming, *Protestants and the Cult of the Saints*, 45.

26. Martin Luther, *Table Talk*, in *Luther's Works*, 55 vols., ed. and trans. Theodore G. Tappert (Philadelphia: Fortress Press, 1967), 54:422.

27. Johannes Lonicer, quoted in Heming, *Protestants and the Cult of the Saints*, 45.

28. William Lambard, *The Duties of Constables, Borsholders, Tithing-men, and Such Other Lowe Ministers of the Peace* (London, 1584), 13.

29. Heather Dubrow, "'In thievish ways': Tropes and Robbers in Shakespeare's Sonnets and Early Modern England," *Journal of English and Germanic Philology* 96, no. 4 (October 1997): 514–44, 519. For extensive discussions of the issue of vagrancy in late-sixteenth-century England, see A. L. Beier's "Vagrants and the Social Order in Elizabethan England," *Past and Present* 64 (1974): 3–29 and *Masterless Men: The Vagrancy Problem in England 1560–1640* (New York: Methuen, 1985). For a consideration of the way vagrancy laws in Catholic nations differed from those in Protestant nations during this period, see Brian Pullan's "Catholics, Protestants, and the Poor in Early Modern Europe," *Journal of Interdisciplinary History* 35:3 (Winter 2005): 441–56.

30. W. H. Frere and W. M. Kennedy, eds., *Visitation Articles and Injunctions*, 3 vols., Alcuin Club, nos. 14–16 (London, 1910), 2:5.

31. Ibid., 2:38–39.

32. Wilkins, *Concilia*, quoted in Lehmberg, *Protestants and the Cult of the Saints*, 70.

33. *Proclamations*, 1:275–76, quoted in Lehmberg, *Protestants and the Cult of the Saints*, 70.

34. Lehmberg, *Protestants and the Cult of the Saints*, 106.

35. Ibid., 128.

36. Ibid., 141–42.

37. Duffy, *Stripping of the Altars*, 192.

38. Ibid., 248; see also David Daniell, *The Bible in English* (New Haven, CT: Yale University Press, 2003), 227.

39. Duffy, *Stripping of the Altars*, 191.

40. Ibid., 195.

41. Ibid.

42. Ibid.

43. From *The Third Eclog* in *Idea. The Shepheards Garland* (1593), excerpted in *Spenser: The Critical Heritage*, ed. R. M. Cummings (New York: Barnes and Noble, 1971), 78.

44. Sumption, *Pilgrimage*, 257.

45. In addition to Dubrow and Beier, see Gámini Salgádo's fascinating *The Elizabethan Underworld* (Gloucestershire, UK: Sutton Publishing, 1997), especially chapter 6, "Low-Life on the Highway."

46. More, *Utopia*, trans. Paul Turner (New York: Penguin Books, 1965), book 1, 47; Shakespeare, *Richard II*, 2.1.40–66. All references to Shakespeare's plays are to *The Riverside Shakespeare*, ed. G. Blakemore Evans (Boston: Houghton Mifflin), 1974.

47. See Salgádo, *Elizabethan Underworld*, Glossary, 207–18.

48. John Bunyan, *The Pilgrim's Progress* (Oxford: Clarendon Press, 1960), 91.

49. For an excellent discussion of the roving press and general tactics of Martin Marprelate, see chapter 5, "Martin Marprelate: Syllogistic Laughter," in Ritchie D. Kendall's *The Drama of Dissent: The Radical Poetics of Nonconformity, 1380–1590* (Chapel Hill: University of North Carolina Press, 1986).

50. Stephen Greenblatt, "Invisible Bullets: Renaissance Authority and Its Subversion," in *Political Shakespeare*, ed. Jonathan Dollimore and Alan Sinfield (Manchester: Manchester University Press, 1985), 18–47.

51. Jean Beaulieu, Secretary to the English Ambassador, quoted in David Riggs, *Ben Jonson* (Cambridge, MA: Harvard University Press, 1989), 190.

52. Peter Greenfield discussed this phenomenon in "The Rise of the Patrons' Companies," paper presented at Shakespeare Association of America annual conference, New Orleans, Louisiana, 2004.

53. See Andrew Gurr's discussion of the effect on players of the 1572 "Acte for the punishment of Vacabondes," in *The Shakespearean Stage 1574–1642* (Cambridge: Cambridge University Press, 1992), 28.

54. See Glynne Wickham, Herbert Berry, and William Ingram, *English Professional Theatre, 1530–1660*, Theatre in Europe: A Documentary History (Cambridge, Cambridge University Press, 2000), 62–64.

55. Jean Howard, "Shakespeare, Geography, and the Work of Genre on the Early Modern Stage," *Modern Language Quarterly* 64, No. 3 (September 2003): 310–11.

56. See Duffy, *Stripping of the Altars*, 193. While Solanio dreams of transglobal commercial pilgrimage, at least one medieval character in Shakespeare's history plays links domestic English pilgrimage with commerce at home. In *1 Henry IV* Falstaff observes to Prince Hal that "there are pilgrims going to Canterbury with rich offerings, and traders riding to London with fat purses" (1.2.125–27). Falstaff's conflation of traders with pilgrims illustrates his own materialistic outlook, of course, but it also suggests early-modern audiences' easy familiarity with the framing of medieval pilgrimage as a kind of commercial adventuring.

57. Richard Hakluyt, *Voyages and Discoveries*, 1589, ed. Jack Beeching (New York: Penguin Books, 1972), 33. See also Michael Drayton's "Ode. To the Virginian Voyage," which praises Hakluyt for "inflam[ing]" Britons' "brave heroic minds" (in

ed. M. H. Abrams, *The Norton Anthology of English Literature*, 7th ed., 2 vols., [New York: W. W. Norton, 2000] 1:968–69).

58. Stephen Greenblatt, *Renaissance Self-Fashioning: From More to Shakespeare* (Chicago: University of Chicago Press, 1980), 194.

59. Hakluyt, *Voyages and Discoveries*, 38, 37.

60. *The Geneva Bible: A Facsimile of the 1560 Edition* (Madison: University of Wisconsin Press, 1969). All biblical references are to the Geneva unless otherwise indicated.

61. Daniel Price, *Sauls Prohibition Staide* (London, 1609), quoted in Stanley Johnson, "John Donne and the Virginia Company," *ELH* 14, no. 2 (June 1947): 128. See also David Daniell's discussion of biblically based religious colonization in *Bible in English*, 417–21.

62. Walter Ralegh, *The Discovery of the Large, Rich, and Bewtiful Empire of Guiana*, 1596, ed. Neil L. Whitehead (Norman: University of Oklahoma Press, 1997), 194–96.

63. Ibid., 194. See Mary C. Fuller's discussion of this passage in her "Ralegh's Fugitive Gold: Reference and Deferral in *The Discovery of Guiana*," in *New World Encounters*, ed. Stephen Greenblatt (Berkeley and Los Angeles: University of California Press, 1993), 232.

64. Henry Parker, *Of a Free Trade* (London, 1648), quoted in Steven Pincus, "John Milton and Commercial Society: The Making of a Republican Conservative," *American Historical Review* 103, no. 3 (June, 1998): 713.

65. Hakluyt, *Voyages and Discoveries*, 37. As David Armitage writes, for Hakluyt, "trade, religion and conquest" were "essential parts of the same enterprise." See *The Ideological Origins of the British Empire* (Cambridge: Cambridge University Press, 2000), 75. See also Blair Worden, *Sound of Virtue: Philip Sidney's* Arcadia *and Elizabethan Politics* (New Haven, CT: Yale University Press, 1996) for a discussion of Protestant imperialism.

66. Eduardo Galeano, *Memoria del Fuego*, 3 vols. (Buenos Aires: Catálogos S. R. L., 2004), 1:68, 98–99.

67. For one discussion of such refurbishments, see pp. 157–59 of Marilyn Stokstad's *Santiago de Compostela in the Age of the Great Pilgrimages* (Norman: University of Oklahoma Press, 1978).

68. John Calvin, *Institutes of the Christian Religion*, ed. John T. McNeill, trans. Ford Lewis Battles, 2 vols. (Philadelphia: Westminster, 1960), 1:693; see also 1:799.

69. Nabil Matar, "Introduction: England and Mediterranean Captivity, 1577–1704," in *Piracy, Slavery, and Redemption: Barbary Captivity Narratives from Early Modern England*, ed. Daniel J. Vitkus (New York: Columbia University Press, 2001), 38.

70. Ibid., 2.

71. Ibid., 36.

72. Joshua Gee, *The Narrative of Joshua Gee of Boston, Mass., while he was captive in Algeria of the Barbary States, 1680–1687*; quoted in ibid., 37.

73. Kendall, *Drama of Dissent*, 25.

74. *The Lanterne of Liyt*, ed. Lillian M. Swinburn, EETS, B.S. 151 (London: Kegan Paul, Trench, Trubner, 1917), 86.

75. John Winthrop, *A Model of Christian Charity*, in *The American Puritans: Their Prose and Poetry*, ed. Perry Miller (New York: Columbia University Press, 1956), 83.

76. Ralegh, *Discovery*, 194.

77. David Daniell, "Shakespeare and the Protestant Mind," *Shakespeare Survey* 54 (2001): 4.

78. John Foxe, *Foxe's Book of Martyrs* (*The Acts and Monuments*, 1563), ed. Marie Gentert King (Old Tappan, NJ: Fleming H. Revell, 1975), 73–74. Foxe's story might instance a common sixteenth-century jest about Romish money hoarding. Shakespeare's King John instructs his cousin, the Bastard, to "shake the bags of hoarding abbots" in English monasteries, and "imprisoned angels"—that is, coins—"set at liberty" (*King John* 3.2.16–18). Both the Foxe and Shakespeare passages would seem to bear out Maryclaire Moroney's claim that in sixteenth-century England, "crucifixes, statues, and beads now assume their true position as objects which have solely material status and value" ("Spenser's Dissolution: Monasticism and Ruins in *The Faerie Queene* and *The View of the Present State of Ireland*," *Spenser Studies* 12 [1991]: 112).

79. Ibid., 886.

80. Fuller, *Ralegh's Fugitive Gold,"* 232.

81. Louis Montrose, "The Work of Gender in the Discourse of Discovery," in *New World Encounters*, ed. Stephen Greenblatt (Berkeley and Los Angeles: University of California Press, 1993), 179.

82. Montrose's "The Work of Gender" includes, for example, an engraving by Jan van der Straet which pictures Amerigo Vespucci's discovery of America as an encounter between a clothed European and a startled, naked female who lounges in a hammock (178).

83. John Donne, "Elegy 19: To His Mistress, Going to Bed," l. 27, "The Canonization," and "The Relic," in *John Donne: The Complete English Poems*, ed. A. J. Smith (New York: Penguin Books, 1987), 125, 47, 75. All references to Donne's poems are to this edition.

84. Robert Herrick, "His Prayer to Ben Jonson," in *Cavalier Poets: Selected Poems*, ed. Thomas Clayton (New York: Oxford University Press, 1978), 127.

85. Andrew Marvell, "Upon Appleton House," in *Andrew Marvell: The Complete Poems*, ed. Elizabeth Story Donno (New York: Penguin Books, 1983), 75.

86. Daniell, "Shakespeare and the Protestant Mind," 4.

87. John Calvin, *Institutes*, 2:880.

88. Miles Coverdale, *Remains*, ed. George Pearson (Cambridge: Cambridge University Press, 1946), 475.

89. William Tyndale, *The Obedience of a Christian Man* (1528), ed. David Daniell (New York: Penguin Books, 2000), 134.

90. William Tyndale, "A Prologue into the Fourth Book of Moses Called Numbers," in *Tyndale's Old Testament*, ed. David Daniell (New Haven, CT: Yale University Press, 1992), 197.

91. Philip Sidney, *Astrophil and Stella*, Number 5, in *The Poems of Philip Sidney*, ed. William Ringler (Oxford: Clarendon Press, 1962), 167.

92. In his Plymouth journal, William Bradford retrospectively complains of the immoral influence Sabbath-scanting Dutch youth exerted on the youth of the English congregation. See Bradford's *Of Plymouth Plantation: 1620–1647*, ed. Francis Murphy (New York: Random House, 1981), 25.

93. From *The Holy Bible* (King James version), 1611 (New York: New American Library, 1974).

94. Daniell, *Bible in English*, 417. See also note 51.

95. Winthrop, *A Model of Christian Charity*, 83.

96. Quoted in Stephanie Hayes-Healey, "Patterns of *Peregrinatio* in the Early Middle Ages," in *Medieval Paradigms: Essays in Honor of Jeremy du Quesnay Adams*, ed. Stephanie Hayes-Healey, 2 vols. (New York: Palgrave Macmillan, 2005), vol. 2, chapter 1.

97. The word would be used in the Vulgate. See *Biblia Sacra: ixta vulgatum versionem*, ed. Robert Weber et al., 3rd ed. (Stuttgart: Deutsche Bibelgesellschaft, 1983).

98. Hayes-Healey "Patterns of *Peregrinatio*," vol. 2, chapter 1.

99. "I am pleased that you make nothing of purgatory. . . . For certainly no one is required to believe that there is a purgatory, because God has said nothing about it" (Martin Luther, "Word and Sacrament," in *Luther's Works*, ed. Tappert, vol. 36, 299). "For what means this purgatory of [Catholics] but that satisfaction for sins is paid by the souls of the dead after their death? Hence, when the notion of satisfaction is destroyed, purgatory itself is straightway torn up the very roots" (John Calvin, *Institutes*, 2:676).

100. *Lanterne of Liyt*, 86.

101. Daniell, *Bible in English*, 113.

102. Thomas Kempis, *Imitation of Christ*, 1328, trans. Aloysius Croft and Harold Bolton (Nashville, TN: Thomas Nelson, 1999), 138.

103. See, for example, Clifford Davidson and Ann Eljenholm Nichols, eds., *Iconoclasm v. Art and Drama*, Early Drama, Art, and Music Monograph Series 11 (Kalamazoo, MI: Medieval Institute Publications, 1989).

104. Daniell, *Bible in English*, 126.

105. Stephen Greenblatt, *Hamlet in Purgatory* (Princeton, NJ: Princeton University Press, 2001), 258.

106. Judith Dundas has written of such narrativizing in Spenser, though her argument about its use is somewhat different than mine. See her "Spenser and the Emblem Books" in *Emblematica* 11 (2001): 293–324.

107. Francesco Petrarca, *For Love of Laura: Poetry of Petrarch*, trans. Marion Shore (Fayetteville: University of Arkansas Press, 1987).

108. In *Measure for Measure* Angelo remarks that Claudio's confession of sexual immorality is "the utmost of his pilgrimage" (2.1.36), but Claudio's sexual "pilgrimage" culminating in marriage to Juliet is finally excused, if not fully celebrated, in the play's comic denouement.

109. Smith, *John Donne: The Complete English Poems*, 47 and 48.

110. Calvin, *Institutes*, 2:973.

111. Ibid., 310.

112. As Su Fang Ng writes, English Protestant reformers, "such as the martyrologist John Foxe in his *Acts and Monuments*, memorialized . . . early translators of the English Bible—John Wyclif and William Tyndale—as Protestant saints to construct a tradition that competes with and is counterposed to Roman Catholic hagiography." See Ng's "Translation, Interpretation, and Heresy: The Wycliffite Bible, Tyndale's Bible, and Contested Origin," in *Studies in Philology* 98, no. 3 (Summer 2001): 315.

113. Bryan Adams Hampton, "'Such Harmony Alone': Performing the Incarnation in Milton's 'Nativity Ode' and 'Lycidas'," in "Repairing the Ruins: Milton,

Proclamation, and Incarnational Poetics" (Ph.D. diss, Northwestern University, 2004).

114. These and all other references to *Paradise Lost* are to John Milton, *Paradise Lost*, ed. Scott Elledge (New York: W. W. Norton, 1975).

115. Milton, *Paradise Lost*, 56.

116. Stanley Fish, *Self-Consuming Artifacts: The Experience of Seventeenth-Century Literature* (Pittsburgh, PA: Duquesne University Press, 1994), 229.

117. Ibid., 24.

118. William Tyndale, *An Answer unto Sir Thomas Mores Dialoge*, ed. Anne M. O'Donnell, S.N.D., and Jared Wicks, S.J., The Independent Works of William Tyndale, 3 vols. (Washington, DC: Catholic University of America Press, 2000), 3:62.

119. Martin Luther, *Works*, ed. Jaroslav Pelikan and Helmut Lehmann, 55 vols. (Philadelphia: Muhlenberg), 23:263.

120. Martin Luther, *Discourse on Free Will*, trans. and ed. Ernst F. Winter (New York: Frederick Unger, 1961), 135–36.

121. John Donne (after Mark 6:44), Holy Sonnet 1, in *Complete English Poems*, 309.

122. George Herbert, "The Pulley," in *The English Poems of George Herbert*, ed. C. A. Patrides (Totowa, NJ: Rowman and Littlefield, 1974), 166–67.

123. T. S. Eliot, "Little Gidding," stanza 5, in *The Four Quartets* (New York: Harcourt, Brace, 1943), 39.

CHAPTER 2. PROTESTANT PILGRIMAGE AND SECULAR STATE

1. Edmund Spenser, *The Vewe of the Present State of Ireland*, in Edmund Spenser, *Works: A Variorum Edition*, ed. Rudolf Gottfried, 10 vols. (Baltimore: Johns Hopkins University Press, 1932–49), 9:223.

2. All references to *The Faerie Queene* come from Edmund Spenser, *The Faerie Queene*, ed. A. C. Hamilton (New York: Longman, 1977).

3. In John King's words, "Like other reformers, Spenser expands upon the late medieval critique of formalistic religion that identified the 'holy' with material places and objects: shrines, relics, and images of saints and the Virgin Mary." King, *Spenser's Poetry and the Reformation Tradition* (Princeton, NJ: Princeton University Press, 1990), 48.

4. Judith Anderson's recent *Translating Investments* discusses an early-seventeenth-century Catholic rewriting of book 1 of *The Faerie Queene* which thematized the conflict between the Christian's obligations to his faith and to his state, an even more vexed question for English Catholics than it was for Spenser. See *Translating Investments: Metaphor and the Dynamic of Cultural Change in Tudor-Stuart England* (New York: Fordham University Press, 2005).

5. The dragon represents Pope Gregory XIII specifically, according to Elizabeth See Watson ("Spenser's Flying Dragon and Pope Gregory," *Spenser Studies* 14 [2000]: 293–301).

6. Gerard de Malynes, *Saint George for England, Allegorically Described* (1601), excerpted in *Spenser: The Critical Heritage*, ed. R. M. Cummings (New York: Barnes and Noble, 1971), 115. See also p. 101 of Samantha Riches's *Saint George: Hero, Saint, and Martyr* (Gloucestershire, UK: Sutton Publishing, 2000).

7. Torquato Tasso, *Jerusalem Delivered*, trans. Edward Fairfax (1600), ed. Roberto Weiss (Carbondale: University of Southern Illinois Press, 1962).

8. Christopher Hodgkins, *Reforming Empire: Protestant Colonialism and Conscience in British Literature* (Columbia: University of Missouri Press, 2002), 77.

9. See Spenser's letter appended to the 1590 edition of *The Faerie Queene*, Longman's edition of his epic, 737; and Fitzgeoffrey's *Sir Francis Drake* and Stradling's "To Edmund Spenser, the British Homer," respectively excerpted and quoted in Cummings, *Spenser*, 89, 123.

10. Dundas, "Spenser and the Emblem Books," 293–324.

11. Moroney, "Spenser's Dissolution," 107–8.

12. John King, *Spenser's Poetry*, 48.

13. Ibid., 67.

14. Moroney, "Spencer's Dissolution," 108.

15. Citing Ernest Gilman, King refers to Spenser's "Protestant shift away from external images of late medieval popular devotion and toward the internalized imagery of metaphor and poetic language" (*Spenser's Poetry*, 67). An earlier—and classic—discussion of Spenser's participation in a general Reformed literary movement away from the veneration of image to the veneration of word is C. S. Lewis's *The Discarded Image: An Introduction to Medieval and Renaissance Literature* (Cambridge: Cambridge University Press, 1964).

16. Ernest B. Gilman, *Iconoclasm and Poetry in the English Reformation: Down Went Dagon* (Chicago: University of Chicago Press, 1986), 65. Gilman cites the *OED*.

17. Ibid, 66.

18. Spenser's letter appended to *The Faerie Queene*, 738.

19. Gilman, *Iconoclasm and Poetry*, 65.

20. Calvin, *Institutes*, 2:970.

21. Spenser's letter appended to *The Faerie Queene*, 738.

22. Calvin, *Institutes*, 1:309.

23. Luther, *Discourse on Free Will*, 136.

24. Jeffrey Fruen, "The Fairy Queen Unveiled? Five Glimpses of Gloriana," *Spenser Studies* 11 (1990): 64.

25. The line is Thomas Kyd's from his *The Spanish Tragedy*, in *The First Part of Hieronimo and The Spanish Tragedy*, ed. Andrew S. Cairncross (Lincoln, NE: Regents Renaissance Drama Series, 1967), 57–176.

26. Kempe, *Book of Margery Kempe*, 68.

27. Martin Luther, *Word and Sacrament*, in *Luther's Works*, 36:169. See also Luther's *Table Talk*, in *Luther's Works*, 54:97.

28. Homer, *Chapman's Homer: The Odyssey*, trans. George Chapman, (1611), ed. Allardyce Nicoll (New York: Pantheon Books, 2000). Spenser would have read this passage in the Greek.

29. Martin Luther, *Civil Righteousness Versus Monastic Piety*, in *Table Talk, Luther's Works*, 54:304. John King concludes that Spenser champions "the active life of lay piety" which "excludes the cloister as a positive ideal" (*Spenser's Poetry*, 58).

30. Philip Sidney, *Astrophil and Stella*, Number 5, 167.

31. See book 2, chapter 2 of Calvin's *Institutes*, entitled "Man Has Now Been Deprived of Freedom of Choice and Bound Over to Miserable Servitude" (1:255).

32. Calvin, *Institutes*, 1:69.

33. *Book of Homilies*, 1.2, in *Certaine Sermons or Homilies Appoynted to be Read in Churches*, 1633, quoted in King, *Spenser's Poetry*, 64.

34. Calvin, *Institutes*, 1:593.

35. Su Fang Ng, "Translation, Interpretation, and Heresy," 331. See also Richard Mallette's discussion of Spenser's stress on mental engagement with the word, in "The Protestant Art of Preaching in Book One of *The Faerie Queene*," *Spenser Studies* 7 (1986): 3–26.

36. William Tyndale, *Prologue to the Prophet Jonas*, quoted in Ng, "Translation, Interpretation, and Heresy," 329.

37. King, *Spenser's Poetry*, 63.

38. William Perkins, *The Workes* (London, 1626–31), quoted in Mallette, "Protestant Art," 5.

39. King, *Spenser's Poetry*, 88.

40. Bryan Crockett, *The Play of Paradox: Stage and Sermon in Renaissance England* (Philadelphia: University of Pennsylvania Press, 1995), 50.

41. Grace Tiffany, "*Hamlet* and Protestant Aural Theater," *Christianity and Literature* 52, no. 3 (Spring 2003): 307–23.

42. John Calvin, *Commentaries*, ed. David W. and Thomas F. Torrance, 23 vols. (Grand Rapids, MI: Calvin Translation Society, 1948–59), 9:15:9.

43. The imaginative blending of Catholicism and Islam was furthered by Shakespeare, whose characters associate both religions with sorcery. King John calls the pope a "meddling priest" who works by "juggling witchcraft" (*King John* 3.1.163, 169), while Brabantio charges Othello—an ethnic Muslim, though a Christian convert—with having bound Desdemona in "chains of magic" (*Othello* 1.2.65).

44. Matar discussed these diplomatic efforts in his talk at the December 2003 Renaissance symposium at Chicago's Newberry Library, *Crossing the Channel*. See also David Armitage, *Ideological Origins of the British Empire*.

45. Calvin, *Institutes*, 2:1486, 1488, 1487.

46. Patrick Cheney, *Marlowe's Counterfeit Profession: Ovid, Spenser, Counter-Nationhood* (Toronto: University of Toronto Press, 1997), 14.

47. Spenser's letter appended to *The Faerie Queene*, 738.

48. See note 5.

49. Greenblatt, *Renaissance Self-Fashioning*, 184.

50. Gregory specifically, according to Watson, "Spenser's Flying Dragon."

51. In *Seeing through Words: The Scope of Late Renaissance Poetry* (New Haven, CT: Yale University Press, 1986), Elizabeth Cook provides a careful discussion of the way Renaissance authors understood the mental processes of enlightenment through reading. See especially her second chapter, "Figured Poetry."

52. Fruen, "Fairy Queen," 79.

53. This portrait is reproduced in François Laroque's *The Age of Shakespeare* (New York: Harry N. Abrams, 1993), 94.

54. Spenser's letter appended to *The Faerie Queene*, 737.

55. Suzanne L. Wofford, "*The Faerie Queene*, Books I–III," in *Cambridge Companion to Spenser*, edited by Andrew Hadfield (New York: Cambridge University Press, 2001), 107.

56. The phrase is Angus Fletcher's ("Complexity and the Spenserian Myth of Mutability," *Literary Imagination* 6, no. 1 [Winter 2004]: 6).

57. Wofford, "*The Fairie Queene*, Books III," 109.

58. Charles Fitzgeoffrey, "To Edmund Spenser," in Cummings, *Spenser,* 110.

CHAPTER 3. IMPERIAL PILGRIMAGE ON SHAKESPEARE'S STAGE

1. John Phillips, *The Reformation of Images: Destruction of Art in England, 1535–1660* (Berkeley and Los Angeles: University of California Press, 1973), 70.

2. From a letter to the doge, quoted in Francis Woodman, *The Architectural History of Canterbury Cathedral* (London: Routledge and Kegan Paul, 1981), 221–22.

3. Erasmus, *Ten Colloquies,* 81–82, 86.

4. See the introduction to the Miller's Tale, ll. 12, 13, and 16, in *The Canterbury Tales,* ed. E. T. Donaldson, 105. See also Donaldson, note 16, on page 105.

5. See, for examples, the introduction to the Clerk's Tale, l. 10; and the epilogue to the Pardoner's Tale, l. 630.

6. "Game," *The Oxford English Dictionary* (Oxford: Clarendon Press, 1988).

7. Anne F. Harris, "Pilgrimage, Performance, and Stained Glass at Canterbury Cathedral," in *Art and Architecture of Late Medieval Pilgrimage,* ed. Sara Blick and Rita Tekippe, 2 vols. (Leiden: E. J. Brill Press, 2004), 243–81.

8. See note 18, chapter 1, above.

9. Charles Wall, *Shrines of British Saints* (London: Methuen, 1905), 159.

10. Lehmberg, *Reformation of Cathedrals,* 51.

11. Clifford Davidson, "Violence and the Saint Play," *Studies in Philology* 98, no. 3 (Summer 2001): 292–314. For a catalogue of holy images of which some became stage properties, see also Davidson's and Jennifer Alexander's *The Early Art of Coventry, Stratford-upon-Avon, Warwick, and Lesser Sites in Warwickshire: A Subject List of Extant and Lost Art Including Items Relevant to Early Drama,* Early Drama, Art, and Music Reference Series 4 (Kalamazoo, MI: Medieval Institute Publications, 1985).

12. Leanne Groeneveld shared the history of this amazing Cross in "The Boxley Rood of Grace: Mechanical Marvel or Miraculous Object?" a paper presented at the 39th Medieval Congress, Kalamazoo, Michigan, May 2004. For another recent discussion of the fusion of religious worship and miracle play attendance in late-medieval England, see Theresa Coletti, *Mary Magdalene and the Drama of Saints: Theater, Gender, and Religion in Late Medieval England* (Philadelphia: University of Pennsylvania Press, 2004).

13. Paul White cites Stokes, *Records* 2:642, in his "Holy Robin Hood! Carnival, Parish Guilds, and the Outlaw Tradition," in *Tudor Drama Before Shakespeare, 1485–1590,* ed. Lloyd Edward Kermode, Jason Scott-Warren, and Martine Van Elk (New York: Palgrave-Macmillan, 2004).

14. See Lehmberg, *Reformation of Cathedrals,* 53.

15. Stanley, *Historical Memorials of Canterbury* (London: John Murray, 1851), 136.

16. These badges and their sale were discussed by Sarah Blick in her presentation, "Thomas Becket in the Chapel of Our Lady of Undercroft, Canterbury Cathedral," at the 40th International Congress on Medieval Studies, Kalamazoo, Michigan, May 2005.

17. Froissart, *Chronicles,* 340.

18. This episode is neatly summarized in Stephen Greenblatt's and George Lo-

gan's introduction, "The Sixteenth Century: 1485–1603," 479–98, in *The Norton Anthology of English Literature*, ed. M. H. Abrams, 7th ed., 2 vols., New York: W. W. Norton, 2000, 1:483.

19. Marc Bloch, *The Royal Touch: Sacred Monarchy and Scrofula in England and France* (London: Routledge and Kegan Paul, 1973), 22.

20. Blick, "Thomas Becket in the Chapel of Our Lady of Undercroft, Canterbury Cathedral."

21. See the Chandos Herald's *Life of the Black Prince* (1397), ed. Mildred K. Pope and Eleanor C. Lodge (Oxford: Clarendon Press, 1910).

22. Stanley, *Historical Memorials*, 137.

23. Duffy, *Stripping of the Altars*, 195.

24. Ibid.

25. Stanley, *Historical Memorials*, 133.

26. James Shapiro, *A Year in the Life of William Shakespeare: 1599* (New York: HarperCollins, 2005), 152.

27. Bloch, *Royal Touch*, 191.

28. Ibid., 65.

29. See Maurice Hunt, "The Hybrid Reformations of Shakespeare's Second Henriad," in *Reformations: Religion, Rulership, and the Sixteenth-Century English Stage*, ed. Grace Tiffany (Kalamazoo, MI: Medieval Institute Publications, 1998), 176–206; Kristen Poole, "Saints Alive! Falstaff, Martin Marprelate, and the Staging of Puritanism," in *Shakespeare Quarterly* 46, no. 1 (Spring 1995): 47–75; and Grace Tiffany, "Puritanism in Comic History: Exposing Royalty in the Henry Plays," *Shakespeare Studies* 26 (1998): 256–87.

30. Catherine Sanok, "Gendering the Past: Anglo-Saxon Saints in Early Modern England," paper presented at the Thirty-Ninth International Congress on Medieval Studies, Kalamazoo, Michigan, May 2004. It should be said that Sanok's larger thesis develops an argument quite different to mine in this book, as she is concerned to demonstrate how actual seventeenth-century books of saints' lives tried to incorporate saints' worship and Catholic history into an early-modern discourse of English nationalism, "against the dominant historiographic conceit of Protestant discourse," which emphasized rupture with the Catholic Church and its saints.

31. In a recent discussion of English Reformation transformations of the idea of sacral kingship, Richard McCoy argues that even the sanctity of the Catholic Eucharist was not so much debunked as reassigned to the English monarch. "Under the Tudors," he writes, "the royal presence acquired some of the awesome sanctity of Christ's real presence in the Eucharist." See Richard C. McCoy, *Alterations of State: Sacred Kingship in the English Reformation* (New York: Columbia University Press, 2002), x.

32. Coverdale, *Remains*, 475.

33. I am indebted to Maurice Hunt for pointing out that Henry is offering his bones as relics (see "Hybrid Reformations," 197).

34. Hunt, "Hybrid Reformations."

35. Graham Holderness, "*Henry IV, Parts 1 and 2*," in *Shakespeare: The Play of History*, ed. Graham Holderness, Nick Potter, and John Turner (Iowa City: University of Iowa Press, 1987), 52.

36. Again, see Hunt, "Hybrid Reformations," for a discussion of parallels between Henry's proposed St. Crispin's Day celebration and holy communion (195).

37. Rachel Koopmans discussed the importance of blood to the cult of St. Thomas in "The Monks of Christ Church and the Beginnings of Thomas Becket's Cult," a paper delivered at the 40th International Congress on Medieval Studies, Kalamazoo, Michigan, May 2005.

38. Shapiro, *A Year in the Life of William Shakespeare*, 164.

39. Kempe, *Book of Margery Kempe*, 69.

40. Richard will trivialize this metaphor in 2.1 when he facetiously calls his finished visit to the deathbed of Gaunt, whom he has treated rudely, a "pilgrimage" [l. 154]).

41. William Tyndale, *Expositions and Notes on Portions of the Holy Scriptures* (1573), ed. Henry Walter, 2 vols., Parker Society 43 (Cambridge: Cambridge University Press, 1848), 1:296.

42. Hakluyt, *Voyages and Discoveries*, 38, 37. Indeed, in the inclusion in Henry's French campaign of London underworld denizens Pistol, Nym, and Bardolph, whose motive for travel abroad is clearly mercenary, we see Shakespeare's Protestant conflation of economic "pilgrimage," military conquest, and wandering roguery. The link between English early-modern war aims and vagabondage in *Henry V* is explored in Linda Bradley Salamon's "Vagabond Veterans: The Roguish Company of Martin Guerre and *Henry V*," in *Rogues and Early Modern Literature*, ed. Craig Dionne and Steve Mentz (Ann Arbor: University of Michigan Press, 2003), 261–93.

43. Anti-Catholic gibes (like anti-Puritan gibes) are numerous in Shakespeare alone, but perhaps the age's most obvious anti-Catholic lampoon is Christopher Marlowe's gluttonous papal assembly in *Doctor Faustus* (1588).

44. See chapter 2, note 44, above.

45. Shapiro, "Revisiting *Tamburlaine*: *Henry V* as Shakespeare's Belated Armada Play," *Criticism* 31 (1989): 351.

46. Shapiro, *A Year in the Life of William Shakespeare*, Chapter 5 (86–103).

47. Indeed, as Tiffany Stern has noted, the 1600 quarto version of *Henry V* "lacks this Essex-promoting chorus. The text seems to have been almost immediately rewritten to take away the embarrassingly wrong prediction" of Essex's victory (Stern, *Making Shakespeare: From Stage to Page* [New York: Routledge, 2004], 51).

48. Numerous studies have been made of the Henry plays' exposure of the theatrical nature of sacred kingship. Some of these are James Calderwood's *Metadrama in Shakespeare's Henriad* (Berkeley and Los Angeles: University of California Press, 1979); Stephen Greenblatt's "Invisible Bullets"; Graham Holderness's *Shakespeare's History* (New York: St. Martin's Press, 1985), and Grace Tiffany's "Elizabethan Constructions of Kingship and the Stage," in *The Iconography of Power*, ed. György E. Szőny and Rowland Wymer (Szeged, Hungary: Institute of English and American Studies, 2000), 89–116.

49. Hughes and Larkin, *Proclamations*, quoted in Lehmberg, *Reformation of Cathedrals*, 70.

50. Franco Moretti, "'A Huge Eclipse': Tragic Form and the Deconsecration of Sovereignty," *Genre* (Spring and Summer 1982): 8.

51. I have argued as much in another discussion of the second Henriad. See Tiffany, "Puritanism in Comic History."

52. Riches, *Saint George,* 102.

53. John Milton, *Eikonoklastes,* in *John Milton: Complete Poems and Major Prose,* ed. Merritt Hughes, 4 vols. (New Haven, CT: Yale University Press, 1962), 3:342–43. I thank Elizabeth Bradburn for calling my attention to this passage.

CHAPTER 4. FOR FIDELIA, FIDELE

1. Miguel de Cervantes, *El Ingenioso Hidalgo Don Quijote de la Mancha,* ed. Luis Andrés Murillo, 2 vols. (Madrid: Clásicos Castalia, 1978), 2:474. This and all other translations from the Spanish are my own.

2. Colin Smith, "The Geography and History of Iberia in the *Liber Sancti Jacobi,*" in *The Pilgrimage to Compostela in the Middle Ages: A Book of Essays,* ed. Maryjane Dunne and Linda Kay Davidson (New York: Garland, 1996), 23.

3. Ibid., 24.

4. The prevalence of this stereotype during the Renaissance is documented not only in the many English plays that make Italy, Spain, or southern France the site of passionate amorous pursuit and encounter, but in sixteenth-century prose that emphasized the hotness of the Mediterranean temperament. See, for example, the anonymous *Comparison of the English and Spanish Nation,* trans. Robert Ashley, London, 1589, *A Short-Title Catalogue of Books Printed in England, Scotland, and Ireland, and of English Books Printed Abroad, 1475–1640,* 2nd ed., ed. A. W. Pollard (London, 1976–91), 81. This *Comparison* described the Spaniard as "insatiable above all other nations." Nor was it only other Europeans who thought Spaniards too hot-blooded. Maureen Flynn has recently shown that sixteenth-century Spanish moralists were themselves deeply concerned with the challenge of controlling anger in social situations. She cites Luis de Granada's counsel that a Christian should never succumb to the temptation to "call people 'dogs' or Moors" (*Libro de Oración* 29, quoted in Flynn, "Taming Anger's Daughters: New Treatment for Emotional Problems in Renaissance Spain," *Renaissance Quarterly* 51, no. 3 [Autumn 1998]: 872).

5. Luis Vázquez de Parga, José María Lacarra, and Juan Uría Ríu, *Las peregrinaciones a Santiago de Compostela, Tomo 1 y 2* (Navarra: Fondo de Publicaciones Gobierno de Navarra, 1997), 121 (my translation).

6. Cervantes, *Don Quijote,* 2:447.

7. Murillo, ed. and intro., *El Ingenioso Hidalgo Don Quijote de la Mancha,* by Miguel de Cervantes, 2 vols. (Madrid: Clásicos Castalia, 1978), 2:447n3.

8. See J. C. Maxwell, who confirms G. K. Hunter's view that Florence was "quite off any possible route between Rossillion [where Helena begins her journey] and Compostella, and Shakespeare's audience would know it" ("Helena's Pilgrimage," *Review of English Studies* 20 [1969]: 191).

9. *Mandeville's Travels* (1400), ed. M. C. Seymour (Oxford: Clarendon Press, 1967), 114–15. Interestingly, North European late-medieval illuminated manuscripts show such fantastic creatures wearing Compostela pilgrims' badges, as Jennifer Lee showed in her presentation, "Pilgrims' Badges as Portable Prototypes, or, Canterbury Gets Around," 40th International Congress on Medieval Studies, Kalamazoo, Michigan, May 2005.

10. Joan Myers, Marc Simmons, and Donna Pierce, *Santiago: Saint of Two Worlds* (Albuquerque: University of New Mexico Press, 1991), 6.

11. See, for example, Cynthia Lewis, "'Derived Honesty and Achieved Goodness': Doctrines of Grace in *All's Well that Ends Well,*" *Renaissance and Reformation* 14, no. 2 (Spring 1990): 147–70; Donna B. Hamilton, *Shakespeare and the Politics of Protestant England* (Lexington: University of Kentucky Press, 1992), and Maurice Hunt, "Words and Deeds in *All's Well that Ends Well,*" *Modern Language Quarterly* 48, no. 4 (December 1987): 320–38 and "Predestination and the Heresy of Merit in *Othello,*" *Comparative Drama* 30 (1996): 346–76; David J. Palmer, "Comedy and the Protestant Spirit in Shakespeare's *All's Well that Ends Well,*" *Bulletin of the John Rylands University Library* 71 (1989): 95–107; Robert N. Watson, "*Othello* as Protestant Propaganda," in *Religion and Culture in Renaissance England,* ed. Claire McEachern and Deborah Shuger (Cambridge: Cambridge University Press, 1997), 234–57; and Eric Griffin, "Un-Sainting James: Or, *Othello* and the 'Spanish Spirits' of Shakespeare's Globe," *Representations* 62 (Spring 1998): 81–86.

12. Griffin also speaks of the misguided "faith Desdemona places in her erring husband" as well as Othello's idealization of Desdemona, calling both mistakes "idolatry" and "'the cause' of the tragedy" ("Un-Sainting James," 83).

13. "If [Eden] may ... yeeld a *bad Wife,* what probability is there, that any *prohibited place* can yeeld a *good?* And if the first man did fall *there,* how can any hope to stand, upon this *un-holy ground?,*" preached the Anglican pastor John Wing in 1620] (*The Crowne Conjugall or, The Spouse Royall* [Middleburgh, 1620, 95–96). As Catherine Belsey writes, "[n]uclear domesticity as a sequel to the Fall and a prelude to violence is [also] not uncommon[ly represented]" in seventeenth-century engravings, including the carved headboards of beds, which often depicted the temptation of Adam by Eve (see Belsey's n22, p. 20, and her article in general, which is "The Serpent in the Garden: Shakespeare, Marriage, and Material Culture," *Seventeenth Century* 21, no. 1 [Spring 1996]: 1–20).

14. See the epigraph to this chapter.

15. Robert Greene, *The Spanish Masquerado* (London, 1589), D–D1.

16. An excellent account of the myth of Santiago can be found in Américo Castro's *The Spaniards: An Introduction to their History* (Berkeley and Los Angeles: University of California Press, 1971). See also Myers, Simmons, and Pierce, *Santiago,* and G. Scott Thomson, *Medieval Pilgrimages* (London: Longman, 1962).

17. See Thomson, *Medieval Pilgrimages,* 67; and Plötz, "La proyección," 57–72.

18. See Thomas Spaccarelli, ed., *Text and Concordance of "El libro de los huéspedes" (Escorial MS. h.I.13),* Madison, Hispanic Seminar of Medieval Studies, 1996; and also Spaccarelli's commentary on that book in his *A Medieval Pilgrim's Companion,* (North Carolina Studies in the Romance Languages and Literatures 261 [Chapel Hill: University of North Carolina Press, 1998]). Also see María Garcia Garcia on the extensive system of hospitals on the road to Santiago, and the relation of these to the tradition of sacred hospitality toward the Compostela pilgrims, in "La hospitalidad y el hospedaje: fundaciones hospitalarias en Asturias," in *Las Peregrinaciones a Santiago de Compostela y San Salvador de Oviedo en la Edad Media, Actas del Congreso internacional celebrado en Oviedo del 3 al 7 de diciembre de 1990* (Oviedo, Servicio Publicaciones, 1993), 211–46.

19. Colin Smith, "Geography and History of Iberia," 24.

20. Thomson, *Medieval Pilgrimages*, 75–76.

21. See Velma Bourgeois Richmond, *Shakespeare, Catholicism, and Romance* (New York: Cassell, 2000), and Peter Milward, *The Catholicism of Shakespeare's Plays* (Tokyo: Renaissance Institute, 1997).

22. David N. Beauregard, "'Inspiréd Merit': Shakespeare's Theology of Grace in *All's Well that Ends Well*," *Renascence* 51, no. 4 (Summer 1999): 221.

23. Ibid., 222–23.

24. See William Elton, *King Lear and the Gods* (San Marino, CA: Huntington Library, 1966), 158. King James is quoted in Elton, 92. Also see Palmer for a Protestant reading of *All's Well That Ends Well*, as well as Grace Tiffany, "Calvinist Grace in Shakespeare's Romances: Upending Tragedy," *Christianity and Literature* 49, No. 4 (Summer 2000): 421–46, which advances a cautious suggestion of the influence of Calvinist preaching and the Geneva Bible on Shakespeare's romances.

25. William Painter, *The Palace of Pleasure*, excerpted in *All's Well That Ends Well*, by William Shakespeare, ed. Sylvan Barnet (New York: Penguin, 1988), 173.

26. Quoted in David Haley, *Shakespeare's Courtly Mirror: Reflexivity and Prudence in "All's Well that Ends Well"* (Newark: University of Delaware Press, 1993), 103.

27. Stanley Wells, *Shakespeare: A Life in Drama* (New York: Norton, 1997), 353.

28. Marco Mincoff, *Things Supernatural and Causeless: Shakespearean Romance* (Newark: University of Delaware Press, 1992), 53.

29. Andrew Gurr, *Shakespearean Stage*, 190.

30. Mincoff, *Things Supernatural and Causeless*, 52.

31. David Bevington, Introduction to *Cymbeline*, in *The Complete Works of Shakespeare*, by William Shakespeare (New York: HarperCollins, 1992), 1437.

32. Mincoff, *Things Supernatural and Causeless*, 55–56.

33. Steve Sohmer, "The 'Double Time' Crux in *Othello* Solved," *English Literary Renaissance*, 32, no. 2 (Spring 2002): 224, 225.

34. Ibid., 220.

35. Ibid., 224.

36. It is Sohmer who calls Othello's journey an "unconsummated pilgrimage" (ibid., 236), since he argues, as would I, that Othello's and Desdemona's marriage is never consummated.

37. Mincoff, *Things Supernatural and Causeless*, 46.

38. Derek Traversi, *An Approach to Shakespeare* (New York: Doubleday, 1939), 132.

39. In chapter 2 of my *Erotic Beasts and Social Monsters: Shakespeare, Jonson, and Comic Androgyny* (Newark: University of Delaware Press, 1995), I discuss Shakespeare's use of animal metaphors to suggest erotic power (76 and 213n14 mention *Othello* specifically). On this point also see Jeanne Addison Roberts, "Animals as Agents of Revelation: The Horizontalizing of the Chain of Being in Shakespeare's Comedies," *New York Critical Forum* (1980): 79–96.

40. Quoted in Griffin, "Un-Sainting James," 60.

41. Ibid., 67, 70–71.

42. Donne, *Complete English Poems*, 75.

43. Giraldi Cinthio, *Hecatommithi*, excerpted in *Othello*, by William Shakespeare, ed. Sylvan Barnet (New York: Penguin, 1986), 171–84.

44. Joel B. Altman, "'Prophetic Fury': *Othello* and the Economy of Shakespearean Reception," *Studies in the Literary Imagination* 26, no. 1 (Spring 1993): 95.

45. Griffin, "Unsainting James," 65.

46. D. Douglas Waters, *Christian Settings in Shakespeare's Tragedies* (Rutherford, NJ: Fairleigh Dickinson University Press, 1994), 189.

47. Quoted in Mark Van Doren, *Shakespeare* (New York: Doubleday, 1939), 194.

48. A. C. Bradley, *Shakespearean Tragedy* (London Macmillan, 1962), 180.

49. Thomas Scott, *Vox Populi, Or Newes from Spayne* (London, 1620), title page.

50. *A Fig for the Spaniard, STC* nos. 1026 and 1027.

51. James Shapiro, *Shakespeare and the Jews* (New York: Columbia University Press, 1996), 41.

52. Peter Milward, "More on the 'Base Judean,'" *Notes and Queries* 38, no. 4 (September 1998): 330.

53. Peter Berek, "The Jew as Renaissance Man," *Renaissance Quarterly* 51, no. 1 (Spring 1998): 135.

54. Ibid., 130–35.

55. Stephen Greenblatt, *Hamlet in Purgatory*, 157.

56. Ibid., 199.

CHAPTER 5. THE PASSIONATE PILGRIM

1. Donne, *Complete English Poems*, 314.

2. Ibid., 346–47.

3. Ibid., 59–60.

4. For an early discussion of the influence of Jesuitism on Donne, see T. S. Eliot, "Donne and the Middle Ages," chapter 2 in *The Varieties of Metaphysical Poetry*, ed. Ronald Shuchard (New York: Harcourt, Brace, 1993).

5. Robert Whalen, "Sacramentalizing the Word: Donne's 1626 Christmas Sermon," *Centered on the Word: Literature, Scripture, and the Tudor-Stuart Middle Way*, ed. Daniel W. Doerksen and Christopher Hodgkins (Newark: University of Delaware Press, 2004), 194. See also N. J. C. Andreason, *John Donne: Conservative Revolutionary* (Princeton, NJ: Princeton University Press, 1967).

6. Richard Strier, "Radical Donne: 'Satire III,'" *ELH* 60, no. 2 (Summer 1993): 286.

7. Mary Arshagouni Papazian, introduction to *John Donne and the Protestant Reformation: New Perspectives*, ed. Papazian (Detroit: Wayne State University Press, 2003), 4.

8. Paul White, "Holy Robin Hood!"

9. T. S. Eliot, "The Conceit of an Idea," chapter 4 in *Varieties of Metaphysical Poetry*, especially pp. 120 and 134.

10. Donne, *Completge English Poems*, 298.

11. Barbara K. Lewalski writes that in "The Progress of the Soul" and other poems, Donne extends biblical typology to accommodate physical symbols in the universe—though, I would add, this accommodation is purely verbal. See Lewalski's "Typological Symbolism and the 'Progress of the Soul,'" in *Literary Uses of Typology from the Late Middle Ages to the Present*, ed. Earl Miner (Princeton, NJ: Princeton University Press, 1977), 82.

12. Donne, *Complete English Poems*, 164.

NOTES

13. Donne, "A Letter to the Lady Carey, and Mistress Essex Rich," from Amiens, in *Complete English Poems*, 234.

14. Donne, "To the Countess of Bedford," in *Complete English Poems*, 225–226.

15. Donne, "Of the Progress of the Soul: The Second Anniversary," in *The Complete English Poems*, 287–301.

16. Donne, *Complete English Poems*, 76.

17. Ibid., 90.

18. Ibid., 215.

19. Richard Lovelace, "To Lucasta, Going to the Wars," l. 2, in *Cavalier Poets*, ed. Thomas Clayton (Oxford: Oxford University Press, 1978), 256.

20. Donne, *Complete English Poems*, 48. Of "The Canonization," Cleanth Brooks writes, "The hermitage of each is the other's body." See "The Language of Paradox: 'The Canonization,'" in *John Donne: A Collection of Critical Essays*, ed. Helen Gardner (Englewood Cliffs, NJ: Prentice-Hall, 1962), 101.

21. Donne, *Complete English Poems*, 68.

22. Ibid., 127.

23. Instance not only Spenser's Archimago but *King John*'s "meddling priest" of Rome, whom Shakespeare's English John accuses of "juggling witchcraft" (3.1.163, 169). In "The Bracelet," Donne imagines that Spanish coins, "as Catholic as their king," are stamped "Like many-angled figures in the book / Of some great conjurer" (ll. 30, 34–35, p. 108).

24. As Nancy E. Wright argues, Donne "calls into question the special religious significance of "martyr" by his representation of his own death in 'The Funeral.'" See "The *Figura* of the Martyr in John Donne's Sermons," *ELH* 56, no. 2 (Summer 1989): 297.

25. Donne, *Complete English Poems*,62.

26. Ibid., 79–80.

27. See Patrick Collinson, *The Elizabethan Puritan Movement* (Berkeley and Los Angeles: University of California Press, 1967), 36. I should note, however, that "A Jet Ring Sent" is more optimistic about the value of wedding rings, which are at least superior to the ring of brittle jet. "Marriage rings are not of this stuff; / Oh, why should aught less precious, or less tough / Figure our loves?" (ll. 5–7, p. 62).

28. Donne, *Complete English Poems*, 82.

29. Ibid., 67.

30. Ibid., 53–56.

31. T. Anthony Perry, *Erotic Spirituality: The Integrative Tradition from Leone Ebreo to John Donne* (Tuscaloosa: University of Alabama Press, 1980), 93.

32. Donne, *Complete English Poems*, 87.

33. Ibid., 75–76. Phillips D. Carleton has argued that Donne's image of the commingled lovers' remains is drawn from a legend of the finding of King Arthur's bones intermingled with Guenevere's hair at Glastonbury, which myth suggests that royal pair's dual burial. See "John Donne's Bracelet of Bright Hair about the Bone," *Modern Language Notes* 56, no. 5 (May 1941): 367.

34. *The Taming of the Shrew* 5.1.124.

35. Stanley Stewart, "Reading Donne: Old and New His- and Her-storicisms," in *Reading the Renaissance*, ed. Marc Berley (Pittsburgh, PA: Duquesne University Press, 2003), 144.

36. Donne, *Complete English Poems*, 86.

37. Ibid., 125.

38. Quoted in A. J. Smith, ed., note 18 to Donne's poem in *Complete English Poems*, 398.

39. Donne, *Complete English Poems*, 77–78, l. 19.

40. Eugene Cunnar, "Donne's Witty Theory of Atonement in 'The Baite,'" *Studies in English Literature* 29 (1989): 85.

41. Donne, *Complete English Poems*, 47–48.

42. An alternative view of this poem's structure is offered by Edward Tayler, who argues that despite Donne's clear shift in tone in stanza 3, all five stanzas of "The Canonization" follow a single progress designed to substitute an erotic for a Catholic enshrinement. He writes, "The linear structure of the five stanzas . . . coincides with the topical (and linear) 'structure' of the ecclesiastical *processus* of canonization: (1) proof of personal sanctity urged against a Devil's Advocate, (2) practice of virtue in heroic degree, (3) examination of alleged miracles, (4) consideration of writings and remains, and (5) canonization." See Tayler's *Donne's Idea of a Woman: Structure and Meaning in the Anniversaries* (New York: Columbia University Press, 1991), 71.

43. Pierre Legouis, "The Dramatic Element in Donne's Poetry," in *John Donne: A Collection of Critical Essays*, ed. Helen Gardner (Englewood Cliffs, NJ: Prentice-Hall, 1962), 46.

44. Ibid.

45. "We two alone will sing like birds i'th'cage; / . . . Talk of court news . . . / Who loses and who wins; who's in, who's out— / And take upon's the mystery of things / As though we were God's spies; and we'll wear out, / In a wall'd prison, packs and sects of great ones, / That ebb and flow by the moon" (Shakespeare, *King Lear* 5.3.9–19).

46. C. S. Lewis, "Donne and Love Poetry in the Seventeenth Century," in *John Donne: A Collection of Critical Essays*, ed. Helen Gardner (Englewood Cliffs, NJ: Prentice-Hall, 1962), 91. See also Belsey, "Serpent in the Garden," 218–39. In fairness it should be noted that, for their part, many mainstream English Protestants, and probably recusant Catholics as well, regarded *Puritans* as lechers. For discussions of this aspect of Elizabethan and Jacobean Puritans' reputation, see Poole, "Saints Alive!" and Tiffany, "Puritanism in Comic History."

47. See Johnson, "John Donne and the Virginia Company," 127–38.

48. Donne, "To the Countess of Bedford," in *Complete English Poems*, 229–31.

49. Donne, *Complete English Poems*, 207.

50. Ibid., 173–75.

51. Ibid., 228–29.

52. For discussions of Donne's military and diplomatic service, see Edmund Gosse's *The Life and Letters of John Donne*, 2 vols. (Gloucester, MA: Peter Smith, 1959) and the outline provided by A. J. Smith on pages 17 through 25 of *Complete English Poems*. For a discussion of his later career as a "diplomat divine," see Paul R. Sellin's *So Doth, So Is Religion: John Donne and Diplomatic Contexts in the Reformed Netherlands, 1619–1620* (Columbia: University of Missouri Press, 1988).

53. Donne, "Eclogue 1613. December 26," in *Complete English Poems*, 139–46.

54. Donne, *Complete English Poems*, 80–81, l. 30.

55. Ibid., 205.

56. Ibid., 126.

57. Brooks, "Language of Paradox," 102.

58. Donne, "Satire 3," in *Complete English Poems*, 161–64.

59. Donne, *Complete English Poems*, 316.

60. Ibid., 323.

61. Luther, *Discourse on Free Will*, 135–36. For a recent discussion of the absolute dependence on God Donne shows in his religious verse, see Catherine Gimelli Martin, "'Unmeete Contraryes': The Reformed Subject and the Triangulation of Religious Desire in Donne's *Annniversaries* and *Holy Sonnets*," in *John Donne and the Protestant Reformation: New Perspectives*, ed. Mary Arshagouni Papazian (Detroit: Wayne State University Press, 2003), 193–220.

62. Calvin, *Institutes*, 1:806.

63. Donne, *Complete English Poems*, 310. See also the discussion of Donne's relation to this Calvinist view in Grace Tiffany, "Calvinist Grace in Shakespeare's Romances," 440–41n7.

64. Donne, "Good Friday, 1613. Riding Westward," in *Complete English Poems*, 329–31. See also Colin Smith's note on this poem, p. 652.

65. Donne, *Complete English Poems*, 310 and 311.

66. Francisco de Quevedo, "A Roma, Sepultada en Sus Ruinas," in *Poesia* (Madrid: Editorial Ebro, 1957), 39. Translations from the Spanish are mine.

67. Quevedo, "Himno a las Estrellas," in *Poesia*, 81–83.

68. Quevedo, *Poesia*, 98.

69. Donne, *Complete English Poems*, 312.

70. Paul Cefalu, "Godly Fear, Sanctification, and Calvinist Theology in the Sermons and 'Holy Sonnets' of John Donne," *Studies in Philology* 100, no. 1 (Winter 2003): 75.

71. Calvin, *Institutes*, 1:788.

72. Cefalu, "Godly Fear," 77.

73. Donne, *Complete English Poems*, 317.

74. Ibid., 314–15.

75. Ibid., 309.

76. Ibid., 84–85.

77. George Herbert, "The Collar," in *The English Poems of George Herbert*, ed. C. A. Patrides (Totowa, NJ: Rowman and Littlefield, 1974), 161–62. Donne's God, whose dauntingly powerful love thwarts rather than inspires the pilgrim's travel, is memorably recaptured in the Victorian poet Francis Thompson's "The Hound of Heaven," wherein God is not a person approached, but himself the pursuer of the fleeing Christian. Like Donne, Thompson conflates time and space in his account of the closing distance between himself and God: "I fled Him, down the nights and down the days; / I fled Him, down the arches of the years" (ll. 1–2). And like Donne, Thompson's sinner finds himself irresistibly drawn back toward the God at his back. "Halts by me that footfall; / Is my gloom, after all, / Shade of His hand, outstretched caressingly?" (ll. 177–79). See Thompson's poem in M. H. Abrams, ed., *The Norton Anthology of English Literature*, 7th ed., 2 vols. (New York: W. W. Norton) 2:1857–60.

78. Cunnar, *"Donne's Witty Theory,"* 78.

79. Donne, "An Anatomy of the World: The First Anniversary," in *Complete English Poems*, 270–83.

80. As Richard F. Hughes has argued, although (in like vein) Donne uses images of the rosary in his sonnet cycle "La Corona" (157), those images' iconicity is eradicated by their translation into language, just as the bead-telling in *The Faerie Queene*'s House of Holiness is divested by narrativization of its iconic threat. The subtitle of Hughes's book—its full title is *The Progress of the Soul: The Interior Career of John Donne*—implies that things Catholic including pilgrimage are absorbed into and transformed by an inner world of language in Donne, befitting Protestant religious tradition. (See Hughes, *The Progress of the Soul* [New York: W. Morrow, 1968].)

81. Donne, *Complete English Poems*, 326.

82. Jorge Luis Borges, *Obras Completas*, 4 vols. (Buenos Aires: Emecé Editores, 1974), 4:135.

83. Donne, *Complete English Poems*, 317.

84. See J. B. Harley and David Woodward, eds., *The History of Cartography: Cartography in Prehistoric, Ancient, and Medieval Europe and the Mediterranean*, 2 vols. (Chicago: University of Chicago Press, 1987), 1:310, where this map is pictured.

85. Ibid.

86. Rosalie Beck argues that Donne's struggle to go west when pulled east, toward Christ's Cross, is in fact entirely a pyschomachia, the war of "two impulses both within the soul" (169). See her "A Precedent for Donne's Imagery in 'Good Friday, 1613, Riding Westward," *Review of English Studies* n.s. 19, no. 74 (May, 1968).

87. Donne, *Complete English Poems*, 307.

88. Donne, "Obsequies to the Lord Harrington, brother to the Lady Lucy, Countess of Bedford," in *Complete English Poems*, 261.

89. Donne, *Complete English Poems*, 309.

90. Ibid., 336.

91. Ibid., 217.

92. Fruen, "Fairy Queen," 79.

93. Donne, *Complete English Poems*, 209.

94. Donne, "Obsequies to the Lord Harrington," 257.

95. In Donne's 1617 accession day sermon, he employs the metaphor of map as body in his description of James I's imminent progress to Scotland. See p. 166 of Mary Morrissey's discussion of this sermon in "John Donne as a Conventional Paul's Cross Preacher," in *John Donne's Professional Lives*, ed. David Colclough (Cambridge, UK: D. S. Brewer, 2003).

96. Gerard Manley Hopkins, "God's Grandeur," in *Chief Modern Poets of Britain and America*, ed. Gerald DeWitt Sanders, John Herbert Nelson, and M. L. Rosenthal (New York: Macmillan, 1970), 60.

97. Edward Wheeler, "Continuing the Conversation," a discussion of Margaret Edson's *Wit*, in *Commonweal* (April 9, 1999), 35.

98. Donne, *Complete English Poems*, 347–48.

99. George Herbert, *English Poems*, 151–52. Abrams's comment is in M. H. Abrams, ed., *The Norton Anthology of English Literature: The Sixteenth Century, The Early Seventeenth Century*, 7th ed., 2 vols. (New York: W. W. Norton, 2000), 1B:1608n4.

100. Nabil Matar, "John Donne, Peter Sterry, and the *Ars Moriendi*," *Explorations in Renaissance Culture* 18 (1992): 56.

101. Donne, *Complete English Poems*, 306.

102. Spenser, *The Faerie Queene*, 1.10.3.

CHAPTER 6. MILTON AND THE PILGRIM READER

1. Martin Luther, *Table Talk*, in *Luther's Work*, 54:238.

2. John Milton, *Areopagitica*, in *Complete Prose Works of John Milton*, ed. Douglas Bush et al., 4 vols. (New Haven, CT: Yale University Press, 1959), 2:514–15. N.B.: For "wayfaring" in this passage, as it was in the original printed versions of *Areopagitica*, Bush has "warfaring," as it was corrected in all four of the first manuscript's presentation copies (see n. 102 on p. 515 of the YP vol. 2). I have retained "wayfaring."

3. Calvin, *Institutes*, 1:183.

4. Ibid., 1:189.

5. Ibid., 2:880.

6. The term "advanced Protestant" replaces "Puritan" in much contemporary Renaissance scholarship. See, for example, Greenfield, "The Rise of the Patrons' Companies," presented at the Shakespeare Association of America's annual meeting in New Orleans, 2004.

7. "I saw Satan fall like lightning from heaven" (Luke 10:18). "[T]herefore the Lord God sent him forth from the garden of Eden. . . . He drove out the man" (Genesis 3:23, 24).

8. As M. H. Abrams writes, Milton "degrad[es] the military glory celebrated in epic tradition in favor of the place-holding 'better fortitude / Of patience and heroic martyrdom.'" See Abrams's introduction to "John Milton" in *The Norton Anthology*, ed. M. H. Abrams, 7th ed., 2 vols. (New York: W. W. Norton, 2000), 1B:1773.

9. On Milton the anti-imperialist, see David Armitage, "John Milton: Poet Against Empire," in *Milton and Republicanism*, ed. David Armitage, Armand Himy, and Quentin Skinner (Cambridge: Cambridge University Press, 1966), 206.

10. Hakluyt, *Voyages and Discoveries*, 38, 37.

11. Milton again links astronomical to maritime exploration in book 5, by a simile that first negatively compares Galileo's to Raphael's powers of vision, then links Galileo's observations to that of an earthly pilot, or ship's captain. Raphael sees "As when by night the glass / Of Galileo, less assured, observes / Imagined lands and regions in the moon: / Or pilot from amidst the Cyclades / Delos or Samos first appearing kens / A cloudy spot" (5.261–66). Raphael sees what Galileo only imagines he sees, and the pilot can discern only clouds.

For Donne's similar habit of linking the new science of astronomy to the older one of global exploration and gently denigrating both, see his "Letter to the Countess of Bedford," which my last chapter discussed: "We have added to the world Virginia, and sent / Two new stars lately to the firmament; / Why grudge we us (not heaven) the dignity / T'increase with ours, those fair souls company?" (ll. 67–70).

Milton's similar skepticism regarding the value of astronomical science is related to his belief, expressed in different ways throughout *Paradise Lost*, that humans should not venture beyond the bounds prescribed to their knowledge. Thus in book 5 Raphael is more forthcoming in his responses to Adam's questions concerning earth and humans' spiritual construction than to those which concern the celestial bodies. God "Did wisely to conceal, and not divulge / His secrets to be scanned by them who ought / Rather admire," says Raphael (8.73–75). For a discussion of Milton's ambivalent attitude toward the discoveries of Galileo, whom he knew, see Judith Scherer Herz, " 'For whom this glorious sight?' Dante, Milton, and the Galileo Question," in *Milton in Italy: Contexts, Images, Contradictions*, ed. Mario A. DiCesare (Binghamton, NY: SUNY Binghamton Press, 1991), 147–57.

12. Quoted in Pincus, "John Milton and Commercial Society," 710.

13. Ibid., 731.

14. My chief source of information regarding Milton's attitudes toward his travels and toward England are Milton's own writings, especially *Areopagitica* and his letters to foreign correspondents, both of which are contained in volume 2 of Milton's *Complete Prose Works*. However, I have also relied on William Riley Parker's excellent *Milton: A Biography*, in 2 vols. (Oxford: Clarendon Press, 1996).

15. An action currently criticized by Philip Pullman's phenomenally popular children's trilogy, the first book in which is titled *The Golden Compass* (New York: Del Rey, 1997).

16. Milton, *Complete Prose Works*, 2:528. All references to Milton's prose are to this edition unless otherwise indicated. I have modernized Milton's spellings and cases.

17. Ibid., 2:520–21.

18. Ibid., 2:543.

19. Kent Lehnof, " 'Impregn'd with Reason': Eve's Aural Conception in *Paradise Lost*," *Milton Studies* 41 (2002): 38–75.

20. Vincent Di Benedetto, "Scripture's Constraint and Adam's Self-Authoring Freedom: A Reading of the Fall in *Paradise Lost*." *Milton Quarterly* 25, no. 1 (March 1991): 2.

21. For a discussion of Milton and Spenser, see John King's "Milton's Cave of Error: A Rewriting of Spenserian Satire," in *Worldmaking Spenser: Explorations in the Early Modern Age*, ed. Patrick Cheney and Lauren Silberman (Lexington: University of Kentucky Press, 2000), 148–55.

22. For a discussion of the self-involvement expressed by the soliloquy as tragedy's fundamental characteristic, see chapter 2 of Tiffany, *Erotic Beasts and Social Monsters*.

23. Anthony Low, "The Fall into Subjectivity: Milton's 'Paradise Within' and 'Abyss of Fears and Horrors,' " in *Reading the Renaissance: Ideas and Idioms from Shakespeare to Milton*, ed. Marc Berley (Pittsburgh, PA: Duquesne University Press, 2003), 208. See also Thomas L. Martin, "On the Margin of God: Deconstruction and the Language of Satan in *Paradise Lost*," *Milton Quarterly* 29, no. 2 (May 1995). Martin calls Satan's language "strained and distorted" (43).

24. Beverley Sherry, "Speech in *Paradise Lost*," *Milton Studies* 8 (1975): 259.

25. Richard Strier, "Milton's Fetters, or, Why Eden is Better than Heaven," *Milton Studies* 38 (2000): 180.

26. Quoted in Thomas Corns, " 'With Unaltered Brow': Milton and the Son of God," in *Milton Studies* 42 (2002): 110.

27. Ibid.

28. *Areopagitica*, in Milton, *Complete Prose Works*, 2:549.

29. For an alternative viewpoint on Miltonic iconoclasm, see Tracy Fessenden, who sees a similar (to *The Faerie Queene*) tension in *Paradise Lost* between "iconoclasm" and "iconophilia" (" 'Shapes of Things Divine' in *Paradise Lost*," *Christianity and Literature* 48, no. 4 [Summer 1999]: 426).

30. "The poetic and pictorial tributes characteristic of the cult of Elizabeth provide the context for understanding Milton's perception of Eve." Albert C. Labriola, "Milton's Eve and the Cult of Elizabeth I," *Journal of English and Germanic Philology* 95, no. 1 (January 1996): 39.

31. In a forthcoming essay, Elizabeth Bradburn demonstrates that the word "amazed" with which Milton describes Eve's response to the serpent (Milton actually says she is "not unamazed" [9.552]) had for early moderns a specific association with the dulling of the intellect, distinct from the meanings associated with the word "wondering." Bradburn's remarks will be published in *Comparative Drama.*

32. Donne, *Complete English Poems*, 309.

33. Ibid., "Holy Sonnet 1," 309.

34. Ibid., 310.

35. Barbara Kiefer Lewalski, "Forum: Milton's *Christian Doctrine*," *Studies in English Literature* 32 (1992): 150. This short essay is largely a defense of Milton's authorship of *De Doctrina Christiana*, a tract which also explicitly attacks the doctrine of predestination. Lewalski defends Milton's authorship of *De Doctrina* at more length in "Milton and *De Doctrina Christiana*: Evidences of Authorship," *Milton Studies* 36 (1998): 203–28. Milton's rejection of Calvin's views have been widely discussed, but for a recent articulation of Milton's opposition to Calvin see Richard Strier, "Milton's Fetters."

36. "I am bringing forward my own resources against free will. Not that I shall produce them all, for who could do that within the limits of this small book, when the whole Scriptures, in every letter and iota, stand on my side? There is no need, because free will lies vanquished and prostrate already." (Martin Luther, *Discourse on Free Will*, 134.)

37. Milton, *Complete Prose Works*, vol. 2, YP, p. 527.

38. Ng, "Translation, Interpretation, and Heresy," 330.

39. Ibid., 323.

40. As Basil Willey has argued, Milton "frees himself from that last infirmity of noble Protestants—subservience to Holy Writ." Willey is quoted in James B. Potts, Jr., "Milton's 'Two-Fold Scripture' and the Seventeenth-Century Search for Certitude," *Explorations in Renaissance Culture* 18 (1992): 93. Potts himself argues that Milton was almost a Quaker in his arguments, framed in *De Doctrina Christiana*, that the Christian's spirit might legitimately prompt him to violate the letter of (even New Testament) scriptural law (97).

41. Milton, *Areopagitica*, 2:529.

42. Ibid., 2:515, 554. See my note 2.

43. Cunnar, "Donne's Witty Theory," 84.

44. Milton, *Areopagitica*, 2:516, 529.

45. Ibid., 2:549.

46. Ibid., 2:521.

47. Donald L. Guss, "Enlightenment as Process: Milton and Habermas," *PMLA* 106, no. 5 (October 1991): 1157.

48. Milton, *Areopagitica*, 2:521.

49. As Bryan Hampton writes, agreeing with John Ulreich, "Jesus . . . performs the Word." "Performing the Incarnation," 5.

50. Milton, *Areopagitica*, 2:556–56.

51. "When I Consider How My Light Is Spent," in Milton, *John Milton: Complete Poems and Major Prose*, 168.

52. Nicholas R. Jones, "'Stand' and 'Fall' as Images of Posture in *Paradise Lost*," *Milton Studies* 8 (1975): 221.

53. Strier, "Milton's Fetters," 187.

54. "When I Consider," 184.

55. Carol Barton, "'They Also Perform the Duties of a Servant Who Only Remain Erect on Their Feet in a Specified Place in Readiness to Receive Orders': The Dynamics of Stasis in Sonnet XIX ('When I Consider How My Light Is Spent')," *Milton Quarterly* 32, no. 4 (December 1998): 109–22. Ronald Levao comments similarly on the significance of Adam's "upright stance" ("'Among Unequals What Society': *Paradise Lost* and the Forms of Intimacy," *Modern Language Quarterly* 61, no. 1 [2000]: 83).

56. Milton, *Areopagitica*, 2:554.

57. John N. King, "Miltonic Transubstantiation," *Milton Studies* 36 (1998): 41. On Milton's disgust with the Catholic Mass, see also Denise Gigante, "Milton's Aesthetics of Eating," in *Diacritics* 30, no. 2 (Summer 2000): 88–112.

58. Bruce Boehrer, "Milton and the Reasoning of Animals," *Milton Studies* 39 (2000): 66.

59. See also Anthony Low, who argues that Raphael's description of transubstantiation shows that to Milton "the hierarchical chain of being is not a static ladder of discrete levels, but vital and dynamic." "Angels and Food in *Paradise Lost*," *Milton Studies* 1 (1969): 135.

60. Hampton, "Performing the Incarnation," 11.

61. Milton, *Areopagitica*, 2:514.

62. Strier, "Milton's Fetters," 30.

63. J. Martin Evans, *The Miltonic Moment* (Lexington: University Press of Kentucky, 1998), 17.

64. Milton, *Areopagitica*, 2:531.

65. Ibid., 2:551.

66. Steven Fallon, "The Spur of Self-Concernment: Milton in His Divorce Tracts," *Milton Studies* 38 (2000): 220–42, 221. Fallon also writes, speaking of the divorce tracts, that "Milton speaks as if alongside God and above the frailties of human beings, as if untouched by human misery (except as a compassionate observer) and as if free from sin". On the related point of Milton's direct infusion with grace, see also William G. Riggs, who writes of Milton's "literal belief in poetic inspiration" ("The Temptation of Milton's Eve: 'Words, Impregn'd / With Reason,'" *Journal of English and Germanic Philology* 94, no. 3 [July 1995]: 366).

67. On Milton as new Moses, see Jason P. Rosenblatt, "The Mosaic Voice in *Paradise Lost*," *Milton Studies* 7 (1975): 207–32.

68. Milton, *Areopagitica*, 2:551, 549.

69. William Tyndale, from *First New Testament*, in *Doctrinal Treatises, and Introductions to Different Portions of the Holy Scriptures*, ed. Henry Walter, Parker Society 42 (Cambridge: Cambridge University Press, 1884), 1:390.

70. "How Soon Hath Time," in Milton, *Complete Poems and Major Prose*, 76.

71. André Verbart, "Measure and Hypermetricality in *Paradise Lost*," *English Studies* 80, no. 5 (1999): 428.

72. Ibid., 431. See also Ernst Häublein's "Milton's Paraphrase of Genesis: A Stylistic Reading of *Paradise Lost*, Book VII," *Milton Studies* 7 (1975): 101–26.

73. Milton, *Areopagitica*, 2:549.

74. For just one such discussion, see Douglas Bush's *Mythology and the Renaissance Tradition in English Poetry* (Minneapolis: University of Minnesota Press), 1932.

75. For a discussion of Milton's Christianization of Urania, see Stevie Davies and William B. Hunter, "Milton's Urania: 'The meaning, not the name I call,'" *Studies in English Literature* 28, no. 1 (Winter 1998). These authors argue that Urania is Christ (95).

76.   Nor is Osiris seen
             In Memphian grove or green,
                 Trampling the unshowered grass with lowings loud,
             Nor can he be at rest
             Within his sacred chest;
                 Naught but profoundest Hell can be his shroud.
             In vain with timbreled anthems dark
             The sable-stoléd sorcerers bear his worshipped ark.
                         ("On the Morning of Christ's Nativity," ll. 213–20,
                           in *John Milton, Complete Poems and Major Prose*, 43–50)

77. In *Paradise Lost and the Genesis Tradition* (Oxford: Clarendon Press, 1968), J. Martin Evans places Milton in the context of other Renaissance writers who modified or expanded Genesis.

78. The most famous example of such condemnation is found in "Lycidas," where corrupt prelates of both the Roman Catholic and English churches are characterized as the "grim wolf with privy paw" (l. 128). See *John Milton, Complete Poems and Major Prose*, 120–25 .

79. I intentionally say "he" rather than "he and she" or (Milton forbid) "she and he." The solitary pronoun is appropriate, in light of *Paradise Lost*'s suggestion that wives receive intellectual sustenance secondhand, from their husbands' accounts (or else directly from dreams) (book 5, especially ll. 52–54).

80. Milton, *Areopagitica*, 2:558.

81. Again I refer my reader to Elizabeth Bradburn's excellent discussion of *Paradise Lost*'s negative uses of the word "amaze" and its variants.

82. Milton, *Areopagitica*, 2:558.

83. Bryan Adams Hampton, "Milton's Parable of Misreading: Navigating the Contextual Waters of the 'Night-Founder'd Skiff' in *Paradise Lost*, 1.192–209," *Milton Studies* 43 (2004): 86–110. See also Jameela Lares, "*Paradise Lost*, Books XI and XII, and the Homiletic Tradition," *Milton Studies* 34 (1996): 99–116.

84. Bryan Crockett, *Play of Paradox*, 50.

85. Milton, *Areopagitica*, 2:543.

86. Again, see Lehnof in "Eve's Aural Conception," on Eve's aural seduction by Satan.

87. M. H. Abrams, introduction to "John Milton," 1774.

88. Milton, *Areopagitica*, 2:515.

89. Ibid., 2:514.

90. Ibid., 2:521.

91. George Herbert, "The Pilgrimage," Norton, vol. 1B, 7th ed., p. 1608.

92. Thomas Festa, "Repairing the Ruins: Milton as Reader and Educator," *Milton Studies* 43 (2004): 35.

93. For this observation I am indebted to William G. Riggs, "Temptation of Milton's Eve, 366.

94. Milton, *Areopagitica*, 2:554.

95. Ibid., 2:558, 552.

96. Ibid., 2:566.

97. Ibid., 2:554.

Chapter 7. Coda

1. John Bunyan, *Pilgrim's Progress*, 1.

2. Milton, *Areopagitica*, 2:565.

3. Ibid., 2:551.

4. Ibid., 2:553.

5. Spenser's letter appended to *The Faerie Queene*, Longman, 737.

6. Bunyan, *Pilgrim's Progress*, 4.

7. Spenser's letter, Longman, 737.

8. Bunyan, *Pilgrim's Progress*, 4. For a recent discussion of Spenser's influence on Bunyan, see chapter 1, "The Allegorical Way," in Kathleen Swaim, *Pilgrim's Progress, Puritan Progress: Discourses and Contexts* (Chicago: University of Illinois Press, 1993).

9. Bunyan, *Pilgrim's Progress*, 7.

10. Ibid., 92–96.

11. Ibid., 116.

12. Milton, *Areopagitica*, 2:543–44.

13. Bunyan, *Pilgrim's Progress*, 77–78.

14. Martin Luther, *Luther's Works*, 54:136 (*Table Talk*).

15. Milton, *Areopagitica*, 2:543.

16. Bunyan, *Pilgrim's Progress*, 65. Richard Greaves gives an account of Bunyan's own uninterest in the threat of "popery" in chapter 7 of his *John Bunyan and English Nonconformity* (London: Hambledon Press, 1992).

17. Bunyan, *Pilgrim's Progress*, 85.

18. Ibid., 41.

19. Ibid., 76.

20. Ibid., 40.

21. Ibid., 89.

22. Ibid., 97.

23. Ibid., 131–32.

24. See Foxe, *Acts and Monuments*, and Calvin's *Institutes*, vol. 2, book 4, chapters 1–2.

25. Milton, "Reason of Church Government," in *Complete Prose Works*, 2:753.

26. For a masterful discussion of Tyndale's importance to the King James Bible, see David Daniell's *Bible in English*, especially part 2.

27. "Prayer (1)," in *English Poems*, 70–71.

28. Russell Fraser, introduction to *Drama of the English Renaissance*, ed. Russell A. Fraser and Norman Rabkin, 1–19, 2 vols. (Berkeley and Los Angeles: University of California Press, 1976), 4.

Bibliography

Primary Sources

Alighieri, Dante. *The Purgatorio*. Translated by John Ciardi. New York: Signet, 1961.

Articles of Religion of the English Church. In *Creeds of the Churches: A Reader in Christian Doctrine from the Bible to the Present*, 3rd ed. edited by John Leith. Atlanta: John Knox, 1982.

Beaumont, Francis. *The Knight of the Burning Pestle*. In *Drama of the English Renaissance*, edited by Russell A. Fraser and Norman Rabkin, 2:517–48. 2 vols. New York: Macmillan, 1976.

Biblia Sacra: ixta vulgatum versionem. Edited by Robert Weber et al. 3rd ed. Stuttgart: Deutsche Bibelgesellschaft, 1983.

Bradford, William. *Of Plymouth Plantation: 1620–1647*. Edited by Francis Murphy. New York: Random House, 1981.

Bunyan, John. *The Pilgrim's Progress*. Oxford: Clarendon Press, 1960.

Calvin, John. *Commentaries*. Edited by David W. and Thomas F. Torrance. 23 vols. Grand Rapids, MI: Calvin Translation Society, 1948–59.

———. *Institutes of the Christian Religion*. Edited by John T. McNeill. Translated by Ford Lewis Battles. 2 vols. Philadelphia: Westminster, 1960.

Cervantes, Miguel de. *El Ingenioso Hidalgo Don Quijote de la Mancha*. Edited by Luis Andrés Murillo. 2 vols. Madrid: Clásicos Castalia, 1978.

The Chandos Herald. *The Life of the Black Prince*. 1397. Edited by Mildred K. Pope and Eleanor C. Lodge. Oxford: Clarendon Press, 1910.

Chaucer, Geoffrey. *The Canterbury Tales. Chaucer's Poetry*, 2nd ed., edited by E. T. Donaldson, 5–583. Glenview, IL: Scott, Foresman, 1975.

Cinthio, Giraldi. *Hecatommithi*. Excerpted in *Othello*, by William Shakespeare, edited by Sylvan Barnet, 71–184. New York: Penguin, 1986.

A Comparison of the English and Spanish Nation. Translated by Robert Ashley. London, 1589.

Coverdale, Miles. *Remains*. Edited by George Pearson. Cambridge: Cambridge University Press, 1946.

Donne, John. *John Donne: The Complete English Poems*. Edited by A. J. Smith. New York: Penguin Books, 1987.

Drayton, Michael. "Ode. To the Virginian Voyage." In *The Norton Anthology of English Literature*, 7th ed., 2 vols., edited by M. H. Abrams, 1: 968–69. New York: W. W. Norton, 2000.

Erasmus. *Ten Colloquies*. Translated by Craig R. Thompson. New York: Liberal Arts Press, 1957.

Foxe, John. *Foxe's Book of Martyrs (Acts and Monuments* 1563). Edited by Marie Gentert King. Old Tappan, NJ: Fleming H. Revell, 1975.

Froissart, Jean. *Chronicles*. 1395, translated by Lord Berners, 1523. Excerpted in *The Literature of Medieval England*, edited by D. W. Robertson, 323–43. New York: McGraw-Hill, 1970.

The Geneva Bible: A Facsimile of the 1560 Edition. Madison: University of Wisconsin Press, 1969.

Greene, Robert. *The Spanish Masquerado*. London, 1589.

Hakluyt, Richard. *Voyages and Discoveries*. London, 1589. Edited by Jack Beeching. New York: Penguin Books, 1972.

Herbert, George. *The English Poems of George Herbert*. Edited by C. A. Patrides. Totowa, NJ: Rowman and Littlefield, 1975.

Herrick, Robert. "His Prayer to Ben Jonson." *Cavalier Poets: Selected Poems*, edited by Thomas Clayton, 127. New York: Oxford University Press, 1978.

Heywood, John. *The Play Called the Four PP*. In *Medieval and Tudor Drama*, edited by John Gassner, 231–62. New York: Bantam Books, 1963.

The Holy Bible (King James Version). 1611. New York: New American Library, 1974.

Homer. *The Odyssey*. Translated by George Chapman, edited by Allardyce Nicoll. New York: Pantheon Books, 2000.

Hopkins, Gerard Manley. "God's Grandeur." In *Chief Modern Poets of Britain and America*, edited by Gerald DeWitt Sanders, John Herbert Nelson, and M. L. Rosenthal, 60. New York: Macmillan, 1970.

Kempe, Margery. *The Book of Margery Kempe*. Edited by Sanford Brown Meech. Early English Text Society, no. 212. New York: Oxford University Press, 1961.

Kempis, Thomas. *Imitation of Christ*. 1328. Translated by Aloysius Croft and Harold Bolton. Nashville, TN: Thomas Nelson, 1999.

Kyd, Thomas, *The Spanish Tragedy. The First Part of Hieronimo and the Spanish Tragedy*, edited by Andrew S. Cairncross, 57–176. Lincoln, NE: Regents Renaissance Drama Series, 1967.

Lambard, William. *The Duties of Constables, Borsholders, Tithing-men, and Such Other Lowe Ministers of the Peace*. London, 1584.

Langland, William. *Piers Plowman: The B Version*. Edited by George Kane and E. Talbot Donaldson. London: Athlone Press, 1975.

The Lanterne of Liyt. Edited by Lillian M. Swinburn. Early English Text Society, o.s. 151. London: Kegan Paul, Trench, Trubner, 1917.

Lovelace, Richard. "To Lucasta, Going to the Wars." In *Cavalier Poets*, edited by Thomas Clayton, 256. New York: Oxford University Press, 1978.

Luther, Martin. *Discourse on Free Will*. Translated by and edited by Ernst F. Winter. New York: Frederick Unger, 1961.

———. *Luther's Works*. Edited by and translated by Theodore G. Tappert. 55 vols. Philadelphia: Fortress Press, 1967.

——. *Works.* Edited by Jaroslav Pelikan and Helmut Lehmann. 55 vols. Philadelphia: Muhlenberg, 1955.

Malynes, Gerard de. *Saint George for England, Allegorically Described,* 1601. Excerpted in *Spenser: The Critical Heritage,* edited by R. M. Cummings, 115. New York: Barnes and Noble, 1971.

Mandeville's Travels. 1400. Edited by M. C. Seymour. Oxford: Clarendon Press, 1967.

Marvell, Andrew, "Upon Appleton House. *Andrew Marvell: The Complete Poems,* edited by Elizabeth Story Donno, 75. New York: Penguin Books, 1983.

Milton, John. *Complete Poems and Major Prose.* Edited by Merritt Y. Hughes. 4 vols. New Haven, CT: Yale University Press, 1962.

——. *The Complete Prose Works of John Milton.* Edited by Douglas Bush et al. 4 vols. New Haven, CT: Yale University Press, 1959.

——. *Paradise Lost.* Edited by Scott Elledge. New York: W. W. Norton, 1975.

More, Thomas. *Utopia.* Translated by Paul Turner. New York: Penguin Books, 1965.

Painter, William. *The Palace of Pleasure.* Excerpted in *All's Well that Ends Well,* by William Shakespeare, edited by Sylvan Barnet, 165–74. New York: Penguin, 1988.

Petrarca, Francesco. *For Love of Laura: Poetry of Petrarch.* Translated by Marion Shore. Fayetteville: University of Arkansas Press, 1987.

Quevedo, Francisco de. *Poesia.* Madrid: Editorial Ebro, 1957.

Ralegh, Walter. *The Discovery of the Large, Rich, and Bewtiful Empire of Guiana.* 1596. Edited by Neil L. Whitehead. Norman: University of Oklahoma Press, 1997.

Scott, Thomas. *Vox Populi, Or Newes from Spayne.* London, 1620.

Shakespeare, William. *The Riverside Shakespeare.* Edited by G. Blakemore Evans. Boston: Houghton Mifflin, 1974.

A Short-Title Catalogue of Books Printed in England, Scotland, and Ireland, and of English Books Printed Abroad, 1475–1640. 2nd ed. Edited by A. W. Pollard. London, 1968–91.

Sidney, Philip. *Astrophil and Stella.* The Poems of Philip Sidney, edited by William Ringler, 167. Oxford: Clarendon Press, 1962.

Spenser, Edmund. *The Faerie Queene.* Edited by A. C. Hamilton. New York: Longman, 1977.

——. *Works: A Variorum Edition.* Edited by Rudolf Gottfried. 10 vols. Baltimore: Johns Hopkins University Press, 1932–49.

Tasso, Torquato. *Jerusalem Delivered.* Translated by Edward Fairfax. 1600. Edited by Roberto Weiss. Carbondale: University of Illinois Press, 1962.

Text and Concordance of "El libro de los huéspedes." Escorial MS. h.I.113. Edited by Thomas Spaccarelli. Madison, WI: Hispanic Seminar of Medieval Studies, 1996.

Thompson, Francis. "The Hound of Heaven." In *The Norton Anthology of English Literature,* 7th ed., 2 vols., edited by M. H. Abrams, 2:1857–60. New York: W. W. Norton, 2000.

Tyndale, William. *An Answer unto Sir Thomas Mores Dialoge.* Edited by Anne M. O'Donnell, S.N.D., and Jared Wicks, S.J. 3 vols. Washington, DC: Catholic University of America Press, 2000.

———. Doctrinal Treatises, and Introductions to Different Portions of the Holy Scriptures. Edited by Henry Walter. Parker Society 42. Cambridge: Cambridge University Press, 1884.

———. *Expositions and Notes on Portions of the Holy Scriptures.* 1573. Edited by Henry Walter. 2 vols. Parker Society 43. Cambridge: Cambridge University Press, 1848.

———. *The Obedience of a Christian Man.* 1528. Edited by David Daniell. New York: Penguin, 2000.

———. *Tyndale's Old Testament.* Edited by David Daniell. New Haven, CT: Yale University Press, 1992.

Visitation Articles and Injunctions. Edited by W. H. Frere and W. M. Kennedy. 3 vols. London: Alcuin Club, 1910.

Wing, John. *The Crowne Conjugall or, The Spouse Royall.* Middleburgh, 1620.

Winthrop, John. *A Model of Christian Charity.* In *The American Puritans: Their Prose and Poetry,* edited by Perry Miller. New York: Columbia University Press, 1965, 79–89.

SECONDARY SOURCES

Abrams, M. H. Introduction to John Milton. *The Norton Anthology of English Literature, The Sixteenth Century, the Seventeenth Century,* 7th ed., edited by M. H. Abrams, 18:1771–74. New York: W. W. Norton, 2000.

Altman, Joel B. "'Prophetic Fury': *Othello* and the Economy of Shakespearean Reception." *Studies in the Literary Imagination* 26, no. 1 (Spring 1993): 85–114.

Anderson, Judith. *Translating Investments: Metaphor and the Dynamic of Cultural Change in Tudor-Stuart England.* New York: Fordham University Press, 2005.

Andreason, N. J. C. *John Donne: Conservative Revolutionary.* Princeton, NJ: Princeton University Press, 1967.

Armitage, David. *The Ideological Origins of the British Empire.* Cambridge: Cambridge University Press, 2000.

———. "John Milton: Poet Against Empire." In *Milton and Republicanism,* edited by David Armitage, Armand Himy, and Quentin Skinner. Cambridge: Cambridge University Press, 1966.

Barton, Carol. "'They Also Perform the Duties of a Servant Who Only Remain Erect on Their Feet in a Specified Place in Readiness to Receive Orders': The Dynamics of Stasis in Sonnet XIX ('When I Consider How My Light Is Spent')." *Milton Quarterly* 32, no. 4 (December 1998): 109–22.

Beauregard, David N. "'Inspiréd Merit': Shakespere's Theology of Grace in *All's Well that Ends Well.*" *Renascence* 51, no. 4 (Summer 1999): 218–39.

Beck, Rosalie. "A Precedent for Donne's Imagery in 'Good Friday, 1613, Riding Westward,'" *Review of English Studies* n.s. 19, no. 74 (May 1968): 166–69.

Beier, A. L. *Masterless Men: The Vagrancy Problem in England 1560–1640.* New York: Methuen, 1985.

———. "Vagrants and the Social Order in Elizabethan England." *Past and Present* 64 (1974): 3–29.

Belsey, Catherine. "The Serpent in the Garden: Shakespeare, Marriage, and Material Culture." *Seventeenth Century* 21, no. 1 (Spring 1996): 1–20.

Berek, Peter. "The Jew as Renaissance Man." *Renaissance Quarterly* 51, no. 1 (Spring 1998): 138–62.

Bevington, David. Introduction to *Cymbeline*. In *The Complete Works of Shakespeare*, by William Shakespeare, edited by David Bevington, 1434–37. New York: Harper-Collins, 1992.

Blick, Sarah. "Thomas Becket in the Chapel of Our Lady of Undercroft, Canterbury Cathedral." Paper presented at the 40th Annual Congress on Medieval Studies, Kalamazoo, Michigan, May 2005.

Bloch, Marc. *The Royal Touch: Sacred Monarchy and Scrofula in England and France*. London: Routledge and Kegan Paul, 1973.

Boehrer, Bruce. "Milton and the Reasoning of Animals." *Milton Studies* 39 (2000): 50–73.

Borges, Jorge Luis. *Obras Completas*. 4 vols. Buenos Aires: Emecé Editores, 1974.

Bradley, A. C. *Shakespearean Tragedy*. London: Macmillan, 1962.

Brooks, Cleanth. "The Language of Paradox: 'The Canonization.'" In *John Donne: A Collection of Critical Essays*, edited by Helen Gardner, 100–103. Englewood Cliffs, NJ: Prentice-Hall, 1962.

Bush, Douglas. *Mythology and the Renaissance Tradition in English Poetry*. Minneapolis: University of Minnesota Press, 1932.

Calderwood, James. *Metadrama in Shakespeare's Henriad*. Berkeley and Los Angeles: University of California Press, 1979.

Cantor, Norman F. *In the Wake of the Plague: The Black Death and the World It Made*. New York: Free Press, 2001.

Carleton, Phillips D. "John Donne's Bracelet of Bright Hair about the Bone." *Modern Language Notes* 56, no. 5 (May 1941): 366–68.

Castro, Américo. *The Spaniards: An Introduction to their History*. Berkeley and Los Angeles: University of California Press, 1971.

Cefalu, Paul. "Godly Fear, Sanctification, and Calvinist Theology in the Sermons and 'Holy Sonnets' of John Donne." *Studies in Philology* 100, no. 1 (Winter 2003): 71–86.

Cheney, Patrick. *Marlowe's Counterfeit Profession: Ovid, Spenser, Counter-Nationhood*. Toronto: University of Toronto Press, 1997.

Chew, Samuel C. *The Pilgrimage of Life*. New Haven, CT: Yale University Press, 1962.

Coletti, Theresa. *Mary Magdalene and the Drama of Saints: Theater, Gender, and Religion in Late Medieval England*. Philadelphia: University of Pennsylvania Press, 2004.

Collinson, Patrick. *The Elizabethan Puritan Movement*. Berkeley and Los Angeles: University of California Press, 1967.

Cook, Elizabeth. *Seeing through Words: The Scope of Late Renaissance Poetry*. New Haven, CT: Yale University Press, 1986.

Corns, Thomas. "'With Unaltered Brow': Milton and the Son of God." *Milton Studies* 42 (2002): 106–21.

Crockett, Bryan. *The Play of Paradox: Stage and Sermon in Renaissance England.* Philadelphia: University of Pennsylvania Press, 1995.

Cummings, R. M., ed. *Spenser: The Critical Heritage.* New York: Barnes and Noble, 1971.

Cunnar, Eugene. "Donne's Witty Theory of Atonement in 'The Baite.'" *Studies in English Literature* 29 (1989): 77–98.

Daniell, David. *The Bible in English.* New Haven, CT: Yale University Press, 2003.

———. "Shakespeare and the Protestant Mind." *Shakespeare Survey* 54 (2001): 1–12.

Davidson, Clifford. "Violence and the Saint Play." *Studies in Philology* 98, no. 3 (Summer 2001): 292–314.

Davidson, Clifford, and Anne Eljenholm Nichols, eds. *Iconoclasm v. Art and Drama.* Early Drama, Art, and Music Monograph Series, 11. Kalamazoo, MI: Medieval Institute Publications, 1989.

Davidson, Clifford, and Jennifer Alexander. *The Early Art of Coventry, Stratford-upon-Avon, Warwick, and Lesser Sites in Warwickshire: A Subject List of Extant and Lost Art Including Items Relevant to Early Drama.* Early Drama, Art, and Music Monograph Series, 4. Kalamazoo, MI: Medieval Institute Publications, 1985.

Davies, Stevie, and William B. Hunter. "Milton's Urania: 'The meaning, not the name I call.'" *Studies in English Literature* 28, no. 1 (Winter 1998): 95–111.

Di Benedetto, Vincent. "Scripture's Constraint and Adam's Self-Authoring Freedom: A Reading of the Fall in *Paradise Lost.*" *Milton Quarterly* 25, no. 1 (March 1991): 1–14.

Dickens, A. G. *The English Reformation.* New York: Schocken Books, 1964.

Dubrow, Heather. "'In thievish ways': Tropes and Robbers in Shakespeare's Sonnets and Early Modern England." *Journal of English and Germanic Philology* 96, no. 4 (October 1997): 514–44.

Duffy, Eamon. *The Stripping of the Altars: Traditional Religion in England 1400–1580.* New Haven, CT: Yale University Press, 1992.

Dundas, Judith. "Spenser and the Emblem Books." *Emblematica* 11 (2001): 293–324.

Eliot, T. S. *Four Quartets.* New York: Harcourt, 1943.

———. *The Varieties of Metaphysical Poetry.* Edited by Ronald Shuchard. New York: Harcourt, Brace, 1993.

Elton, William. *King Lear and the Gods.* San Marino, CA: Huntington Library, 1966.

Evans, J. Martin. *The Miltonic Moment.* Lexington: University of Kentucky Press, 1998.

———. *Paradise Lost and the Genesis Tradition.* Oxford: Clarendon Press, 1968.

Fallon, Steven. "The Spur of Self-Concealment: Milton in His Divorce Tracts." *Milton Studies* 38 (2000): 220–42.

Fessenden, Tracy. "'Shapes of Things Divine in *Paradise Lost.*" *Christianity and Literature* 48, no. 4 (Summer 1999): 425–43.

Festa, Thomas. "Repairing the Ruines: Milton as Reader and Educator." *Milton Studies* 43 (2004): 35–63.

Fish, Stanley. *Self-Consuming Artifacts: The Experience of Seventeenth-Century Literature.* Pittsburgh, PA: Duquesne University Press, 1994.

Fletcher, Angus. "Complexity and the Spenserian Myth of Mutability." *Literary Imagination* 6, no. 1 (Winter 2004): 1–22.

Flynn, Maureen. "Taming Anger's Daughter's: New Treatment for Emotional Problems in Renaissance Spain." *Renaissance Quarterly* 51, no. 3 (Autumn 1998): 864–86.

Fraser, Russell. Introduction to *Drama of the English Renaissance,* edited by Russell A. Fraser and Norman Rabkin, 1–19. 2 vols. Berkeley and Los Angeles: University of California Press, 1976.

Fruen, Jeffrey. "The Fairy Queen Unveiled? Five Glimpses of Gloriana." *Spenser Studies* 11 (1990): 53–88.

Fuller, Mary C. "Ralegh's Fugitive Gold: Reference and Deferral in *The Discovery of Guiana.*" In *New World Encounters,* edited by Stephen Greenblatt, 218–40. Berkeley and Los Angeles: University of California Press, 1993.

Galeano, Eduardo. *Memoria del Fuego.* 3 vols. Buenos Aires: Catálogos S. R. L., 2004.

Garcia Garcia, María. "La hospitalidad y el hospedaje: fundaciones hospitalarias en Asturias." In *Las Peregrinaciones a Santiago de Compostela y San Salvador de Oviedo en la Edad Media, Actas del Congreso internacional celebrado en Oviedo del 3 al 7 de diciembre de 1990,* 211–46. Oviedo: Servicio Publicaciones, 1993.

Gigante, Denise. "Milton's Aesthetics of Eating." *Diacritics* 30, no. 2 (Summer 2000): 88–112.

Gilman, Ernest B. *Iconoclasm and Poetry in the English Reformation: Down Went Dagon.* Chicago: University of Chicago Press, 1986.

Greenblatt, Stephen. *Hamlet in Purgatory.* Princeton, NJ: Princeton University Press, 2001.

———. "Invisible Bullets: Renaissance Authority and Its Subversion." In *Political Shakespeare,* edited by Jonathan Dollimore and Alan Sinfield, 18–47. Manchester: Manchester University Press, 1985.

———. *Renaissance Self-Fashioning: From More To Shakespeare.* Chicago: University of Chicago Press, 1980.

Greenblatt, Stephen, and George Logan. "The Sixteenth Century: 1485–1603." *The Norton Anthology of English Literature,* 7th ed., 2 vols. Edited by M. H. Abrams, 1:469–98. New York: W. W. Norton, 2000.

Greenfield, Peter. "The Rise of the Patrons' Companies." Paper presented at the Shakespeare Association of America, New Orleans, 2004.

Griffin, Eric. "Un-Sainting James: Or, *Othello* and the 'Spanish Spirits' of Shakespeare's Globe." *Representations* 62 (Spring 1998): 58–99.

Groeneveld, Leanne. "The Boxley Rood of Grace: Mechanical Marvel or Miraculous Object?" Paper presented at 39th Annual Congress for Medieval Studies, Kalamazoo, Michigan, May 2004.

Gosse, Edmund. *The Life and Letters of John Donne.* 2 vols. Gloucester, MA: Peter Smith, 1959.

Greaves, Richard. *John Bunyan and English Nonconformity.* London: Hambledon Press, 1992.

Gurr, Andrew. *The Shakespearean Stage 1574–1642*. Cambridge: Cambridge University Press, 1992.

Guss, Donald L. "Enlightenment as Process: Milton and Habermas." *PMLA* 106, no. 5 (October 1991): 1156–69.

Haley, David. *Shakespeare's Courtly Mirror: Reflexivity and Prudence in "All's Well that Ends Well."* Newark: University of Delaware Press, 1993.

Hamilton, Donna B. *Shakespeare and the Politics of Protestant England*. Lexington: University of Kentucky Press, 1992.

Hampton, Bryan Adams. "Milton's Parable of Misreading: Navigating the Contextual Waters of the 'Night-Founder'd Skiff' in *Paradise Lost*, 1.192–209." *Milton Studies* 43 (2004): 86–110.

———. "'Such harmony alone': Performing the Incarnation in Milton's 'Nativity Ode' and 'Lycidas.'" Repairing the Ruins: Milton, Proclamation, and International Poetics." Ph.D. dissertation, Northwestern University, 2004.

Harley, J. B., and David Woodward. *The History of Cartography: Cartography in Prehistoric, Ancient, and Medieval Europe and the Mediterranean*. 2 vols. Chicago: University of Chicago Press, 1987.

Harris, Anne F. "Stained Glass and Popular Culture at Canterbury Cathedral." Paper presented at 40th Annual Congress for Medieval Studies, Kalamazoo, Michigan, May 2005.

Häublein, Ernst. "Milton's Paraphrase of Genesis: A Stylistic Reading of *Paradise Lost*, Book VII." *Milton Studies* 7 (1975): 101–26.

Hayes-Healey, Stephanie. "Patterns of *Peregrinatio* in the Early Middle Ages." *Medieval Paradigms: Essays in Honor of Jeremy du Quesnay Adams*, 2 vols. Edited by Stephanie Hayes-Healey, vol. 2; ch. 1. New York: Palgrave Macmillan, 2005.

Heming, Carol Piper. *Protestants and the Cult of the Saints in German-Speaking Europe, 1517–1531*. Kirksville, MO: Truman State University Press, 2003.

Herz, Judith Scherer. "'For whom this glorious sight?' Dante, Milton, and the Galileo Question." In *Milton in Italy: Contexts, Images, Contradictions*, edited by Mario A. DiCesare, 147–57. Binghamton, New York: SUNY Binghamton Press, 1991.

Hodgkins, Christopher. *Reforming Empire: Protestant Colonialism and Conscience in British Literature*. Columbia: University of Missouri Press, 2002.

Holderness, Graham. "*Henry IV, Parts 1 and 2*." *Shakespeare: The Play of History*, edited by Graham Holderness, Nick Potter, and John Turner, 41–61. Iowa City: University of Iowa Press, 1987.

———. *Shakespeare's History*. New York: St. Martin's Press, 1985.

Howard, Jean. "Shakespeare, Geography, and the Work of Genre on the Early Modern English Stage." *Modern Language Quarterly* 64, no. 3 (September 2003): 299–322.

Hughes, Richard F. *The Progress of the Soul: The Interior Career of John Donne*. New York: W. Morrow, 1968.

Hunt, Maurice. "The Hybrid Reformations of Shakespeare's Second Henriad." In *Reformations: Religion, Rulership, and the Sixteenth-Century English Stage*, edited by Grace Tiffany, 176–206. Kalamazoo, MI: Medieval Institute Publications, 1998.

———. "Predestination and the Heresy of Merit in *Othello.*" *Comparative Drama* 30 (1996): 346–76.

———. "Words and Deeds in *All's Well that Ends Well.*" *Modern Language Quarterly* 48, no. 4 (December 1987): 320–38.

Johnson, Stanley. "John Donne and the Virginia Company." *ELH* 14, no. 2 (June 1947): 127–38.

Jones, Nicholas R. "'Stand' and 'Fall' as Images of Posture in *Paradise Lost.*" *Milton Studies* 8 (1975): 221–46.

Kendall, Ritchie D. *The Drama of Dissent: The Radical Poetics of Nonconformity, 1380–1590.* Chapel Hill: University of North Carolina Press, 1986.

King, John. "Miltonic Transubstantiation." *Milton Studies* 36 (1998): 41–58.

———. "Milton's Cave of Error: A Rewriting of Spenserian Satire." In *Worldmaking Spenser: Explorations in the Early Modern Age,* edited by Patrick Cheney and Lauren Silberman, 148–55. Lexington: University of Kentucky Press, 2000.

———. *Spenser's Poetry and the Reformation Tradition.* Princeton, NJ: Princeton University Press, 1990.

Koopmans, Rachel. "The Monks of Christ Church and the Beginnings of Thomas Becket's Cult." Paper presented at the 40th International Congress on Medieval Studies, Kalamazoo, MI, May 2005.

Labriola, Albert C., "Milton's Eve and the Cult of Elizabeth I." *Journal of English and Germanic Philology* 95, no. 1, (January 1996): 38–51.

Lares, Jameela, "*Paradise Lost,* Books XI, and XII, and the Homiletic Tradition," *Milton Studies* 34 (1996): 99–116.

Laroque, François. *The Age of Shakespeare.* New York, Harry N. Abrams, 1993.

Lee, Jennifer, "Pilgrims' Badges as Portable Prototypes, or, Canterbury Gets Around." Paper presented at the 40th International Congress on Medieval Studies, Kalamazoo, MI, May, 2005.

Legouis, Pierre. "The Dramatic Element in Donne's Poetry." In *John Donne: A Collection of Essays,* edited by Helen Gardner, 36–51. Englewood Cliffs, NJ: Prentice-Hall, 1962.

Lehmberg, Stanford E. *The Reformation of Cathedrals: Cathedrals in English Society, 1485–1603.* Princeton, NJ: Princeton University Press, 1988.

Lehnof, Kent. "'Impregn'd with Reason': Eve's Aural Conception in *Paradise Lost.*" *Milton Studies* 41 (2002): 38–75.

Levao, Ronald. "'Among Unequals What Society': *Paradise Lost* and the Forms of Intimacy." *Modern Language Quarterly* 61, no. 1 (2000): 79–107.

Lewalski, Barbara K. "Forum: Milton's *Christian Doctrine.*" *Studies in English Literature* 32 (1992): 150.

———. "Milton and *De Doctrina Christiana:* Evidences of Authorship." *Milton Studies* 36 (1998): 203–28.

———. "Typological Symbolism and the 'Progress of the Soul.'" In *Literary Uses of Typology from the Late Middle Ages to the Present,* edited by Earl Miner, 79–114. Princeton, NJ: Princeton University Press, 1977.

Lewis, C. S. *The Discarded Image: An Introduction to Medieval and Renaissance Literature.* Cambridge: Cambridge University Press, 1964.

———. "Donne and Love Poetry in the Seventeenth Century." In *John Donne: A Collection of Critical Essays*, edited by Helen Gardner, 90–99. Englewood Cliffs, NJ: Prentice-Hall, 1962.

Lewis, Cynthia. "'Derived Honesty and Achieved Goodness': Doctrines of Grace in *All's Well that Ends Well.*" *Renaissance and Reformation* 14, no. 2 (Spring 1990): 147–70.

Low, Anthony. "Angels and Food in *Paradise Lost.*" *Milton Studies* 1 (1969): 135–45.

———. "The Fall into Subjectivity: Milton's 'Paradise Within' and 'Abyss of Fears and Horrors.'" *Reading the Renaissance*, edited by Marc Berley, 205–32. Pittsburgh, PA: Duquesne University Press, 2003.

Mallette, Richard. "The Protestant Art of Preaching in Book One of *The Faerie Queene.*" *Spenser Studies* 7 (1986): 3–26.

Martin, Catherine Gimelli. "'Ummeete Contraryes': The Reformed Subject and the Triangulation of Religious Desire in Donne's *Anniversaries* and *Holy Sonnets.*" In *John Donne and the Protestant Reformation: New Perspectives*, edited by Mary Arshagouni Papazian, 193–220. Detroit: Wayne State University Press, 2003.

Martin, Thomas L. "On the Margin of God: Deconstruction and the Language of Satan in *Paradise Lost.*" *Milton Quarterly* 29, no. 2 (May, 1995): 41–47.

Matar, Nabil I. *Crossing the Channel.* Presentation at The Newberry Library, December 2003.

———. "Introduction: England and Mediterranean Captivity, 1577–1704." In *Piracy, Slavery, and Redemption: Barbary Captivity Narratives From Early Modern England*, edited by Daniel J. Vitkus, 1–52. New York: Columbia University Press, 2001.

———. "John Donne, Peter Sterry, and the *Ars Moriendi.*" *Explorations in Renaissance Culture* 18 (1992): 55–70.

Maxwell, J. C. "Helena's Pilgrimage." *Review of English Studies* 20 (1969): 189–92.

McCoy, Richard C. *Alterations of State: Sacred Kingship in the English Reformation.* New York: Columbia University Press, 2002.

Milward, Peter. *The Catholicism of Shakespeare's Plays.* Tokyo: Renaissance Institute, 1997.

———. "More on the 'Base Judean.'" *Notes and Queries* 38, no. 4 (September 1998): 329–31.

Mincoff, Marco. *Things Supernatural and Causeless: Shakespearean Romance.* Newark: University of Delaware Press, 1992.

Montrose, Louis. "The Work of Gender in the Discourse of Discovery." In *New World Encounters*, edited by Stephen Greenblatt, 177–217. Berkeley and Los Angeles: University of California Press, 1993.

Moretti, Franco. "'A Huge Eclipse': Tragic Form and the Deconsecration of Sovereignty." *Genre* (Spring and Summer 1982): 7–40.

Moroney, Maryclaire. "Spenser's Dissolution: Monasticism and Ruins in *The Faerie Queene* and *The View of the Present State of Ireland.*" *Spenser Studies* 12 (1991): 105–32.

Morrissey, Mary. "John Donne as a Conventional Paul's Cross Preacher." In *John Donne's Professional Lives*, edited by David Colclough, 159–78. Cambridge, UK: D. S. Brewer, 2003.

Murillo, Luis Andrés, ed. *El Ingenioso Hidalgo Don Quijote de la Mancha*, by Miguel de Cervantes. 2 vols. Madrid: Clásicos Castalia, 1978.

Myers, Joan, Marc Simmons, and Donna Pierce. *Santiago: Saint of Two Worlds*. Albuquerque: University of New Mexico Press, 1991.

Ng, Su Fang, "Translation, Interpretation, and Heresy: The Wycliffite Bible, Tyndale's Bible, and Contested Origin," *Studies in Philology* 98, no. 3, (Summer 2001): 315–38.

The Oxford English Dictionary. Oxford: Clarendon Press, 1988.

Palmer, David J. "Comedy and the Protestant Spirit in Shakespeare's *All's Well that Ends Well.*" *Bulletin of the John Rylands University Library* 71 (1989): 95–107.

Papazian, Mary Arshagouni. Introduction to *John Donne and the Protestant Reformation: New Perspectives*, edited by Mary Arshagouni Papazian, 1–11. Detroit: Wayne State University Press, 2003.

Parker, William Riley. *Milton: A Biography*. 2 vols. Oxford: Clarendon Press, 1996.

Perry, T. Anthony. *Erotic Spirituality: The Integrative Tradition from Leone Ebreo to John Donne*. Tuscaloosa: University of Alabama Press, 1980.

Phillips, John. *The Reformation of Images: Destruction of Art in England, 1535–1660*. Berkeley and Los Angeles: University of California Press, 1973.

Pincus, Steven. "John Milton and Commercial Society: The Making of a Republican Conservative." *American Historical Review* 103, no. 3 (June 1998): 705–36.

Plötz, Robert. "La proyección del culto jacobea en Europa." In *Las Peregrinaciones a Santiago de Compostela y San Salvador de Oviedo en la Edad Media, Actas del Congreso Internacional celebrado en Oviedo del 3 al 7 de diciembre de 1990*, coord. Juan Ignacio Ruiz de la Peña, 57–72. Oviedo: Servicio Publicaciones, 1993.

Poole, Kristen. "Saints Alive! Falstaff, Martin Marprelate, and the Staging of Puritanism." *Shakespeare Quarterly* 46, no. 1 (Spring 1995): 47–75.

Potts, James B., Jr. "Milton's 'Two-Fold Scripture' and the Seventeenth-Century Search for Certitude." *Explorations in Renaissance Culture* 18 (1992): 93–110.

Pullan, Brian. "Catholics, Protestants, and the Poor in Early Modern Europe," *Journal of Interdisciplinary History* 35, no. 3 (Winter 2005): 441–56.

Pullman, Philip. *The Golden Compass*, New York: Del Rey, 1997.

Riches, Samantha. *Saint George: Hero, Saint, and Martyr*. Gloucestershire, UK: Sutton Publishing, 2000.

Richmond, Velma Bourgeois. *Shakespeare, Catholicism, and Romance*. New York: Cassell, 2000.

Riggs, David. *Ben Jonson*: Cambridge, MA: Harvard University Press, 1989.

Riggs, William G. "The Temptation of Milton's Eve: 'Words, Impregn'd / With Reason,' " *Journal of English and Germanic Philology* 94, no. 3 (July 1995): 365–92.

Roberts, Jeanne Addison. "Animals as Agents of Revelation: The Horizontalizing of the Chain of Being in Shakespeare's Comedies." *New York Critical Forum* (1980): 79–96.

Rosenblatt, Jason P. "The Mosaic Voice in *Paradise Lost.*" *Milton Studies* 7 (1975): 207–32.

Salamon, Linda Bradley. "Vagabond Veterans: The Roguish Company of Martin Guerre and *Henry V.*" In *Rogues and Early Modern Literature*, edited by Craig Dionne and Steve Mentz, 261–93. Ann Arbor: University of Michigan Press, 2003.

Salgádo, Gámini. *The Elizabethan Underworld.* Gloucestershire, UK: Sutton Publishing, 1997.

Sanok, Catherine. "Gendering the Past: Anglo-Saxon Saints in Early Modern England." Paper presented at the 39th Congress for Medieval Studies, Kalamazoo, Michigan, May 2004.

Sellin, Paul R. *So Doth, So Is Religion: John Donne and Diplomatic Contexts in the Reformed Netherlands, 1619–1620.* Columbia: University of Missouri Press, 1988.

Shapiro, James. "Revisiting *Tamburlaine: Henry V* as Shakespeare's Belated Armada Play." *Criticism* 31 (1989): 351–66.

———. *Shakespeare and the Jews.* New York: Columbia University Press, 1996.

———. *A Year in the Life of William Shakespeare: 1599.* New York: HarperCollins, 2005.

Sherry, Beverley. "Speech in *Paradise Lost.*" *Milton Studies* 8 (1975): 247–66.

Smith, A. J., ed. John Donne: *The Complete English Poems.* New York: Penguin Books, 1987.

Smith, Colin. "The Geography and History of Iberia in the *Liber Sancti Jacobi.*" In *The Pilgrimage to Compostela in the Middle Ages: A Book of Essays*, edited by Maryjane Dunne and Linda Kay Davidson, 23–42. New York: Garland, 1996.

Smith, R. A. L. *Canterbury Cathedral Priory.* Cambridge: Cambridge University Press, 1943.

Sohmer, Steve. "The 'Double Time' Crux in *Othello* Solved." *English Literary Renaissance* 32, no. 2 (Spring 2002): 214–38.

Spaccarelli, Thomas. *A Medieval Pilgrim's Companion.* North Carolina Studies in the Romance Languages and Literatures 261. Chapel Hill: University of North Carolina Press, 1998).

Stanley, Arthur. *Historical Memorials of Canterbury.* London: John Murray, 1851.

Stern, Tiffany. *Making Shakespeare: From Stage to Page.* New York: Routledge, 2004.

Stewart, Stanley. "Reading Donne: Old and New His- and Her-storicisms." In *Reading the Renaissance*, edited by Marc Berley, 130–52. Pittsburgh, PA: Duquesne University Press, 2003.

Stokstad, Marilyn, *Santiago de Compostela in The Age of the Great Pilgrimages.* Norman: University of Oklahoma Press, 1978.

Strier, Richard. "Milton's Fetters, or, Why Eden is Better than Heaven." *Milton Studies* 38 (2000): 169–97.

———. "Radical Donne: 'Satire III.' " *LH* 60, no. 2 (Summer 1993): 283–322.

Sumption, Jonathan. *Pilgrimage: An Image of Medieval Religion.* London: Faber and Faber, 1975.

Swaim, Kathleen. *Pilgrim's Progress, Puritan Progress: Discourses and Contexts.* Chicago: University of Illlinois Press, 1993.

Tayler, Edward. *Donne's Idea of a Woman: Structure and Meaning in the Annniversaries.* New York: Columbia University Press, 1991.

Thomson, G. Scott. *Medieval Pilgrimages.* London: Longman, 1962.

Tiffany, Grace. "Calvinist Grace in Shakespeare's Romances: Upending Tragedy." *Christianity and Literature* 49, no. 4 (Summer, 2000): 421–46.

———. "Elizabethan Constructions of Kingship and the Stage." In *The Iconography of Power,* edited by György E. Szőny and Rowland Wymer, 89–116. Szeged, Hungary: Institute of English and American Studies, 2000.

———. *Erotic Beasts and Social Monsters: Shakespeare, Jonson, and Comic Androgyny.* Newark: University of Delaware Press, 1995.

———. "*Hamlet* and Protestant Aural Theater." *Christianity and Literature* 52, no. 3 (Spring 2003): 307–23.

———. "Puritanism in Comic History: Exposing Royalty in the Henry Plays." *Shakespeare Studies* 26 (1998): 256–87.

Traversi, Derek. *An Approach to Shakespeare.* New York: Doubleday, 1939.

Van Doren, Mark. *Shakespeare.* New York: Doubleday, 1939.

Vázquez de Parga, Luis José; María Lacarra; and Juan Uría Ríu. *Las peregrinaciones a Santiago de Compostela, Tomo 1 y 2.* Navarra: Fondo de Publicaciones Gobierno de Navarra, 1997.

Verbart, André. "Measure and Hypermetricality in *Paradise Lost.*" *English Studies* 80, no. 5 (1999): 428–48.

Wall, Charles. *Shrines of British Saints.* London: Methuen, 1905.

Waters, D. Douglas. *Christian Settings in Shakespeare's Tragedies.* Rutherford, NJ: Fairleigh Dickinson University Press, 1994.

Watson, Elizabeth See. "Spenser's Flying Dragon and Pope Gregory." *Spenser Studies* 14 (2000): 293–301.

Watson, Robert N. "*Othello* as Protestant Propaganda." In *Religion and Culture in Renaissance England,* edited by Claire McEachern and Deborah Shuger, 234–57. Cambridge: Cambridge University Press, 1997.

Wells, Stanley. *Shakespeare: A Life in Drama.* New York: Norton, 1997.

Whalen, Robert. "Sacramentalizing the Word: Donne's 1626 Christmas Sermon." In *Centered on the Word: Literature, Scripture, and the Tudor-Stuart Middle Way,* edited by Daniel W. Doerksen and Christopher Hodgins, 193–223. Newark: University of Delaware Press, 2004.

Wheeler, Edward. "Continuing the Conversation." *Commonweal* 35. April 9, 1999.

White, Paul. "Holy Robin Hood! Carnival, Parish Guilds, and the Outlaw Tradition." In *Tudor Drama before Shakespeare, 1485–1590,* edited by Lloyd Edward Kermode, Jason Scott-Warren, and Martine Van Elk, 67–89. New York: Palgrave-Macmillan, 2004.

Wickham, Glynne, Herbert Berry, and William Ingram. *English Professional Theatre, 1530–1660.* Theatre in Europe: A Documentary History. Cambridge: Cambridge University Press, 2000.

Wofford, Suzanne L. "*The Faerie Queene,* Books I–III." In *Cambridge Companion to Spenser,* edited by Andrew Hadfield, 124–42. New York: Cambridge University Press, 2001.

Woodman, Francis. *The Architectural History of Canterbury Cathedral.* London: Routledge and Kegan Paul, 1981.

Worden, Blair. *Sound of Virtue: Philip Sidney's* Arcadia *and Elizabethan Politics.* New Haven, CT: Yale University Press, 1996.

Wright, Nancy E. "The *Figura* of the Martyr in John Donne's Sermons." *ELH* 56, no. 2 (Summer 1989): 293–309.

Index